Yucatán
at the Time of the
Spanish Encounter

Relación de las cosas de
Yucatán

Diego de Landa

Translated & Edited by
Louis E.V. Nevaer

Bilingual Edition / *Edición Bilingüe*

Yucatán at the Time of the Spanish Encounter

Relación de las cosas de Yucatán

Diego de Landa

Translated & Edited by Louis E.V. Nevaer

Yucatán at the Time of the Spanish Encounter / Relación de las cosas de Yucatán

ATTENTION UNIVERSITIES, COLLEGES, PROFESSIONAL, AND CHARITABLE ORGANIZATIONS: Quantity discounts are available on bulk purchases of this book for educational and gift purposes, or as premiums in fundraising efforts. Inquiries should be addressed to
Published by Hispanic Economics, Inc.
P.O. Box 140681
Coral Gables, FL 33114-0681
info@hispaniceconomics.com
HispanicEconomics.com

ISBN: 978-1-939879-02-8

Publication date: June, 2013.

Cover and Interior Design by John Clifton
john@johnclifton.net

CONTENTS / CONTENIDO

CONTENTS / CONTENIDO

CONTENTS / CONTENIDO

CONTENTS / CONTENIDO

CONTENTS / CONTENIDO

Dedico este libro a su santidad el papa Francisco

Acknowledgments

Christine Valentine, Estela Keim and Alberto Huchim, who encouraged me to translate and edit Diego de Landa's original manuscript, were instrumental in making this work possible. To them, I am grateful.

Yucatán
at the Time of the
Spanish
Encounter

Diego de Landa

Translated & Edited by Louis E.V. Nevaer

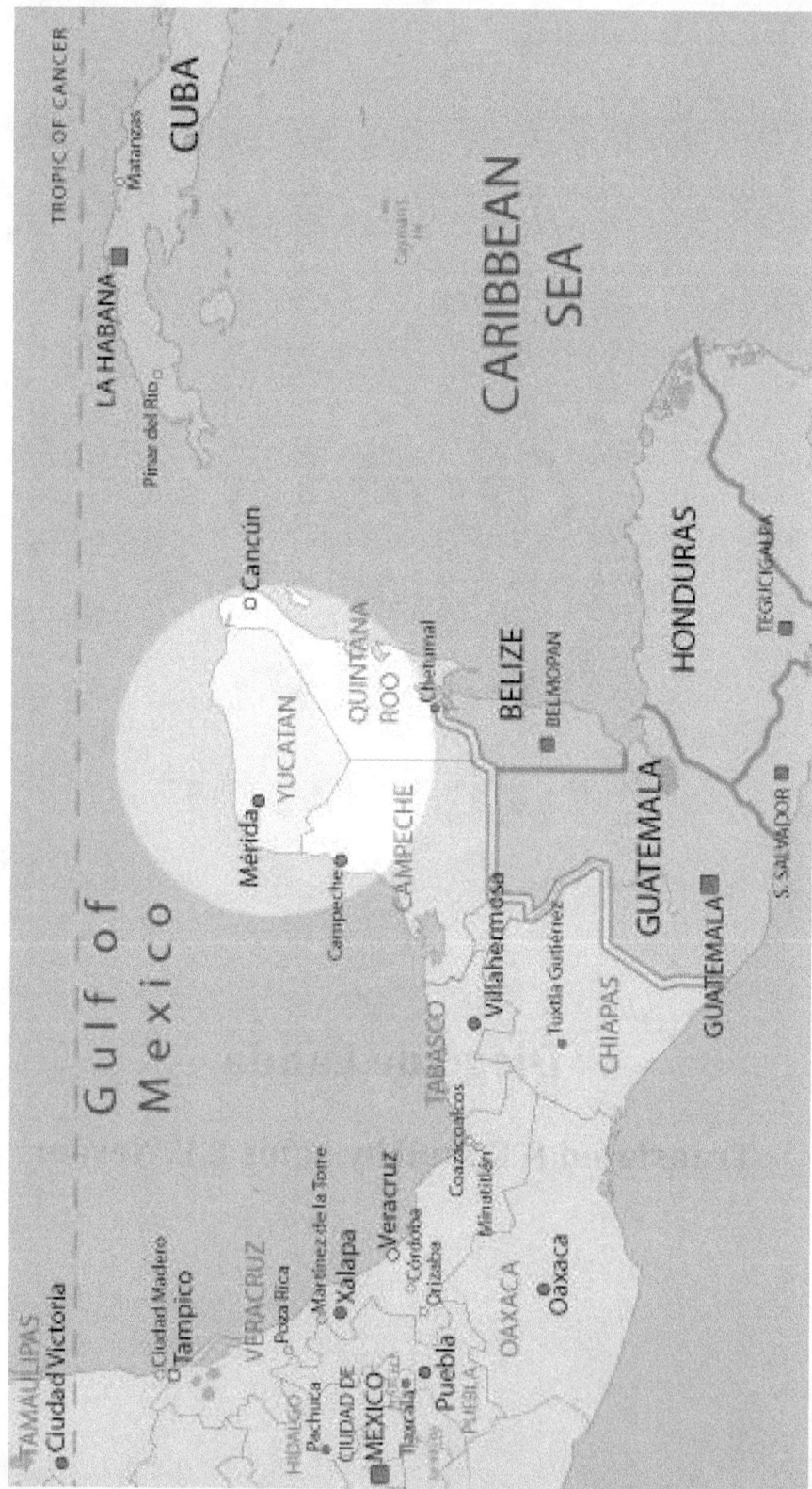

Franciscan friars and Maya converts battling the devil in Yucatán in the sixteenth century, mural at Izamal.

Introduction

There was a time when most people believed that the devil walked amongst us. There was a time when people accepted the proposition that our souls were so precious and beautiful that the devil would do anything to lead us astray in order to deprive God of the precious beauty of our souls. There was a time when people, based on these assumptions, carried on with their lives, ever mindful of the possibility that the devil would appear amongst us.

These beliefs, primarily Christian and based on biblical teachings, were shared by Jews and Muslims; Judaism and Islam overflow with angels and demons, with competing temptations and dangers that lurk in the world around us.

In Salem, Massachusetts, between February 1692 and May 1693 people accused of witchcraft—and consorting with the devil—were put on trial. Nineteen people were executed during these events, which today are remembered as an early episode of mass hysteria in colonial New England.

A century before Salem, the devil is believed to have visited Yucatán, then a remote province of colonial New Spain.

During renovations carried out in the first decade of this century at the great Franciscan monastery at Izamal, frescoes were uncovered depicting the faithful battling the devil. The murals portray Franciscan friars, along with Maya converts to Christianity, standing together, fighting the devil and his minions. The murals, long lost to history and human memory, but now recovered, illuminate one of the most compelling episodes in colonial Yucatán, and one that documents how European interpreted the world around them in the wilderness of the Americas.

In sixteenth century Yucatán, Francisco Toral, who would be appointed the first bishop of Yucatán, disagreed with Diego de Landa, who would become the second bishop of Yucatán. The men were at odds over the question of the devil's appearance in Yucatán. That murals depicting an epic battle exist, however, indicates that, upon becoming bishop, Landa's views prevailed.

Of course today, with our modern sensibilities, belief that the devil incarnate walks amongst us has subsided. We prefer to invoke the notion or idea of "evil," however one wishes to understand that concept. There is, after all, a universal consensus that, last century, Adolph Hitler was a man possessed by "evil," however that came to be. In this century, it was George W. Bush, president of the United States who, on the evening of September 11, 2001, addressed the world from the Oval Office to declare that "our nation saw evil today," thereby declaring himself a "wartime president" and launching into a military campaign against "terror."

The depiction of the devil in the murals at Izamal has generated a great reappraisal of our understanding of colonial Yucatán, and the sweeping theological debates that consumed the Franciscan missionaries sent to this isolated province of New Spain.

Did the devil, in fact, visit Yucatán?

This question calls for a reexamination of the landmark account of the things of Yucatán written by Diego de Landa. This new translation, published for the first time with the Spanish-language original, offers the contemporary reader a more fluid prose of the sixteenth century document. In the same way that throughout Europe and colonial New England, witchcraft, distinctions between "white magic" and "black magic," and rigorous protocols were in place to establish "proof" of demonic presences, the events in Yucatán must be examined in the same context.

What evidence was presented to Diego de Landa that compelled him to believe the devil was present in Yucatán? Why was this evidence insufficient for Francisco Toral? How did the conflict between the two men rise to the level where Francisco Toral denounced Diego de Landa before the Council of the Indies?

It is important to recall that, at this time, throughout Europe and the colonial possessions in the Americas, courts accepted "spectral evidence" in legal proceedings. Spectral evidence is testimony based upon dreams and visions: if two witnesses had the same dream, or reported having the same vision, this was entered as legal evidence. Although pioneered by Catholics, it was widely accepted by Protestants. The most famous instance of spectral evidence being used in the English-speaking world at the time was during the Bury St. Edmunds witch trials held in England between 1599 and 1694.

Diego de Landa believed in spectral evidence; Francisco Toral did not.

What role did the Maya themselves play in this episode? How were the Maya who had converted to Christianity challenged by the Maya who resisted the new religion? How did Spaniard and Maya understand each other, and come to a consensus, if they did, on one set of standards for determining whether or not was faithful and true to Christianity?

How does one recognize the devil? How does one recognize evil?

This is the question that transcends the centuries, from Izamal, Yucatán to Salem, Massachusetts; from your house to the White House.

Louis E.V. Nevaer
Mérida, Yucatán

Yucatán at the Time of the Spanish Encounter

Yucatán is not an island, nor is it a point entering the sea, as some have thought, but firm land. This misconception came about from the fact that the sea goes from Cape Cotoch along the Bay of Ascension passage to the Golfo Dulce on one side, and facing Mexico, by the Desconocido, before coming to Campeche, and there encounters the lagoons by Puerto Real and Dos Bocas.

The land is very flat and free of ranges [*sierras*], so that it is not seen from ships until they come very close; except between Campeche and Champotón, where there are some low ranges and a headland that are called Los Diablos.

As one arrives from Veracruz toward Cape Cotoch, one finds himself at less than 20 degrees, via the mouth of the Puerto Real, at more than 23 degrees. From one point to the other it should be over 130 leagues (390 miles or 593 kilometers), on a direct road.

The coast is low-lying, so that large ships must stay at some distance from the shore.

The coast is very full of rocks and rough points that wear the ship's cables badly. There is, however, much mud, so that even if ships run aground, they lose few people.

The tides run high, especially in the Bay of Campeche, and the sea often leaves, at some places, half a league (1.5 miles or 2.3 kilometers) exposed.

As a result of these tides, many small fish are left in the seaweed, mud, and tide pools that are the source of nourishment for many people.

A small range crosses Yucatán from one corner to the other, starting near Champotón and running to the town of Salamanca in the opposing angle.

This range divides Yucatán into two parts; to the south, toward Lacandón and Taiza, is uninhabited for lack of water, except when it rains. The northern part is inhabited.

The land is very hot and the sun burns fiercely, although there are fresh breezes like those from the northeast and east, which are frequent, together with an evening breeze from the sea.

People live long in the land, and men of 140 years of age have been found.

The winter begins on Saint Francis Day [October 4] and lasts until the end of March. During this time the north winds prevail and cause severe colds and catarrh from the insufficient clothing the people wear.

The end of January and February bring a short hot spell, when it does not rain except at the change of the moon.

The rains begin in April and last through September, during which time the crops are sown and mature despite the constant rain. On Saint Francis, a certain kind of maize is also sown, which is harvested early.

II
Etymology of the Name of This Province. Its Location.

This province is called in the language of the First People *Ulumil cutz yetel ceh*, which means "the land of the pheasant and the deer." It is also called Petén, meaning "island," an error arising from the gulfs and bays we have mentioned.

When Francisco Hernández de Córdoba came to this land and landed at the point he named Cape Cotoch, he met certain First People [who were] fishermen whom he asked what land this was, and they answered Cotoch, which means "our homes" and "our homeland." This is the reason he gave that name to this cape. When he then asked by signs how this land was theirs, they replied *Ci uthan*, meaning "They say it," and from that the Spaniards gave the name *Yucatán*. This was learned from one of the early conquistadors, Blas Hernández, who arrived here with the Admiral on the first voyage.

In the southern part of Yucatán are the rivers of Taiz and the *sierras* of Lacandón, and between the south and west lies the province of Chiapas. To reach it, one must cross four streams that descend from the mountains and unite with others to form the San Pedro y San Pablo River, discovered by [Juan de] Grijalva in Tabasco. To the west lie Xicalango and Tabasco, one and the same province.

Between this province of Tabasco and Yucatán there are two sea mouths [gulfs] breaking the coast; the largest of these forms a vast lagoon, while the other is of lesser extent. The sea enters these mouths with such fury as to create a great lagoon abundant in fish of all kinds. The islets are so many that the First People put signs on the trees to mark the way going or coming by boat from Tabasco to Yucatán. These islands with their shores and sandy beaches have so great a variety of seabirds as to be a matter of wonder and beauty. There is an infinite amount of game: deer, hare, the wild boars of the land, and monkeys, which are not found in Yucatán.

The number of iguanas is frightening. On one of these islands is a town called Tixchel.

To the north is the island of Cuba, with Havana facing at a distance of 60 leagues (180 miles or 274 kilometers); somewhat farther on is a small island belonging to Cuba, which they call Pines [Isla de Pinos, currently Isla de la Juventud].

At the east lies Honduras, between which and Yucatán is a great arm of the sea that [Juan de] Grijalva called Ascension Bay. This is filled with islets on which many boats are lost, especially those engaged in the trade between Yucatán and Honduras. Fifteen years ago a ship laden with many people and goods foundered, and all were drowned save one Majuelas and four others, who seized hold of a great piece of wood [ship's plank] from the ship, and thus went three or four days without reaching any of the islets until their strength gave out and all sank except for Majuelas. He came out half dead and recovered himself by eating snails and shellfish. Then from the islet he reached the mainland on a raft which he made as best he could out of branches. Making landfall, and while hunting for food, he came upon a crab that bit off his thumb at the first joint, and caused him intense pain. Then he set out through difficult bush to try to reach Salamanca. When night came, he climbed a tree from which he saw a great tiger [jaguar] waylay and kill a deer. When the following morning arrived, he ate what the [jaguar] had left.

In front of Yucatán, somewhat below Cape Cotoch, lies Cuzmil [Cozumel], across a 5 league (1.5 miles or 2.3 kilometers) channel where the sea runs with a strong current between the mainland and the island.

Cuzmil [Cozumel] is an island 15 leagues (45 miles or 68 kilometers) long by five wide (15 miles or 22.8 kilometers). The First People are few in number, and of the same language and customs as those of Yucatán. It lies at the 20th degree of latitude.

The Isle of Women [Isla de Mugeres, or Isla de Mujeres], is 13 leagues (39 miles or 59.3 kilometers) below Cape Cotoch; 2 leagues (6 miles or 9.1 kilometers) off the coast opposite Ekab.

III
Captivity of Gerónimo de Aguilar. Expedition of Hernández de Córdoba y [Juan de] Grijalva to Yucatán.

It is said that the first Spaniards to come to Yucatán were Gerónimo de Aguilar, a native of Écija, and his companions. In 1511, upon the break-up at Darien resulting from the dissensions between Diego de Nicueza and Vasco Núñez de Balboa, these men followed Valdivia on his voyage in a caravel to Santo Domingo, to report to the Admiral and the governor, and to deliver 20,000 ducats due the king. This caravel, arriving in Jamaica, ran aground on the shoals known as Víboras, where all of it was lost, save for 20 men. These men went with Valdivia in a lifeboat, without sails, with some poor oars and with no provisions. They were at sea for 13 days. After almost half the survivors died of hunger, they reached the coast of Yucatán, at a province called of the Maya, where the language of Yucatán is called Mayathan, which means the Maya language.

These poor souls fell into the hands of an evil [Maya leader], who sacrificed Valdivia and four others to their idols, and then served [their flesh] in a feast to his people. He saved Aguilar and Guerrero and five or six others to fatten them up. These escaped from their imprisonment and they fled through the forests. They came upon another community leader who was an enemy of the first, and more merciful. He made use of them as his slaves, and his successor treated them with much kindness. The men, however, died of grief, save only Gerómino de Aguilar and Gonzalo Guerrero. Of these, Aguilar was a good Christian and had a breviary, by which he knew [and kept count of] the feast days. And he was saved with the arrival of the Marquis Hernán Cortés in 1519.[1]

Guerrero, as he understood the [Maya] language, went to Chectemal [Chetumal], which is the Salamanca of Yucatán. He was received by a community leader named Nachancán, who placed him in charge of military affairs. In this, he did well and vanquished his lord's enemies many times. He taught the First People to fight, showing them how to make use of barricades and bastions. Through [these achievements], and by living like [a native], he gained a great reputation and married a [Maya] woman of great standing, with whom he had children. He, for this reason, made no attempt to escape as Aguilar had done. He decorated his

---

[1] Note: Diego de Landa writes "Hernando Cortés," but the contemporary English translation is generally accepted as "Hernán Cortés."

body [with tattoos], let his hair grow, pierced his ears in order to wear rings like the [First People], and it is believed he became an idolater like them.

During Lent of 1517, Francisco Hernández de Córdoba sailed from Cuba with three vessels to procure slaves for the mines, as the [First People] population of Cuba was diminishing. Others say he sailed to discover new lands, taking Alaminos as a pilot, since he had landed on Isla de Mugeres, to which he gave this name because of the idols he found there, which were of the goddesses of that land, Aixchel, Ixchebeliax, Ixhunic, Ixhunieta. These were dressed from the waist down, and had their breasts covered in the manner of the [First People]. The building was made of stone, such as to astonish them; and they found certain objects of gold, which they took. Arriving at Cape Cotoch, there they turned and set their course to the Bay of Campeche, where they disembarked on Lazarus Sunday, and so they named the place Lazarus. They were well received by the community leader, and the [First People] marveled at seeing the Spaniards, touching their beards and persons.

At Campeche they found a building in the sea, near to land, square shaped and with stairs. Atop they found an idol with [stone carvings of] two fierce animals devouring its sides. There was also a stone [sculpture] of a great, thick serpent swallowing a lion [jaguar]; the animals were covered with the blood of sacrificial victims.

At Campeche they learned of a large town nearby, which was Champotón. Upon landing there they learned that the community leader was named Mochcouoh. He was a bellicose man who called his people to rise against the Spaniards. Francisco Hernández regretted this, seeing how this would end. But so as to not show any less valor, he organized his own men, and fired artillery from the ships. And although the noise, smoke, and fire of the guns was new to the [First People], they did not desist from attacking with great cries. The Spaniards resisted, inflicting severe wounds and killing many [First People]. The community leader [Mochcouoh] so inspired his people that they forced the Spaniards to retreat, killing 20, wounding 50, and taking alive two whom they sacrificed afterward. Francisco Hernández himself suffered 33 wounds and returned to Cuba dispirited, [yet] he reported that the land was good and wealthy because of the gold he had found on the Isla de Mugeres.

These accounts excited Diego Velázquez, Governor of Cuba, as well as many others, so that he sent his nephew, Juan de Grijalva, with four ships and 200 men. He was accompanied by Francisco de Montejo, who was owner of one of the ships, and they set sail on 1 May 1518.

They took with them as pilot the same Alaminos, and landed on the island of Cuzmil [Cozumel], from where the pilot could see Yucatán. As he had done before with Francisco Hernández, he sailed along on the right hand, going south, wishing to see whether it was an island. They turned left and followed the bay they named Ascension, because they entered it on that day. Then, turning back, they followed the entire coast until they reached Champotón again. Landing there for fresh water, one man was killed and 50 were wounded, among them [Juan de] Grijalva, who suffered two arrow wounds, and had a tooth and half fractured. In this manner, they departed and named the harbor the Puerto de la Mala Pelea [Port of the Bad Battle]. On this voyage, they discovered New Spain, Panuco, and Tabasco, where they stayed for five months. They attempted to make landfall in Champotón. The [First People] resisted with much courage; they approached close to the ships in their canoes, allowing them to shoot their arrows. So they [the Spaniards] set sail and left them.

When [Juan de] Grijalva returned [to Havana] from his [voyage of] discovery and barter in Tabasco and Ulua, the great captain Hernán Cortés was in Cuba. Upon hearing of the news of a land of such size and vast riches, he [Cortés] desired to see them, and even to acquire them for God, for his king, for himself, and for his friends.

IV
Expedition of Cortés to Cuzmil [Cozumel]. Letter to Aguilar and His Companions.

Hernán Cortés sailed from Cuba with 11 ships, the largest being of 100 tons burden, placing in them 11 captains, and himself being one of among them. He took 500 men and some horses [and] goods for barter. Francisco Montejo, as a captain, and Alaminos, as chief pilot of the armada, were aboard. On the Admiral's ship [Cortés] placed a banner of white and blue, in honor of Our Lady, whose image, along with the cross, he placed wherever he removed idols. On the banner was a red cross surrounded by the legend that read *Amici sequamur crucem* [sic], *& si habuerimus fidem in hoc signo vincemus.*

With this fleet, and no additional equipment, he set sail and arrived at Cuzmil with ten ships, because one became separated during a storm; this one was subsequently recovered along the coast. The [fleet's] approach to Cuzmil was to the north, where they encountered fine stone buildings for idols, and a fine village. The [First People], upon seeing so grand a fleet of vessels and the soldiers disembarking, fled into the scrub forests.

On entering the village, the Spaniards ransacked it, and took possession of it. Searching for the people who had fled into the forests, they came upon the community leader's wife and children. Through Melchior, the [native Maya] interpreter, who had been with Francisco Hernández and [Juan de] Grijalva, they learned she was the community leader's wife. Cortés presented her, and the children, many presents and had them send for the community leader [to return]. He treated him [the community leader] very well upon his return, giving him small presents, and handed over his wife and children, and all the things that had been taken from the town. He begged him to order the [First People] to return to their homes. Upon their return, he ensured that everything that had been taken from their houses was returned to the rightful owners. After reassuring them, he preached to them about the vanity of idols. He persuaded them to worship the cross, and he placed one in their temples with an image of Our Lady, and with this, public idolatry ceased.

Cortés then became informed that there were bearded men six days' journey away, in the custody of a [rival] community leader, and he persuaded the [First People] to send messengers to summon them to him. He found [some] willing to go, although with difficulty because of the fear they had of the community leader [holding] the bearded men. He wrote this letter:

> Noble sirs: I left Cuba with a fleet of 11 vessels and 500 Spaniards, and laid upon Cuzmil, from where I write this letter. Those of the island have assured me that there are in the land five or six men with beards and resembling us in all manner of things. They are unable to give me other indications, but from [what I am told] I conjecture that you are Spaniards. I and these gentlemen who accompany me to settle and discover these lands urge that, within six days of receiving this [letter], you come to us, without making further delay or excuse. Should you come, we will make due acknowledgment, and reward the good act which this armada shall receive from you [by your presence]. I am sending a brigantine for you to return in, and two boats for your safety.

The [First People] took this letter, wrapped in their hair, and gave it to Aguilar. The [First People], however, were delayed beyond the appointed time; those on the ships believed they had been killed, and returned to the port of Cuzmil. Cortés, upon seeing that neither the [First People] nor the bearded men returned, set sail the following day. On that day, however, a vessel sprang a leak and it was necessary to return to port. While the ship was undergoing repairs, Aguilar, having received the letter, crossed the channel between Yucatán and Cuzmil, and, when [the Spaniards] of the armada saw him approach, they went to see who it was. Aguilar asked if they were Christians. The Spaniards answered yes. [Aguilar] wept for joy and, falling to his knees, gave thanks to God. He then asked the Spaniards if it was Wednesday.

The Spaniards took him naked as he had arrived to Cortés. Cortés clothed him and treated him with much affection. Aguilar told his story [of his shipwreck], of his being lost and his labors, and the death of his companions, and how it was impossible to notify Guerrero in so short a time; he was more than 80 leagues (240 miles or 365 kilometers) away.

With Aguilar, who was an excellent interpreter, Cortés renewed the preaching for the adoration of the cross, and he removed the idols from the temples. It is said that Cortés's preaching made such an impression on the people of Cuzmil that they came to the beaches [shore] and to the Spaniards who passed by said, "María, María; Cortés, Cortés."

Cortés departed from there and arrived in Campeche in passing, but he did not stop until he reached Tabasco. It was here that, among other presents and [women] given to him, was a woman he later named Marina [who is remembered in history as La Malinche]. She was from Xalisco, a daughter of noble parents, kidnapped as a small child, and sold in Tabasco. [She was] later sold in Xicalango and Champotón, where she learned the language of Yucatán [Yucatec Maya]. [Through knowledge of this language] she was able to understand Aguilar, and it is thus that God provided Cortés with good and faithful interpreters, through whom he acquired news [knowledge] and intimacy [details] with Mexican things, about which Marina knew much. [She] had interacted with [First People] merchants and leading people who spoke of [news of the affairs of the Mexica-Aztec empire] every day.

V
Province of Yucatán. Its Principal Ancient Structures.

Some old men of Yucatán say that they heard from their ancestors that this land was settled by people who came from the East, whom God delivered by opening 12 roads for them through the sea. If this is true, all the inhabitants of the Indies must be of Jewish descent because, passing the Straits of Magellan, they must have spread over more than 2,000 leagues (6,000 miles or 9,120 kilometers) of territory Spain today governs.

The language of this land is all the same, and this aids greatly in conversion, although along the coasts there are some differences in words and accents. Those living on the coast are more polished in their manners and language; and the women cover their breasts, which those farther inland do not.

The land is divided into provinces subject to the nearest Spanish settlement. The province of Chectemal and Bacalar is subject to Salamanca. The provinces of Ekab, of Cochuah, and of Kupul are subject to Valladolid. Those of Ah Kin Chel and Izamal, Zotuta, Hocabai Humun, Tutul Xiú, Cehpech, and Chakan are subject to the city of Mérida. Camol, Campech, Champutun, and Tixchel are assigned to San Francisco de Campeche.

There are in Yucatán many buildings of great beauty, these being the most outstanding of all the discoveries in the Indies. They are constructed of finely ornamented stone, though there is no metal found in the land for this cutting.

These buildings are very close to each other and resemble temples. The reason there are so many is that the people have moved many times. In each town they erected a temple, out of the abundance of stone and lime and of a certain white soil that is excellent for buildings.

These structures are not the work of other peoples, but of the [First People] themselves, and are decorated with stone carvings of men, bare-chested, but with the midriffs and groins covered by certain long strips of cloth which in their language are called *ex*, together with other distinguishing details worn by the [First People].

While this cleric, the author of this account, was in that land, a large urn with three handles, painted on the outside with silvered colors, was found in a demolished building. It contained the ashes of a cremated body and some bones of the arms and legs, of an unbelievable size, and with three fine beads of the kind the [First People] use as currency.

At Izamal there were 11 or 12 of these buildings in all, with no memory of who had built them. On the site of one of these, at the suggestion of the [First People], the monastery of San Antonio was established in 1549.

The second most important buildings are those of Tikoch and of Chicheniza [Chichén Itzá], which will be described later.

Chicheniza is a fine center ten leagues (30 miles or 45 kilometers) from Izamal and 11 leagues (33 miles or 50 kilometers) from Valladolid, which is said to have been ruled by three lords, brothers who came to that land from the West. These [brothers] were very devout and were thus able to build very beautiful temples. They lived unmarried and most honorably. One of them either died or departed, whereupon the others conducted themselves unjustly and dishonestly, for which they were put to death. Later on we shall describe the decorations of the main building, also describing the well [a natural sinkhole in the limestone karst topography] into which they cast living men as sacrifices; and also other precious objects. The well is over seven stages [the height of a man] (approximately 45 feet or 15 meters) down to the water, over a hundred feet across (33 meters) and, marvelously cut round in the sliced rock. The water appears green: they say it is caused by the forests that surround it.

VI
Kukulkán. Foundation of Mayapán.

It is the opinion of the First People that the Yzaes, who settled Chichenizá, were ruled by a great leader named Kukulkán. As proof, the principal building is called Kukulkán. They say that he came from the West, but do not agree as to whether he came before or after the Yzaes, or with them. They say that he was of good disposition, that he had no wife or children, and that after his return [to his homeland in the Valley of Mexico] he was regarded in Mexico as one of their gods, and called Cezalcohuati [Quetzalcóatl]. In Yucatán he was also revered as a god because of his great services to the nation. This is seen in the order he established in Yucatán after the death of the [previous] community leaders, and how he settled the discord caused in the land by their deaths.

This Kukulkán entered into an agreement with the community leaders native to this land and undertook the founding of another city in which he and they would live and attend to all matters and affairs. For this purpose he chose a fine site eight leagues (24 miles or 36.5 kilometers) farther inland from where Mérida now lies, and some 15 or 16 leagues (42 miles or 71 kilometers) from the sea. They enclosed the place with a very broad wall of dry stone some eighth of a league (2.4 miles or 3.7 kilometers) in length, leaving only two narrow doorways. The wall itself was low. In the middle of the enclosure they built their temples. The largest, as is the case at Chichenizá, they named Kukulkán. They built another circular temple, different from all others in the land, and with four entrances. They also built many others around them, each one connected to the other. Within the enclosure they built houses for the elite families within the compound. They divided the land into parcels, assigning villages to each according to the antiquity of his lineage and the character of his person. Kukulkán did not name the city after himself, as was done by the Ahizaes [Itzaes] at Chichenizá, which means the Well of the Ahizaes, but called it Mayapán, meaning the Standard of the Mayas. The language of the land was known as Maya. The First People today call the city Ychpa, meaning Within the Fortifications.

Kukulkán lived for some years in this city with the community leaders, and then left them, full of peace and friendship, returning by the same road to Mexico. On the way he stopped in passing at Champotón. There, in memory to himself and his departure, he constructed in the sea, at a good stone's throw from the shore, a fine building similar to those at Chichenizá. And thus Kukulkán left a permanent legacy in Yucatán.

VII
Government, Priesthood, Sciences, Literature, and Books of Yucatán.

After Kukulkán's departure, the community leaders agreed that for the nation to endure that the House of the Cocoms should exercise primary authority, since it was the oldest and wealthiest clan, and because, at that time, it was headed by a man of great valor. This settled, they decreed that within the enclosure there should only be temples and residential compounds of the community leaders and the High Priest. Outside the walls they would build residences where each of the community leaders might house their servants, and where the people from their villages might assemble [and be housed] whenever they had business in the city. In these houses each community leader placed his majordomo [steward], who carried, as his sign of authority, a short, thick baton, which was called the Caluac. This steward supervised the villages and those in charge of each one. The steward would send messages [to the villages] concerning the things needed in the community leader's residence, such as birds, maize, honey, salt, fish, game, clothing, and other things. The Caluac always attended to the household needs the community leader, seeing what needed replenishment and providing it promptly: his residence functioned as the warehouse of his community leader.

It was the custom to identify the impoverished and the blind [in the villages] and to provide for their necessities [and general welfare].[2]

The community leaders appointed the governors [for the villages] and, those who proved faithful could pass their offices to their sons. The leaders entrusted their appointed governors with the good treatment of the villagers, community peace, and that all should be diligent in supporting themselves and [providing] for the community leaders.

It was the duty of all the community leaders to honor, visit, and entertain the Cocom, accompanying him and hosting festivities for him, and turning to him in difficult matters. They lived in harmony with one another. There were many diversions according to their customs, consisting of dances, feasts, and hunting.

The First People of Yucatán were so intrigued by matters of religion that the government had a High Priest whom they called Ah Kin May, and also Ahau Can May, meaning the Priest May, or the High Priest May. He

---

[2] The "impoverished" were, for the most part, individuals who were "differently-abled."

was held in reverence by the community leaders. He had no allotment of [servants] for himself [and therefore depended] on the presents the community leaders gave him, in addition to the contributions the local priests sent him. He was succeeded in [office] by his sons or nearest heirs. The key to their sciences was entrusted to him, the study to which he most devoted himself. He counseled the community leaders and answered their questions. As to the matter of sacrifices, he rarely took part, except during festivals or on very important occasions. He and his colleagues appointed priests to serve the towns when there were vacancies, [after] testing [their knowledge] in their sciences and ceremonies; and entrusting to them the affairs of their office; and the setting of a good example to the people. He provided them with books. He sent them in turn to attend in service to the temples, teaching their sciences and writing about [their learning].

They taught the sons of the other priests, and the second sons of the community leaders, who were brought to them as young children for this purpose, if it was evident that they were inclined toward this career.

The sciences that they taught were the reckoning of the years, months and days and epochs; the festivals and ceremonies; the administration of their sacraments; the omens of the days; their methods of prophecies [divinations]; remedies for sicknesses; antiquities [histories]; and reading and writing using the letters and the characters [glyphs] by which they wrote, which illustrated their writings.

They wrote their books on a long sheet, doubled in folds, which was then enclosed between two finely ornamented boards. The writing was on one side and the other, according to the folds. The paper was made from the roots of a tree, which gave it a white finish well-suited for writing. Some of the principal community leaders were learned in these sciences out of self-interest, and because of these skills, they were held in greater esteem, although they did not make use of [reading and writing] in public.

VIII
Arrival of the Tutul Xiués and the Alliance They Made with the Community Leaders of Mayapán. The Tyranny of Cocom, the Ruin of His Power and of the City of Mayapán.

The First People relate that many tribes came with their community leaders to Yucatán from the south. It seems they came from Chiapas, although the First People cannot say with certainty. This writer so conjectures because many words and verbal constructions are the same in Chiapas and in Yucatán, and from substantial indications of places that have been abandoned. They say that these people wandered 40 years through the wilderness of Yucatán, having during this time no water other than from the rains, and that at the end of this period they reached the range [*sierra*] that lies about ten leagues' distance (30 miles or 45 kilometers) opposite the city of Mayapán. From here they began to settle and build many fine structures in many places; that the inhabitants of Mayapán held most friendly relations with them, and were pleased that they worked the land as if they were native to [Yucatán]. In this way the people of Tutul Xiués became subject to the laws of Mayapán. They intermarried, and so the community leader Xiú of the Tutul Xiués came to be held in great esteem by all.

These peoples lived in such peace that they had no conflicts whatsoever. They neither used arms nor bows, not even to hunt, although now [today] they are excellent archers. They only used snares and traps, with which they used to secure much game. Their priests were artful in throwing darts with the aid of a stick as thick as three fingers, hollowed out for a third of the way, and six palms long; with this and cords they threw with force and accuracy.

They had laws against delinquents which they enforced with rigor; such as [laws] against adultery. [An adulterer was] turned over to the injured party that he might be put to death by dropping a large stone down upon his head, or [the injured party] might forgive him if he chose. For the adulteress there was no penalty other than infamy, which was a very grave thing among them. One who raped a virgin was stoned to death, and they tell of a case of a community leader of the Tutul Xiués who, having a brother accused of this crime, had him stoned. Afterward he covered [his corpse] with a great heap of rocks. They also say that before the founding of the city they had another law providing for the punishment of adulterers by cutting out their intestines through the navel.

There came a time when the governing Cocom began to covet riches, and to this end he negotiated with the [Emperor] of Mexico based in Tabasco and Xicalango that he would hand over the city. In this manner he introduced the Mexicans into Mayapán, oppressed the poor, and made slaves of many of them. The community leaders would have slain him but for their fear of the Mexicans. The community leader of the Tutul Xiués never gave his consent to this, and, seeing the people of Yucatán oppressed, learned from the Mexicans the art of warfare. In time [the Maya] then became masters of the bow and arrow, of the lance, the ax, the shield, and strong sacks made of quilted cotton together with other accoutrements of war. So they no longer admired, or feared, the Mexicans, but rather held them with little regard. Several years passed in this manner.

This Cocom was the first who introduced slavery, but from this evil came the use of arms to defend themselves, so that they might not all become slaves.

Among the successors of the House of Cocom one emerged, very proud and an imitator of Cocom, who made another alliance with the Tabascans, placing more Mexicans within the city. He began to act with tyranny and to enslave the common people. Community leaders then banded together with the Tutul Xiués, a patriot, like his ancestors, and they plotted to kill the Cocom. They did so, slaying him at the same time as all of his sons, save one who was absent. They sacked his residence and took possession of all his property, his stores of cacao and other fruits, saying that thus they so repaid themselves what had been stolen from them. The conflicts among the Cocoms, who claimed that they had been unjustly expelled, and the Xiués, went on to such an extent that, after having been residents of in this city for more than 500 years, they [both clans] abandoned the place and left it uninhabited, each going to his own land.

IX

Chronological Monuments of Mayapán. Founding of the Kingdom of Zotuta. Origin of the C[h]iles. The Three Principal Kingdoms of Yucatán.

According to the First People's chronology, it has been 120 years since Mayapán was abandoned. On the site of the city one finds seven or eight stones, each ten feet in height (three meters), round on one side, well carved and displaying several lines of the characters they use, so worn away by the water that they are now unreadable. They are believed to be a monument to the founding and destruction of that city.[3] Other similar ones are located at Zilán, a town on the coast, although these are taller. When asked what they were, the First People answered that it was the custom to erect one of these stones every 20 years, that being the number by which they count the passage of time. It would seem that this explanation is without warrant, for if that were the case, there would have to be many others; there are no other of these stones other than at Mayapán and Zilán.

The books of their sciences were the most important thing that the community leaders who abandoned Mayapán [ensured to take with them]. They were always very faithful to the counsels of their priests, which is the reason there are so many temples in those provinces.

The son of Cocom, who had escaped death by being away on a trading expedition in the land of Ulna, which is beyond the city of Salamanca, upon learning of his father's death and the destruction of the city, returned in haste and joined his relatives and vassals. They settled in a place which he named Tibulón, meaning "we have been swindled." They built many other towns in those forests, reuniting many of these Cocoms' families. The province where this community leader rules is called Zututa.

The community leaders of Mayapán took no vengeance on the Mexicans who aided Cocom because they had been persuaded by the governor of that land, and because they were foreigners. As such, they left them undisturbed, granting them leave to settle in a town apart just for themselves, or to leave that land. Unable to intermarry with the indigenous [Maya], they were left among themselves. These decided to remain in Yucatán, and not return to the lagoons and mosquitoes of

---

[3] By the time the Spanish arrived in Yucatán in the sixteenth century, the Maya had become illiterate; no one was left who could read or write in their the Maya language.

Tabasco. They settled in the province of Canul, which was assigned to them. They remained there until the second war with the Spanish.

They say that among the 12 priests of Mayapán, there was a very wise one who had an only daughter. He married her off to a young nobleman named Ah Chel. They had sons who were named after their father, as was the custom of the land. They say that this priest advised his son-in-law of the fall of the city. The priest, they say, inscribed certain important characters on the broad part of his [son-in-law's] arm so he would be held in high esteem. With this distinction conferred on him, he traveled, with a great number of people following him, along the coast, establishing the settlement at Tikoch. And so arose the renowned families of the Cheles. They peopled the most famous province of Yucatán, which they named, after themselves, the province of Ah Kin Chel. It is Ytzamal, where the Cheles resided. They multiplied throughout Yucatán until the arrival of the Admiral Montejo.

There were constant feuds and enmities among the three principal Houses of the Cocoms, Xiués and Cheles, which still continue to this day, even after they have become Christians. The Cocoms said the Xiués were foreigners and traitors for murdering their own leader and plundering his hacienda [possessions]. The Xiués said they were as fine as the others, as ancient and as noble [as the others]; that they were not traitors but liberators of their land, having slain a tyrant. The Chel said that his lineage was as good as the others', being the grandson of a priest, the most renowned in Mayapán. As for himself, he was better than they, having known how to conduct himself as much as a gentleman as they did. The quarrel extended even to their food supply, for the Chel, living on the coast, would not give fish or salt to the Cocom people, forcing them travel a long distance for it; the Cocom people would not allow the Chel people to hunt game or gather fruit.

These clans enjoyed more than 20 years of abundance and health, and they multiplied so that the whole land seemed like a town. It was during this that time they raised temples in great number, as is today seen everywhere. Traveling through the forests [today] one can see in the forests the remains of residences and structures marvelously worked.

After this period of prosperity, there came on one winter night, at about six o'clock in the evening, a storm that grew into a hurricane of the four winds. The wind blew down all the high trees, causing great loss of all kinds of game. It overthrew the high houses, which being constructed of thatched roofs and containing fires inside because of the cold, caught fire and burned great numbers of people. Those who escaped were crushed by the falling trees. The hurricane lasted through noon the next day. They found that those who lived in small houses had escaped, as well as the newly married couples whose custom it was to live for a few years in cabins in front of their father's or fathers-in-law's houses. The land then lost the name it had borne, that "of the pheasant and the deer." It was left so treeless that today it looks as if planted at the same time; all mature trees appear to be of one size. To look at the forests from heights it looks as if all [the trees were] trimmed with a pair of shears.

Those who escaped took heart and resigned themselves to rebuilding and cultivating the land. They multiplied greatly during 16 years of health and abundance, the last year being the most fertile one of all. Then as they were about to begin harvesting the crops an epidemic of pestilential fevers that lasted for 24 hours arrived. When the fever disappeared, the bodies of those infected swelled and broke out full of maggot-filled sores. Many people died of this pestilence and most of the crops were not harvested.

After the passing of the pestilence they enjoyed another 16 good years during which they renewed their passions and feuds, so that 150,000 men were killed in battles. With this slaughter they ceased and made peace and rested for 20 years. After this period, another pestilence fell upon them. [Those infected suffered] great boils that rotted the body, were foul in odor, and their limbs fell off within four or five days.

Since this last plague more than 50 years have now passed. The mortality of the wars was 20 years prior, and the pestilence of the swelling was 16 years before the wars, and 22 or 23 after the destruction of the city of Mayapán. Thus, according to this count, it has been 125 years since its collapse during which time the people of this land have passed through the calamities described, apart from many others after the Spaniards began to enter, both by wars and other afflictions sent by God.[4] It is a marvel there are any of the people left, few in number as they are.

---

[4] Diego de Landa refers to epidemics that afflicted the First Peoples who had no natural immunity to diseases that, in previous centuries, had similarly decimated the populations of Europe. In fact, the Black Death is considered one of the most devastating pandemics in human history. It reached its peak between 1348 and 1350 in Western Europe and is believed to have killed between 100 and 200 million people. The surviving generations of Europeans developed immunity to many of these infections, and when they arrived in the New World they encountered multitudes that had no natural immunity. It is believed that similar scores of millions of people throughout the Americas also perished.

XI
Prophecies of the Arrival of the Spaniards. Biography of Francisco de Montejo, the First Admiral of Yucatán.

[In the same way] the Mexican people had signs and prophecies of the coming of the Spaniards and the end of their power and religion, so also did the peoples of Yucatán some years before they were conquered by the Admiral Montejo. In the district of Maní, located in the province of Tutul Xiú, a [Maya] named Ah Cambal, whose office was of *Chilán*, who is the one in charge of giving out the responses of the demon, publicly stated that they would soon be ruled by a foreign race who would preach a God and the virtue of a wood post, which in their tongue he called Vahom Ché, meaning a tree lifted up possessing great power against the demons.

The successor of the Cocoms, called Don Juan Cocom after he became a Christian, was a man of great reputation. He was very learned in matters and affairs of the land, very wise and well informed. He was on familiar terms with the author of this book, Fray Diego de Landa, who recounted to him many ancient things, and showed him a book which had belonged to his grandfather, the son of the Cocom whom they killed in Mayapán. A deer was painted in this book and his grandfather had told him that when there should come into the land large deer (for so they called the cows), the worship of their own deities would cease. This had been fulfilled, because the Spaniards brought along large cows.

The Admiral Francisco de Montejo was a native of Salamanca and came to the Indies after the settling of the city of San Domingo, on the Island of Española. After having lived for a time in Sevilla, where he left an infant son whom he had there, he went to the island of Cuba, where he earned a living and made many friends because of his fine qualities. Among them was Diego Velázquez, the governor of the island, and Hernán Cortés. The governor decided to send his nephew Juan de Grijalva to trade in the land of Yucatán and to discover new lands, after the news brought by Francisco Hernández de Cordova that this was a rich land. He decided to have Montejo go with [Juan de] Grijalva. Since [Montejo] was wealthy, he supplied one of the ships and much provisioning, and was thus one of the second party of Spaniards that discovered Yucatán. Once he saw the coast of Yucatán he resolved to make his fortune there instead of in Cuba. Learning of Hernán Cortés's determination, he placed himself and his fortune at Cortés's disposal. [Cortés] gave him command of a ship and made him her captain. In Yucatán they met with Gerónimo de

Aguilar, through whom Montejo learned the language of the land and its affairs. Cortés, upon landing in New Spain, began at once to found settlements, calling the first town Vera Cruz, after the blazon of his banner. Montejo was appointed as one of the king's magistrates of the town. He conducted himself with discretion, and Cortés publicly named him as a Magistrate when [Cortés] returned from the trip he made around the coast. For this reason he was sent to Spain as one of the representatives of the state of New Spain and to take the king the royal fifth due him, along with an account of the lands discovered, and the things that were unfolding there.

When Francisco de Montejo arrived at the Court of Castile, Juan Rodríguez de Fonseca, Bishop of Burgos, was president of the Council of the Indies. He was wrongly prejudiced against Cortés [because of information] Diego Velázquez, the governor of Cuba, who also claimed the governorship of New Spain, [had said about Cortés]. The majority of the Council was [also hostile to] Cortés, falsely believing him to be asking the king for money instead of sending payments. Montejo, finding that the emperor was away in Flanders, his mission went poorly. Montejo persevered for seven years from the time he left the Indies (which was in 1519) until he re-embarked in 1526. His perseverance [was such that] he challenged the president and Pope Adrian [VI], who was regent for the kingdom, and spoke with the emperor himself. [This proved successful and] and he gave his approval [to Cortés's initiative] and settled Cortés's request in a just manner.

XII

Montejo Sails to Yucatán and Takes Possession of the Land. The Chels Cede to Him the Site of Chicheniza. The First People Force Him to Leave.

During the time that Montejo was at court he secured for himself the commission to conquer Yucatán, although he might have had other things, and he was given the title of Admiral and Captain General. He next went to Sevilla and took with him a nephew 13 years of age, who bore his own name. [In Sevilla] he found his son, now 28 years of age, and took him along. He arranged a marriage with a rich widow of Sevilla and was thus able to assemble 500 men with whom he embarked in three ships. Setting sail he made port at Cuzmil, an island of Yucatán. The First People there did not oppose him [and his men], having been made friendly by the Spaniards under Cortés. There he learned many words of their language, and how to communicate with them. He then sailed to Yucatán and took possession of it with one of his standard-bearers saying, banner in hand: "In the name of God I take possession of this land for God and for the King of Castile."

Then he sailed down the coast, which was then well populated, until he landed at Conil, a town of the same coast. The First People became alarmed at seeing so many horses and men and sent word throughout the land of what was happening, watching to see what the Spaniards' intentions were.

The community leaders of the First People of the province, the Chicaca, came to visit the Admiral in peace and were well received. Among them came a man of great strength who, taking a cutlass [a short sword used by sailors] from a young Negro who bore it, tried to kill the Admiral with it.[5] He defended himself, and the other Spaniards came up and stopped the trouble. They learned that it was necessary to proceed on their guard.

The Admiral made inquires to identify the largest city and learned it was Tekoch [Tikoch], a city of the Chels, located on the coast farther down along the course the Spaniards were taking. The First People, thinking they were on their way out of their land, were not hostile, nor did they oppose their march. In this way they reached Tekoch and found it a much larger and finer city than they had supposed. [The Admiral]

---

[5] This is the first mention of the arrival of blacks among the Maya. In a few decades, blacks would outnumber Spaniards throughout New Spain.

found it fortunate that the community leaders of that land were not the Couohes of Champotón, who were always braver [more hostile] than the Chels. The [Chels], with their priesthood, which still exists today, were not as arrogant as the others. [For this reason] they allowed the Admiral to establish a settlement for his men, giving him the site of Chichenizá for the purpose, an excellent place seven leagues (21 miles or 32 kilometers) away. From this location he set out to the conquest of the land, a task rendered easy by the nonresistance of the people of Ah Kin Chel and the assistance of those of Tutul Xiú. As a result the others offered little resistance.

In this way the Admiral asked [the Maya] for men to build at Chichenizá, and in a short time he built a town, making the houses of wood and the roofs of certain palm leaves and long grass as were used by the First Peoples. And so, realizing that the First People served without ill will, he conducted a census, which was well populated, and he divided the towns among the Spaniards. They say the smallest allotment [per officer] was 2,000 or 3,000 villagers. He also began to fix rules for the natives, rendering their services to the Spaniards' towns. This [turn of events] did not sit well with the First People, although they concealed their displeasure for the time being.

XIII
Montejo Leaves Yucatán with His Men and Returns to Mexico. His Son Francisco de Montejo Afterward Pacifies the Land.

The Admiral Montejo did not construct defenses against enemies in his settlement because it was quite far from the sea for invasion from Mexico City or for receiving provisions from Spain. The First People felt it a humiliation that they [were now made] to serve strangers where they had been the rulers of this land. They began to launch hostile attacks on all sides, although [Montejo] defended himself with his horses and men and killed many. The First People were reinforced every day, so that he [Montejo] found provisions running out. At last, one night [the Spaniards] left the city, leaving a dog tied to the clapper of a bell, near some bread placed just out of his reach. The preceding day [Montejo had fought the Maya and] had exhausted [them] in skirmishes [with the purpose of tiring them out so they would need to rest and] that they might not follow [the Spaniards, who planned to abandon their settlement]. The dog, in trying to reach the bread kept the bell ringing, keeping the First People uncertain and expecting an attack. When they discovered that a trick had been played upon them, the First People were furious and decided to pursue the Spaniards in all directions because they did not know which direction they had taken. The men who followed in the direction [the Spaniards] had taken caught up with them, making a great hue and cry as if chasing fugitives. Six of the horsemen waited for them out in the open and ran many of them down. One of the First People seized hold of a horse by the leg and stayed him as if he were a sheep. The Spaniards reached Zilán [Dzilán], a beautiful place, whose community leader was a youth of the Chels. He had become a Christian and a friend of the Spaniards; he treated them well. This was near Tikoch, which with all the other towns of that region [along the coast] was under the rule of the Chels. Here [Montejo and his men] remained some months in safety.

The Admiral, realizing that here they would be unable to receive aid from Spain, and that in case of an uprising by the First People they would be lost, resolved to go with all his men to Campeche and from there to Mexico City, leaving Yucatán without Spaniards. Campeche is located 48 leagues (144 miles or 219 kilometers) from Zilán through densely populated [towns] so that when he disclosed his plans to Namux Chel, the community leader of Zilán, the latter offered to make the road safe and to accompany the Spaniards. The Admiral also arranged with the community leader of Yobain, who was [Namux Chel's] uncle, for the company of his two sons, well-disposed youths. Thus with these three youthful cousins, he of Zilán on one horse and the other two *en croupe*, they arrived safely at Campeche and were received there in peace. The Chels took their leave and returned to their homes, though the community leader of Zilán died on the way. From there, they departed for Mexico City, where Cortés had set aside an allotment of First People for the Admiral, notwithstanding his absence.

On arriving in Mexico with his son and nephew, the Admiral learned that his wife, Doña Beatriz de Herrera, whom he had married secretly at Sevilla, and a daughter he had had by her, named Beatriz de Mendoza, had arrived in search of him. Some say he refused to receive her, but Don Antonio de Mendoza, the Viceroy of New Spain, intervened and reconciled them. The same Viceroy [then] sent him as governor of Honduras, where he married his daughter to Alonso Maldonado, a lawyer and president of the Audiencia of the Confines. Some years later they removed to Chiapas, and from there he sent his son, duly empowered, to Yucatán, to conquer and pacify [that land].

This Don Francisco, son of the Admiral, had been raised at the court of the Catholic king [Ferdinand V] and was brought along by his father on his return to the Indies for the conquest of Yucatán; and from there he accompanied him to Mexico City. The Viceroy and the Marquis Don Hernán Cortés thought well of him, and he went with the Marquis on a journey to California. On his return the Viceroy made him governor of Tabasco and he married a lady named Doña Andrea del Castillo, who had come to Mexico as a young girl with her parents.

XIV
State of Yucatán After the Departure of the Spaniards. Don Francisco, Son of the Admiral, Reestablishes Spanish Rule in Yucatán.

After the departure of the Spaniards from Yucatán, there was a drought throughout the land and because the corn had been exhausted during the wars with the Spaniards, they suffered much from famine. They were reduced to eating the bark of trees, especially of a certain kind called *cumché*, the inside of which is soft and mellow. On account of this famine the Xiú of Maní resolved to make a solemn sacrifice to the idols, taking certain male and female slaves to cast into the well at Chicheniza. To do this, however, they had to pass by the town of the Cocom, their mortal enemies, but thinking that ancient quarrels would be forgotten in such times they sent to ask permission to pass through their land. The Cocoms deceived them by giving them a favorable answer, but once they had lodged them all together in one great building, they set fire to it, and slew those who escaped. As a result of this, great wars followed [among the Maya].[6] [To exacerbate the situation] there was also a plague of locusts for five years, so great that no green thing was left. Such a famine ensued that they fell dead along the roadsides. When the Spaniards returned they did not recognize the land. After four good years [that] followed the end of the locusts, the situation improved somewhat.

This Don Francisco set out for Yucatán following the rivers of Tabasco and entered the region by the lagoons of Dos Bocas. The first town he reached was Champotón, whose leader, Mochcouoh, had caused much trouble to Francisco Hernández and [Juan de] Grijalva. That community leader having, however, died, Don Francisco then met no resistance. To the contrary, he was supported along with his men for two years by the people of the place. During this time he could not advance farther because of the resistance he encountered. Later he went to Campeche, where he found the inhabitants very friendly. With their assistance and that of the people of Champotón, he concluded the conquest. For their loyalty, he had promised that the king would reward them, a promise which up to the present time the king has not fulfilled.

The light resistance he did encounter was not strong enough to prevent Don Francisco from reaching T'ihó with his men; here he

---

[6] Diego de Landa refers to the constant internecine warfare among the Maya that characterized their civilization, from the apogee of their dominance, to their collapse in the ninth century, and on for six centuries until the European arrival.

founded the city of Mérida. Leaving his pack of animals there, he set out to continue the conquest [of the peninsula], sending captains in different directions. Don Francisco sent his cousin Francisco de Montejo to Valladolid to pacify the natives, who had mounted a slight rebellion, and to establish the city as it is now. In Chectemal [Chetumal] he founded the city of Salamanca [de Bacalar]; Campeche he already had settled [with Spaniards]. He established in orderly manner the duties of the First People and the government by the Spaniards, in anticipation of his father, the Admiral, to arrive and to assume control. The latter on arriving from Chiapas with his wife and household was welcomed at Campeche and gave his own name to the city: as San Francisco [de Campeche]. Then he continued on to the city of Mérida.

XV
Cruelties of the Spaniards Against the First People. How They Justified Themselves.

The First People accepted the yoke of servitude reluctantly. The Spaniards held the towns comprising the land well partitioned [among them], but there were some among the First People who kept stirring them up [to rebel]. Very severe punishments were administered in consequence, resulting in the diminishment of the population. They burned alive several principal men of the province of Cupul. Others were hanged. Accusations were levied against the people of Yobain, a town of the Chels. The leading men accused were put in stocks in a building and then fire was set to the house, burning them alive with the greatest inhumanity that can be imagined. And I, Diego de Landa, say that I saw a great tree near the village upon the branches of which a captain had hanged many women, with their young children hung from their feet. At this town, and another two leagues (6 miles or 9 kilometers) away called Verey, they hanged two [Maya] women, one a maiden and the other recently married, for no other crime than their beauty, and because of fear that [they might cause sexual jealousies] among the soldiers on their account. [They also wanted] the Maya to believe the Spaniards were indifferent to their women. The memory of these two still remains vivid among the First People and Spaniards, both on account of their great beauty and because of the cruelty with which they were killed.

The First People of the provinces of Cochuah and Chectemal rebelled. The Spaniards suppressed them in such manner that from being the most settled and populous they became the most wretched of the whole land. Unheard-of cruelties were inflicted: they cut off their noses, hands, arms, and legs, and the breasts of their women; threw them into deep water with gourds tied to their feet; and speared the children because they could not go as fast as their mothers.[7] If some of those who had been put in chains fell sick or could not keep pace with the rest, they would cut off their heads among the rest rather than stop to free them. They also kept great numbers of women and men prisoner to serve them, subject to similar treatment. It is affirmed that Don Francisco de Montejo did not carry out any of these cruelties nor approved them, but condemned them severely, yet he was unable to do anything [to stop them].

---

[7] The gourd is made from the fruit of the calabash (*Lagenaria siceraria*) plant.

35

In their defense the Spaniards argue that being so few in numbers they could not have subdued so populous a land save through the fear of such terrible punishments. They offer the example from history of the passage of the Hebrews to the Promised Land who committed great cruelties as commanded by God. On the other hand, the First People were right in defending their liberty and trusting to the valor of their community leaders. They believed they would [succeed in their resistance] against the Spaniards.

They tell of a Spanish crossbowman and a [Maya] archer who, being both very skilled, sought to kill each other but neither could take the other off guard. The Spaniard, pretending to drop his guard, put one knee to the ground, whereupon the Maya shot an arrow that entered his hand, and going up the arm separated the bones from each other. At the same moment, the Spaniard shot his crossbow and struck the Maya in the chest. He, feeling himself mortally wounded, cut a liana, which is like an osier only much longer, and hanged himself with it in sight of all. [This way] it could not be said that a Spaniard had killed him. There are many instances of such valor.

XVI
State of the Land Before the Conquest. Royal Decree in Favor of the First People. Death of the Admiral [Montejo]. His Descendants.

Before the Spaniards subdued the land the First People lived together in well ordered communities. They kept the ground in excellent condition, free from weeds and planted with fine trees. The layout [of their communities] was as follows: in the center of the town were temples, with beautiful plazas, and around the temples stood the houses of the community leaders and the priests, followed by those of the elite families. Adjacent to these were the houses of the wealthiest and most esteemed. At the edges of the town were the houses of the common people. The wells, if they were few, were near the houses of the community leaders. Their plantations were set out in the trees for making wine [pulque], and sown with cotton [trees], pepper [believed to be allspice, *Pimenta officinalis*] and maize. They lived in these communities out of fear of their enemies, lest they be taken captive. After the wars with the Spaniards[, however,] many dispersed through the forests.

The First People of Valladolid, either because of their evil nature or from their bad treatment by the Spaniards, plotted to slay the Spaniards when they separated to collect tribute. In one day they killed 17 Spaniards and 400 servants belonging to those [Spaniards] they killed. They spared other [Maya servants]. Then they sent [severed] arms and feet through the whole land as a sign of what they had done in order to arouse the rest [to rebellion]. These, however, would not follow suit and so the Admiral was able to send aid to the Spaniards of Valladolid and to punish the First People [responsible for the massacre].

The Admiral had trouble with [the Spaniards] of Mérida particularly because of royal decree that deprived the governors of the First People [they held in slavery or servitude]. An actuary was sent to Yucatán [and he] took the First People from the Admiral and placed them under royal protection. After this a Residencia [Residency] was instituted before the Royal Audience in Mexico City, which [accused the Admiral of wrongdoing and] ordered him before the Royal Council of the Indies in Spain.[8] There he died, burdened by the years and his labors, leaving his

---

[8] The system of "checks and balances" established in New Spain sought to hold accountable governors and administrators. Oftentimes petty jealousies and rivalries resulted in accusations and cross-accusations. This kept the Council of the Indies in Spain

wife Doña Beatriz richer than himself. His son Don Francisco de Montejo married in Yucatán. His daughter Doña Catalina married to Alonso Maldonado in Honduras, who was an attorney and president of the Audience of Honduras and San Domingo on the Island of Hispaniola. [He was also survived by] Don Juan de Montejo, a Spaniard, and Don Diego, a son he had with a Maya woman.[9]

Don Francisco, after leaving the government to his father the Admiral, lived in his home as a private citizen and ended his public life. He was much respected by all as having conquered, apportioned and governed the land. He went to Guatemala with his position of Residencia and returned to his home. The children he had were Don Juan de Montejo, who married Doña Isabel a native of Salamanca; Doña Beatriz de Montejo, who married her uncle, his father's first cousin; and Doña Francisca de Montejo, who married Don Carlos de Arellano, a native of Guadalajara. He died after a long illness, having seen all of his children married.

---

busy arbitrating disputes and conducting trials. Although he himself was absolved of most of the serious accusations levied against him, Montejo was found "responsible" for the excesses of the men who reported to him.

[9] This marks the first mention of the Spanish elite engaging in miscegenation, and welcoming mixed-race people into the higher social classes. This Catholic impulse of welcoming others would stand in sharp contrast to the Protestant disdain at the intermingling of the races. Centuries later, for instance, Abraham Lincoln, in the Lincoln-Douglas debates, would characterize Mexico as "a race of mongrels." Did you hear that Barack Obama? Did you hear that Halle Berry?

XVII
Arrival of the Spanish Franciscan Friars in Yucatán. Protection they Dispenses to the First People. Their Struggles with Spanish Civilian Authorities.

Friar Jacobo de Testera, a Franciscan, arrived in Yucatán and began to instruct the [Maya] children. The Spanish soldiers, however, wanted to employ the services of the youths to such an extent that it left no time for them to learn their catechism. They also were angered at the friars for rebuking their wrongs they did toward the First People. As a result of this friar Jacobo returned to Mexico, where he died. Later, Friar Toribio Motolinia sent two friars from Guatemala. Friar Martín de Hojacastro sent other friars from Mexico City. All the friars settled in Campeche and Mérida with the approval of the Admiral and his son Don Francisco. [These friars] built a monastery at Mérida, as has been stated. They undertook to learn the [Maya] language, which was a very difficult task.

The one who learned the best was Friar Luis de Villalpando, who began to learn it through signs and small stones. He reduced it to a certain manner of grammar and wrote a Christian catechism in the language. But he encountered many hindrances, both on the part of the Spaniards who, being absolute masters, wanted everything directed to their own profit and tributes. He also [encountered resistance] on the part of the First People who wanted to continue in their idolatries and debaucheries [of drunken festivals].[10] [Furthermore,] the task [of teaching the Maya] was difficult because of the First People were so scattered through the forests.

The Spaniards [also] resented that the friars built monasteries. The [Spanish colonists] drove the young Maya from their estates in order that they might not go [learn] catechism. On two occasions [the Spaniards] in Valladolid burned the monastery and its church which were constructed of wood and straw. [In consequence] it became necessary for the friars to go and live among the First Peoples. When the Maya of that province rebelled [in protest to the destruction of the monastery and church], they

---

[10] This marks the first documentation of the fundamental conflict between the secular Spanish colonists and the religious missionaries in New Spain. The tensions, and rivalries, between the Church and State would characterize the entire colonial period in Yucatán as well as throughout the whole of New Spain. The rivalries that unfolded became so complicated that among the religious, parish priests grew to resent the Franciscan friars, who were held in higher esteem by the First Peoples and who enjoyed greater influence over the new converts.

wrote to the Viceroy Don Antonio stating it was because of their fondness for the friars [that the Spanish colonists destroyed the monastery and church]. The Viceroy ordered an investigation and [it was] proved that the friars had not yet come into the province at the time of the uprising. [The Spanish colonists] watched [and spied on] the friars at night causing great scandal among the First People. The Spanish colonists pried into the friars' lives and deprived them of alms.

In the face of this [perceived] danger [from the Spanish colonists] the friars sent one of their own to a very distinguished judge, Cerrato, Chief Magistrate of Guatemala, to whom he reported what was happening. The latter, seeing the disorder and unchristian conduct of the Spanish colonists—how they took all the tribute they possibly could against the king's orders, required [the Maya] to provide personal service of every sort of labor even hiring them to transport of burdens [as if they were beasts of burden]—established a specific scale of taxation, which while exhaustive was still tolerable. In it, [these taxes] specified what property belonged to the Maya after he paid his master the tribute due him, rather than everything belonging absolutely to the Spaniards. [The Spanish estate owners] appealed this and out of fear of the tax they took more from the Maya than they had before. They returned once again to the Audiencia [of Guatemala] and also sent an appeal to Spain. They succeeded so far that the Audiencia of Guatemala sent an Auditor [to Yucatán] who established the land tax and abolished personal service. He ordered some [of the Spanish colonists] to marry, breaking up the houses full of women they had. This man was Tomás López who was a lawyer and a native of Tendilla. All this caused [the Spanish colonists] to increase greatly their animosity against the friars. [The Spanish colonists] spread infamous libels against them, and the men ceased to attend masses.

This hatred [between the Spanish colonists and Franciscan friars] caused the First People to harbor goodwill toward the friars. They saw the troubles [the friars] took in order to secure their freedom without a thought to their personal gain. So much did this [goodwill] go that [the First People] undertook nothing without consulting the friars and getting their counsel. And all this aroused further bitterness against the friars on the part of the Spaniards who declared they did all this to govern over all of the Indies for themselves and enjoy all the things they had taken from them [the Spanish colonists].

XVIII
Vices of the First People. The Friars Study the Language of the Land. Their Teachings to the First People. Punishments of the Apostates.

The vices of the First People were idolatry, repudiation of their wives [divorce], public drunkenness, and the buying and selling of slaves. And because the friars kept them from [engaging in these] things they came to hate [the friars]. Apart from the Spanish colonists, however, the ones most averse to the friars were the priests, since they were the class [of the religious] who had lost social standing and privileges.

The method taken for teaching [Christianity to] the First People was to assemble the small children of the families of the community leaders and elite households and establishing [boarding schools] adjacent to the monasteries in residences each town built for this purpose. In each town, all the children were gathered together, and their parents and relatives would bring them food. Then among these children they assembled [the adults] to teach them catechism as well. [As a result of] frequent visits [to see their children and attendance in adult-education classes] many [adults] asked for baptism with much devotion. The children, after being instructed informed the friars of idolatries and licentiousness [among adult members of their families]. [The children] would break up idols, even those belonging to their own fathers. They exhorted divorced women and any orphans that were enslaved [either by the Spanish colonists or the Maya] to avail themselves to the friars. Even when they were threatened by their own [families] they were not deterred. They answered that it was for their honor, since [what they were doing] was for the good of their souls. The Admiral and the king's judges always provided the friars with assistants in gathering the First People for catechism and in punishing those who returned to their old life [of praying to idols]. At first the community leaders were reluctant to hand over their children [to the friars], fearing that they wished to make little slaves of them as the Spanish colonists had done. [In consequence] they sent many young slaves in place of their own children. When they understood[, however,] the arrangement they sent [their own children] with good grace. In this way the children and the others [adults] both made remarkable progress in school [learning to read and write Spanish], and in learning [Catholic] catechism.

They learned to read and write in the Maya language, forming a grammatical system, in order to study it in the same manner as Latin.

They found that six of our letters, specifically D, F, G, Q, R, and S, were not used or needed at all. Others, however, they had to double, and some add some other, in order to understand the many meanings of some words. Consider that *pa* means "to open," and *ppa*, spoken by tightly compressing the lips, means "to break;" tan means "lime," or "ashes," and *than* (*t'an*) spoken forcibly between the tongue and upper teeth means "word," or "to speak," and so forth with other words. Because they had different characters for these things, there was no need for inventing new forms of letters, but only to make use of the Latin ones, common to all. They also gave orders [to the Maya] that they should leave their homes in the forests and gather as formerly in proper communities. In this way, it would be easier to teach them and would alleviate [the difficulties] that the friars encountered [having to travel to them]. To provide [for the friars] they also gave alms during Christmas and at other festivals and [the Maya] also contributed to maintaining the churches through two elder First People who were appointed for the purpose of [collecting donations]. With this [practice] they provided for the needs [of the friars] whenever they went visiting among them and also [provided for the furnishing and] ornamentation of the churches.

After the people had been thus instructed in [the Christian] religion, and the young made good progress as we have said, they were perverted by their priests and community leaders to return to their idolatry. They did this by making sacrifices not only by incense [to their idols], but also of human blood.[11] The friars set up a court of inquiry [or an Inquisition] to review this situation and called upon the Magistrate for aid. [Many Maya] were arrested and put on trial. They celebrated an Auto-da-fé. Many were placed on scaffolds, capped [with conical hats], [their hair] shorn and beaten. Some were [forced to wear] penitential robes for a time. Some of the Maya, out of grief and deluded by the devil, hanged themselves. In general [, however,] they all showed great repentance and willingness to be good Christians.[12]

---

[11] Diego de Landa's claim here is important to his defense of the Inquisition. Under Catholic teachings of the time, unless an individual was a Catholic, he was not subject to the jurisdiction of the Inquisition. Francisco Toral challenged Diego de Landa's assertion that the Maya, upon baptism, were "proper" Catholics, and subject to the jurisdiction of the Inquisition.

[12] Diego de Landa became astounded at the Mayas' awareness that the devil was all around them. He believed Satan had deceived these innocent people and that their practice of human sacrifice was a manifestation of a demonic presence in the Yucatán.

XIX
Arrival of Bishop Toral. The Release of First People Arbitrarily Imprisoned. Landa's Journey to Spain to Justify the Conduct of the Franciscans.

At this point fray Francisco Toral, a Franciscan friar, and a native of Úbeda, who had been for 20 years in Mexico and then was appointed [first] Bishop of Yucatán, arrived at Campeche. He, listening to reports of the charges against the Spaniards [civilian and clerical alike] and the complaints of the Maya, undid the friars' work and ordered the [Maya] prisoners released. The provincial [Diego de Landa, the highest-ranking religious authority in Yucatán,] feeling himself aggrieved [by Toral's actions] determined to go to Spain after first lodging a complaint in Mexico.[13] He thus arrived at Madrid, where the Council of the Indies censured him severely for having usurped the office of bishop and Inquisitor. In defense he asserted the privileges held by his order in those territories by the grant of Pope Adrian [VI] at the request of the emperor and at the support the Royal Audience of the Indies [in Guatemala] ordered he receive as bishop. These defenses infuriated the members of the Council even more and they decided to refer him, and his papers, as well as those which had been sent by the bishop [Toral] against the friars, to fray Pedro de Bobadilla, Provincial of Castile, to whom the king wrote commanding investigation and to render justice. Fray Pedro, being ill, entrusted the examination of the affair to Fray Pedro de Guzmán, who belonged his own [Franciscan] order, a man learned and experienced in inquisitorial matters. The opinions of seven authorities from the kingdom of Toledo were presented to him, namely: Fray Francisco de Medina and Fray Francisco Dorantes, of the Franciscan order; Master Teacher Fray Alonso de la Cruz, an Augustinian friar who had spent 30 years in the Indies; Tomás López, a lawyer who had been an Magistrate in Guatemala in the New Kingdom and a judge in Yucatán; Don Hurtado, professor of canon law; D. Méndez, professor of the Holy Scriptures; and D. Martínez, Scottish professor at Alcalá. These declared that the Provincial [Diego de Landa] had acted correctly in the matter of the Auto-da-fé and other things to castigate the First Peoples. After fray Francisco de Guzmán

---

[13] In this paragraph Diego de Landa refers to himself in the third person.

reviewed the matter, he [Francisco de Guzmán] wrote fully upon it to the Provincial, Fray Pedro de Bobadilla.[14]

The First Peoples of Yucatán deserve that the king should favor them for many things, especially for the willingness they have shown to serve him. When he was occupied in Flanders his sister the princess Doña Juana, who was then regent of the kingdom, wrote a letter asking the assistance of those in the Indies. A Magistrate of Guatemala carried [this request] to Yucatán and, having assembled the community leaders together, he directed a friar to preach about what they owed to his majesty, and what [his majesty] asked of them. When he finished his speech, the First People rose to their feet and said that they recognized their obligation to God for having given them so noble and most Christian a king and how they regretted they did not to live where they might serve him in person. [This notwithstanding, they vowed that despite] their poverty all they had they placed at his [majesty's] service. If that did not suffice, they would sell their children and wives.

---

[14] Diego de Landa was, in effect, prevented from returning to Yucatán, a practice often employed to remove controversial officials who had engaged in improper or scandalous actions.

XX
Manner of Constructing Houses in Yucatán. Obedience and Respect of the First People to Their Community Leaders. Headwear and the Wearing of Garments.

The manner of building their houses was to cover them with an excellent thatch they have in abundance or with the leaves of a palm well adapted to that purpose. Their roofs are very steep slopes to prevent the raining from leaking. Then they build a wall lengthways of the whole house, leaving certain doorways dividing the space into what they call the back of the house, where they keep their beds. The other half they paint white with a very fine whitewash. The community leaders have beautiful frescos on these walls. This part serves for the reception and lodging of guests and has no doorway but is open along the whole length of the house. The eaves drops very low in front as a protection against sun and rain; also, they say, the better to defend themselves against enemies in case of necessity. The common people build the community leaders' dwellings at their own expense. Since the houses have no doors, it is held a serious offense to do any wrong to another's house. They have a small doorway, however, in the back used for household needs. They sleep on beds made of small rods, covered with mats, and with their cloaks of cotton as covering. In the summer they sleep in the front part of the house on the mats, especially the men. Away from their residences the entire village sows the fields of the community leader. The villagers tend them and harvest what is required for their needs and their household. Whenever they hunt and fish or gather salt, they always give a part to the community leader. In these matters everything is always in [held in] common. If the community leader should die, his eldest son would succeed him, but the others [heirs] would always be much respected, favored and held as leaders.

The leading men [of] lower [rank] than community leader are also favored in all these matters depending on who they are, or [depending on] the esteem shown them by the community leader. The priests live by means of their profession and offerings.

The community leaders govern the town, settling disputes, ordering and arranging the affairs of the commonwealths with the help of the leading men. These leading men [of elite families] are much honored and obeyed, especially the wealthy. The community leaders visit them and hold court at their houses for the settlement of matters and business which is principally done at night. Whenever the community leaders leave town they do so with a great company in attendance and the same when they leave their houses.

The First People of Yucatán are people of good physique. They are tall, well-built and of great strength, and they are usually all bow-legged from having been carried astride the mother's hip when they are taken somewhere in their infancy. They consider it elegant to be cross-eyed and this was artificially brought about by the mothers who, in infancy, suspended a small plaster from the hair down between the eyebrows. [As it moved about] they would life their eyes to it [and in time] they finally became cross-eyed. They also had their heads and foreheads flattened by their mothers in infancy. Their ears were pierced for ornaments and much mutilated from the sacrifices.[15] They did not grow beards and say that their mothers were used to scorch their faces with hot cloths to prevent the growth. Nowadays they grow beards, although they are very rough, like hogs' bristles.

They allowed their hair to grow like the women: on top they ringed it, making a good tonsure. In essence, they grow it short on the crown, but long down the sides. They braided their locks and wound around the head, with an end left behind like a tassel. All the men used mirrors, but not the women. To call a man a cuckold they said his wife had put the mirror in his hair behind his head.

They bathed often, not troubling to cover themselves from women, except such as they might do with the hand.

They were fond of perfumes, having bouquets of flowers and fragrant herbs arranged with much care and skill.

They painted their faces and bodies red, which was unflattering, although it seemed handsome to them.

Their clothing was a strip of cloth one hand wide that served for breeches and drawers and which they wrapped several times about the waist. [They did this in such fashion that they] left one end hang in front and one behind. These ends were embroidered by their wives with much care and with feather work. They wore large square cloaks, which they threw over their shoulders. They wore sandals of hemp or deerskin tanned dry, and no other garments.

---

[15] The Maya pierced their ears to draw blood in ritual sacrifices to their gods.

XXI
Food and Drink of the First People of Yucatán.

Their principal food is maize [corn], from which they prepare various dishes and drinks. Even when drunk as [as a porridge as] they do, it serves as both their food and drink. The Maya women put maize to soak overnight in a lime and water [solution] and in the morning it is soft and half-cooked. It is then easier to remove the husk and nib. Next, they grind it on stones and when half ground they make it into great balls and loads for the use of laborers, travelers and sailors. In that form it keeps for several months except that it sours. They will take a lump and thin it in a vessel or gourd formed by the rind of a fruit that grows on a tree whereby God has provided them with vessels. They drink of this preparation and then eat the rest. It is of excellent taste and very nourishing. From the more finely ground maize they obtain a milky liquid and boil it down [to thicken it] over a fire, making a sort of gruel that they drink in the mornings as a hot beverage. What is left over from the morning they pour water for drinking through the day, since they are not accustomed to drink plain water. They also toast the maize, grind it and mix it with water, adding a little pepper or cacao to make a very refreshing beverage.[16]

They make a delicious, frothy beverage out of maize and ground cacao with which they celebrate their festivals. From the cacao they extract a fat [cacao butter] that is much like butter and from this together with maize, they prepare another agreeable and much-esteemed beverage. Yet another beverage is made from the substance of the ground maize, raw [maize paste], which is also fresh and flavorful.

They make many kinds of bread, good and healthful, except that it is not appetizing to eat when cold. This keeps the Maya women busy [because] they have to make it twice a day. They have not learned how to make flour [from corn] that can be kneaded like wheat flour. When they do make it as one makes wheat bread, it is [unsuitable for eating].

They make ragouts of vegetables and venison and of both wild and domesticated birds of which there are many, and of fish which are plentiful. As such, they have good provisions, especially since they are beginning to raise pigs and fowl introduced from Spain.

---

[16] The pepper to which Diego de Landa refers is believed to be allspice (*Pimenta officinalis*), although he also mentions that corn and cacao are combined to make a nourishing porridge.

In the mornings they take their hot drink with pepper [cacao and spices?] as we have mentioned. Throughout the day [they drink] cool beverages and in the evening the cooked ragouts. When they have no meat they make stews of pepper and vegetables. It is not their custom for men and women to eat together, but rather apart, sitting on the floor or at the most with a mat serving for a table. They eat well when they have food, and bear hunger equally well when they do not have [food] getting by on very little.

After eating they wash their hands and rinse their mouths.

XXII
[Body] Painting and Tattooing of the First People. Their Drunkenness, Banquets, Farces, Music and Dancing.

They tattoo their bodies and are considered valiant and brave the more [tattoos] they have, since the process is very painful. In [creating these tattoos] the craftsman first covers the body he wishes [to tattoo] with color and then he delicately pierces the image on the skin, so that the blood and pigment drains [from the incisions] the [permanent] image remains on the body. [Tattooing] is performed a little at a time on account of the pain. People often became ill afterward. The skin often became inflamed and festered [with infection]. Despite this, they ridiculed those who are not tattooed. They flatter themselves on their refinement and the showing of graces and good manners; now they eat and drink as we do [using utensils and tables].

The First People are very dissolute, in drinking and becoming intoxicated. Many ills follow as a result of these excesses. They kill each other, violate their beds (the poor women thinking they are receiving their own husbands), and they mistreat their own fathers and mothers as if they were enemies. They set fire to their houses. They destroy themselves in their drunkenness. When the carousing is general and on occasion of [human] sacrifices all participants contribute to it. When [drunkenness is a] private [affair], the cost is borne by the host with the aid of his relatives. They make a wine [pulque] from honey and water and the root of a certain tree they grow for the purpose. This wine [pulque] is of great strength but has a very disagreeable odor[17]. At their dances and festivities, they eat seated two by two, or in fours. After the meal the wine [pulque] bearers, who abstain and remain sober, help themselves from great bowls until they are overcome and their wives have great trouble in getting their drunken husbands home.

They often spend on one banquet all they have earned in many days of trading or scheming. They have two methods of giving these feasts. In the first of these (given by community leaders and leading men) requires each guest to return an invitation to his host. The host must give each guest a roast bird and cacao beverages in abundance. After the banquet it is the custom to present each [guest] with a cloak to wear, a small stool and the most elegant drinking vessel that the host can afford. If one of the

---

[17] Diego de Landa refers to *pulque*, a fermented alcoholic drink.

guests dies [during the festivities], it is the obligation of his household or relatives to provide the feast he would have owed. The other fashion is among relatives and [these festivities] are given when they marry their children or to commemorate the deeds of their ancestors. This does not require a feast in returned, except that if one has invited scores of individuals to a feast, all are then invited by him when he hosts a banquet or marries his children. They think highly of friendship and remember these invitations even when separated far from each other. At these banquets the drink is served by beautiful women who, after handing the vessel, turn the back on the man until it is emptied.

The First People have amusing ways with entertainment, especially their comic actors who perform with much grace. In fact, they will hire Spaniards for [no other reason] than to observe the jests the Spaniards make of their servants, their wives, and on themselves over their good or bad service [they receive]. Later the Maya performer will imitate [what they observed] in theatrical performances with as much grace [of impersonation] as attentive [as any] Spaniard could.[18] They have small drums which they beat with [an open] hand and another drum [made of] of hollow wood that gives a deep, mournful sound. This [latter drum] they beat with a longish stick at the end of which is a ball of a certain gum that exudes from a tree.[19] They have long, slim trumpets [made] of hollow wood, the end of which is formed of a large twisted gourd. They have another instrument made of a whole turtle with its shells, once the flesh has been removed. This they beat with the palm of the hand, giving a doleful, sad sound.

They have whistles [made] of deer bones, large conches and reed flutes. They accompany the dancers with these instruments. Two of their dances are especially virile and worth seeing. The first one is a game of reeds, which they call *colomché*, the word means ["to play with reeds"]. To perform it they form a large circle of dancers, who are accompanied by music. Keeping in time [with the music] two individuals enter the circle. One of these dances upright, holding a handful of reeds while the other dances squatting. Both keep time with the circle. The one [holding] a bundle of reeds throws them with all his force at the other who with great skill catches them [in midair] with a small rod. After this they are all thrown they return into the circle, keeping time, and others come out to do the same [in their turn]. There is another dance in which 800 [dancers], or more or less, take part. Holding small flags and with music

---

[18] Among the Maya, theater involves comic imitations, farces, mimicking and cross-dressing. Performances mock the vanities of their leaders and elites.

[19] Diego de Landa is describing rubber from the rubber tree, which was unknown in Europe.

and long steps they perform [a kind of] Great War dance. This they perform without one being out of step. They dance very slowly and they do not cease [to rest] dancing for the entire day. Food and drink are brought to them. It is not their custom that men dance with women.

XXIII
Industry, Commerce and Currency. Agriculture and Seeds. Justice and Hospitality.

Among the occupations of the First People were pottery and wood-working craftsmen. They earned much from forming idols of clay and wood, for they observed many fasts and many [religious] rituals. There were also physicians, or better said, sorcerers, who treated people through the use of herbs and many superstitious. It was also the same with all their other professions. The occupation they favored most was being a merchant, trading in salt, clothing and slaves from the regions of Ulúa and Tabasco. In their transactions they used cacao and stone counters [beads] for money with which they bought slaves and other fine and beautiful stones which the community leaders wore as jewels on festive occasions. They also used certain red seashells they used both as currency and wore as jewels. They carried these shells in knitted purses. In their markets they traded in many products of the region. They gave credit, lent and paid promptly and without charging interest. The most common occupation was [family farming] agriculture and the cultivation of maize and the other seeds. These they kept in well-constructed granaries and cribs for sale in due time. Their mules and oxen were the people themselves. For each married man and his wife it was their custom to sow an area comprised of 400 feet (approximately 135 meters) which was called *hum uinic* [meaning, "one person"]. A [standard] plot measured with a 20-foot (approximately 7 meters) rod, 20-foot (approximately 7 meters) in breadth and 20-foot (approximately 7 meters) in length.

The First People have the generous custom of helping one another in all their work. At the time of planting, those who have no people of their own to help them are joined together by others in groups of 20, more or less. All labor together to complete the task [assigned to] each, all duly measured. They do not rest until all the tilling is completed. The lands today are held in common and whoever occupies a place first, possesses it. They sow crops in different places, so that if the crop fails in one area, another will compensate elsewhere. When they work the land they do little more than gather the brush and burn it before sowing. From the middle of January through April they tend the land and then sow it when the rains come. They carry a small sack over their shoulders they make a hole in the ground with a pointed stick, dropping five or six seeds, covering them with the same stick. When it rains, it is frightening to see how [the plants] grow. In hunting, they likewise unite in bands comprised of 50 men, or more or less. The meat of the deer they roast over sticks to keep it from spoiling. Upon returning to town they first make bestow gifts to the community leader and then distribute all as between friends. They do the same with the fishing catch.

When visiting others the First People always take a gift according to their station [and means]. The one visited responds with another gift. During these visits other persons [who are] present speak and listen attentively to those talking. They have due regard for their social rank; although they all address one another as "thou." Those of lower rank must, however, in the course of the conversation, repeat the title or position of the one higher in rank. When speaking, they have the custom of assisting one who brings a message by responding with a cadence of the voice, a sort of breathing or aspiration in the throat, as if to say "and then," or "and so." The women are brief in what they say and are not in the habit of negotiating on their own account, especially if poor. For this [reason] the community leaders scoffed at the friars for listening to poor and rich without distinction.

Offenses committed by one [community] against another were redressed by the community leader of the town seeking that justice to be rendered by the town of the aggressor. If this was refused it became the cause for more trouble. If they were of the same town they presented their case before the judge who arbitrated [the dispute] and ordered a satisfactory solution. If the offender lacked the means for this, his relatives or friends helped him out [with compensation]. The cases in which they were accustomed to demand amends [or compensation] were in instances of involuntary manslaughter; the suicide of either husband or wife occasioned by other's fault; the accidental burning of homes; and disputes over lands of inheritance, beehives or granaries. Other injuries committed with malice [wickedness] were settled through blood or fighting.

The Yucatecans are most generous and hospitable. No one enters their homes without being offered food and drink. Guests are offered drink during the day or food in the evening.[20] If they have none, they ask of their neighbors. And when they encounter one another on the road, all join in sharing what they have, even if they have little for their own need as a result.

---

[20] This marks the first time that the people who live in Yucatán are called "Yucatecans," a different ethnic group from the "Mexicans."

XXIV
Method of Counting of the Yucatecans. Genealogies. Inheritances and the Welfare of Orphans. Succession of the Community Leaders.

They count by fives up to 20, by 20s up to a 100, and by 100s to 400; then by 400s up to 8,000. This method of counting is used in the buying and selling of cacao [beans]. They have other very long counts, extended to ad infinitum, counting 20 times 8,000, or 160,000; then they multiply this 160,000 again by 20, and continue so until they reach an uncountable figure.[21] They make their calculations on the ground or a flat surface.

They make much of knowing the origin of their lineages, especially if they belong to one of the houses of Mayapán. This they can learn from their priests, since [genealogy is] one their sciences. They boast much if a man of their lineages has distinguished himself. The father's name is passed on to his sons, but not to his daughters. Sons and daughters both are called by the name of their father and their mother, the father's as the proper name, and the mother's as the given one. And so, the son of *Chel* and *Chan* was called *Na-Chan Chel*, meaning the son of these people. For this reason the First People consider all who have the same name as relatives, and treat them accordingly. [In consequence, it is the custom that] when they go to a part of the land where they are unknown and find themselves in need, they will quickly make their names known, and if there are any who bear the same name, they will receive and treat them with goodwill and affection. Also no man or woman married another of the same name, because this was considered a great wickedness. Today they use their baptismal names, and their own [pre-Christian names].

Daughters did not inherit equally with their brothers, except out of pity or goodwill, in which case they received something, with the balance being divided equally among the brothers. The exception [existed] where one [son] had done more in the accumulation of property, in which case he received his reward before the division [of the balance of the estate]. If the children were all female, then the cousins or other nearest male kin inherited. In cases where the heir was not of sufficient age to receive the property, they entrusted it to the nearest male relative as guardian or tutor. [This trustee] supplied the mother with what she needed for his bringing up; for it was not their custom to place any property under the

---

[21] This astounded the Spaniards who were accustomed to the practice of the ancient Greeks who described anything larger than 10,000 as "infinite."

mother's control. Moreover, [on occasion] they even removed the children from her care, especially when the trustees were the brothers of the deceased. When the heirs reached their majority, the guardians turned over to them the property; if this was not done it was considered a great injustice and became the reason of violent quarrels. The transfer was made in the presence of the community leaders and leading men, deducting what had been spent for their care. The heirs received nothing from the harvests, or the products of the hives or cacao trees, because of the labor involved in maintaining them.

When the community leader died, if he left no sons of age to succeed him but left brothers, it was the eldest or most capable one who ruled. [During this regency] the heir was educated in the customs, the ceremonies, and everything he would need to know when he became of age. These brothers, even when the heir was ready to govern, still controlled the affairs throughout his life. Should there be no brothers [of the deceased community leader], the priests and leading men chose a man capable to be entrusted with this position.

XXV
Marriages. Divorces Are Frequent Among the Yucatecans. Nuptial Customs.

In previous times they married at the age of 20, but now they do so at of 12 or 13. For this reason they divorce more readily, because they marry without love, or ignorant of [the demands of] married life and the duties of married men. If their parents could not persuade them to return to their wives, they would find them another, and then another and another. Men with children left their wives with equal ease and no fear lest another [man] might take them as wives, or that they themselves might later return to them. Nevertheless, they are very jealous, and do not tolerate infidelity on their wives' part lightly. Now that they see how the Spaniards kill their wives for this reason [of adultery], they are beginning to mistreat and even to kill them [their own wives for infidelity]. In cases of divorce, small children remained with their mothers, while older boys went with their father, but the girls remained with their mother.

Although divorce was so common and familiar a thing, the elders and those of better customs [disapproved of it], and there were many who never had but a single wife. They did not marry one bearing their own name on the father's side, for this was considered a wicked thing. It was considered equally wrong for a man to marry his sister-in-law, or the widow of a brother. Neither did they marry their stepmothers, their wives' sisters, nor their mother's sisters (aunts). All these [marriages] were considered wrong. They could marry all other kinsmen on their mother's side, even first cousins, [practices that were] held legitimate.

The fathers took great care to seek [suitable] wives for their sons, [who were] of equal rank and position. It was regarded as undignified for men to seek their own wives, as well as for the parents of the woman to make advances. In these matters they left the negotiations in the charge of other persons to attend; these terms thus negotiated [included] discussions regarding the dowry or the settlement, which was not large. The young man's father made payment to the prospective father-in-law, while the girl's mother prepared garments for the bride and for the groom. When the day of the marriage arrives, they all assemble at the house of the fiancée's father, where a meal had been prepared. The guests meet with the young couple and their relatives; the priest makes sure they are both in agreement to the marriage and that they have given the matter all due consideration. [The priest] makes sure the girl's parents have considered the young man [suitable for their daughter]. If settled, [the young man is given the young woman and he would] receive her that night; and after [this communal affirmation], the banquet and celebrations take place. From that day forward, the son-in-law remained at his father-in-law's house for five or six years, working for him. If he did not do this, he was driven from the house. Mothers made sure the [young] wife provided her husband with his food, which was a sign of marriage. Marriages between widowers and widows took place without any feasts or ceremonies. The man simply went to the woman's house, was admitted and given to eat, and with this it was then a marriage. The result of this was that they separated as easily as they came together. The Yucatecans never took more than a single wife, although in other places [of New Spain the First Peoples] frequently took many wives at the same time. On occasion, parents contracted marriages for their children even when they were youngsters, and [these families] regarded each other as parents-in-law until their children came of age [and married].

Baptism is not found in any part of the Indies save here in Yucatán. It is even called a word meaning "to be born anew" or a second time, the same as the Latin *renascer*. In the language of Yucatán *zihil* means "to be born anew" or "a second time," but only in composition: *caputzihil* means "to be reborn."

We have not been able to learn the origin of baptism, only that it is a custom they have always used and for which they have had such devotion that no one fails to receive it. They had such reverence for it that those who are sinful, or who knew they were about to commit a sin, were required to confess to the priest in order to receive baptism. They had such faith in this ceremony that they would never repeat the sin. They believed that with it, however, they acquired a predisposition to engage in good conduct and ways and [enjoy] protection against being harmed by demons in their earthly matters.[22] [They believed] that through [baptism] and by living a good life they would gain paradise in the hereafter, like that of Mahomet, which consisted of enjoying plentiful eating and drinking. This was their custom for preparing for baptism: women raised the children to the age of three. They placed a large white branch on the heads of the boys, fastened to the tonsure on their heads. The girls wore a thin cord with a small seashell tied to cover their private parts. It was considered a sin and disgraceful to remove these two items until the time of the baptism, which was performed between the ages of three and twelve. They never married before baptism. When one wished to have his child baptized, he went to see the priest and made his request known to him. The priest then announced it to the community. The day was chosen, which they made sure would be a good omen. When this was done, the supplicant, responsible for giving the banquet, selected, at his discretion, some leading man of the community to assist him in the matter. It was customary to choose four other old and honored men to assist the priest on the day of the ceremony. They were chosen with the priest's counsel. Those selected involved the fathers of all the children eligible to receive baptism, since the ceremony was the concern of all. The men chosen were called *chacs*. For the three days prior to the

---

[22] Diego de Landa speaks of the beliefs, both among the Maya and the Spaniards, that the world was filled with "demons" who enticed humanity to sinful ways on a daily basis.

ceremony, the fathers of the children, along with the officials, fasted and abstained from [sexual relations with] their wives.

On the day, they all gathered at the house of the one giving the feast and assembled all the children who were to be baptized. They placed them in the court or courtyard of the house, which had been all cleaned and scattered with fresh leaves; the boys together in a line on one side, and the girls the same on the other side. An elder woman acted as matron for the girls, and a man was placed in charge of the boys.

When this was done the priest proceeded to the purification of the house, casting out the devil. To accomplish this, he placed four small benches in the four corners of the courtyard, on which the four chacs sat, connected to each other with a long cord tied in such manner that the children were confined in the middle. Then the parents, who had fasted, entered the enclosure by stepping over the cord. Either before or after, they placed another bench in the middle for the priest to sit on. He carried a brazier and a little ground maize and incense. Then the boys and girls approached him in a line, and he put a little of the ground maize and incense into the hand of each one. They threw it into the brazier. This done, they took up the brazier and the cord held by the chacs. They also poured a little wine [pulque] in a drinking vessel and then gave it all to a celebrant to carry away from the village, warning him not to drink the wine [pulque] or to look behind him on his return. They said that in this manner the devil had been exorcised. They then swept the courtyard and took away the leaves, which were of a tree called *cihom*, and scattered other leaves, these of a tree called *copó*. They laid down mats while the priest changed his ceremonial attire. He returned dressed in a tunic embroidered with red feathers and long plumes hanging from the edges. He wore on his head a sort of cone decorated with the same feathers. Beneath his tunic were strips of cotton ribbons like tails. He held a water sprinkler made of a short, richly carved rod and the tassels of certain serpents like rattlesnakes. He bore, neither more nor less, the dignity of a pope about to crown an emperor. The awesome serenity was a marvel to behold. Then the chacs approached the children and placed on the heads of each one white cloths that their mothers had brought for the purpose. They asked of the oldest ones [first] if they had committed any sin, or [engaged] in lewd conduct. Any who had done so confessed their [trespasses] and were separated from the others.

This done, the priest called on all to be silent and seated. He then blessed the children, with many incantations, and he sanctified them with sprinkles [of water], all with great serenity. After this benediction, he sat himself down. The man the parents had chosen as director of the feast took a bone the priest had given him, went to the children, and tapped each one with it nine times on the forehead. Then he dipped the bone in a jar of water he carried on his person and anointed them on the forehead, the face, and between the fingers of their hands and the bones of their feet, without saying a word. This water was scented with certain flowers and ground cacao, dissolved in "virgin water," as they call it, taken from the hollows of trees or of rocks in the forest.

After this anointment the priest stood and removed the white cloths from their heads as well as others they wore over their shoulders that contained a few feathers of very beautiful birds and some cacao beans, all of which one of the chacs had collected. Then, using a stone knife, the priest cut off the small beads each of the boys had worn on their heads. After this, the priest's assistants brought a bouquet of flowers and a pipe such as the Maya used for smoking. With these, they threatened each child nine times. Then they gave each child the bouquet to smell and the pipe to smoke. After this they gathered the presents the mothers had brought, which consisted of foods to eat, and gave these to each child to eat there. Then they brought out a fine chalice of wine [pulque] and offered the remaining gifts [of food and wine] to the deities, entreating them with devout prayers to receive this small gift on behalf of the children. They then handed this chalice to another official, called *cayom*, so that he might empty it at a single sitting; it was considered a sin if he took a break to catch his breath.

When this [ceremony] was done, the girls took their leave first, after their mothers removed the cord and seashells they had worn about the hips in sign of their virginity. This was a sign that they could [now] be married, whenever their parents thought best. Then the boys took their leave. The fathers approached the pile of cloaks they had brought and distributed them with their own hands to the assistants and the officials. The ceremony then concluded with a long [feast of] eating and drinking. This banquet was called *em-ku*, which means "the descent of the deity." Then the one who had been responsible for and borne the cost of the celebrations, in addition to the three previous days of abstinence and fast, was now required to continue [in abstinence and fasting] for yet other nine days; this was observed inviolably.

XXVII
Kind of Confessions Among the First Peoples. Abstinences and Superstitions. Diversity and Abundance of the Idols. Duties of the Priests.

The Yucatecans naturally knew when they had done wrong, and because they believed that death, disease, and misfortunes would befall them because of wrongdoing and sin, they had the custom, when these things visited them, of confessing to their priests. As such, when they feared death from illness or from another cause was at hand, they would confess their sins, and if they neglected to do so, their nearest relatives or friends would remind them of it. They would then [avail themselves] and confessed their sins to the priest if he was available; or if not, then [they would confess] to their mothers and fathers, women to their husbands, and the men to their wives.

The sins of which they commonly accused themselves were theft, homicide, of the flesh, and bearing false witness; in this way they considered themselves to be saved. Many times, after they had escaped death [or recovered from an illness], there were quarrels between spouses, or with others, because of any dishonor they had brought on them, or with others who had been the cause [of their sinning].

Men confessed their transgressions, except those committed with their female slaves, should they have any, since they held it a man's right to dispose of his own property as he wished. They did not confess sins of intention [and not yet committed], although they considered these as evil, and in their counsels and sermons advised against them.

When abstaining, they refrained from consuming salt and pepper in their meals, something that was difficult for the men. In some of the fasts observed for their festivals they neither ate meat nor did they have sexual relations with their wives.

Those widowed did not marry for a year thereafter, nor did widows or widowers have sexual relations with either another man or a woman during this time. Those who violated this custom [of celibacy] were deemed intemperate, and they believed some ill would befall them.

During some fasts for their celebrations they would neither eat meat nor have sexual relations with their wives. They undertook their duties for these fasts as solemnly as their civic obligations [to the state], and some fasts were so long they lasted three years, and it was a grave sin to break them.

They were so devoted to their idolatrous practices that in times of necessity even the women and youths and maidens understood that it was incumbent on them to burn incense and pray to a deity that they be freed from evil and overcome the demon that caused it.

Even some travelers along the roads carried incense with them, and a little plate on which to burn it. As such, at night, wherever they arrived [to rest] they were able to set up three small stones [as an offering], placing a little incense on each. They placed three flat stones in front of these, on which they burned incense, praying to the deity they called Ek-chuah that he bring them safely back to their homes. They performed this ceremony every night until they returned home, unless there was someone else, or even more [individuals], who could do this on their behalf.

They had a great number of idols and many temples that were, in their own style, sumptuous. In addition to these public temples, their community leaders, priests, and elite families also had shrines and idols in their houses for their private offerings and prayers. They held Cuzmil and the [sacred] well at Chicheniza in such great veneration as we [ourselves] have in our pilgrimages to Jerusalem and Rome. They embarked on pilgrimages to offer gifts, especially at Cuzmil, as we do at our holy places. When they did not [themselves] make a pilgrimage they sent offerings. Those who made the journey had the habit, upon passing an abandoned temple, of entering to pray and burn copal incense.

They have so many idols that their deities were not enough for them. There was no animal or reptile of which they did not make graven images, and in the form of their deities. They had a few idols of stone; others more numerous of wood; but the greatest number by far were of terra-cotta. The wooden idols were especially esteemed; they were passed down as the most valuable part of an inheritance. They had no metal statues because there are no metals in the land. Regarding these graven images, they knew perfectly well that they were made by human hands, perishable, and not divine; but they were much revered because of what they represented. There were many ceremonies and rituals associated with their fabrication, especially the wooden ones.

The most idolatrous of them were the priests, the *chilanes*, sorcerers, physicians, *chacs*, and *nacones*. It was the obligation of the priests to deal in and teach their sciences; to anticipate calamities and to identify remedies for them; to preach during the festivals; to officiate during sacrifices; and to administer their sacraments. The *chilanes* were responsible for announcing to all those in their town the oracles of the deity; they were held in such esteem that, when they left their homes, they were carried upon litters borne on the shoulders [of townspeople].

The sorcerers and physicians cured the area afflicted through bleeding [by incisions or leeches] and would cast lots for divination in performing their work in this and other matters.

The *chacs* comprised four old men, specially elected on occasion, to assist the priest in carrying out celebrations and festivals properly. The *nacones* consisted of two officials: one was permanent and carried little honor, since it was his obligations to cut open the chests of those who were sacrificed; the other was a leader chosen to serve as a general for the wars and to preside over certain festivals. This office was for a three-year period and was held in great honor.

XXVIII
Sacrifices and Self-Mortifications, both Cruel and Obscene, Among the Yucatecans. Human Victims Slain by Arrow, and Others.

At times the men made sacrifices of their own blood, cutting all around their ear[lobes] in strips that they left as a sign [of their devotion]. On other occasions they pierced their cheeks or lower lips, made incisions in other parts of the body, or would pierce the tongue from side to side and pass straw through the incisions, causing themselves extreme pain. At times, they cut away the superfluous part of the member [foreskin], leaving the flesh in the form of shreds, as was the case of their ears. It was this [sacrificial] custom that led the historian of the Indies to claim incorrectly that they practiced circumcision.[23]

On other occasions they practiced a foul and tedious sacrifice. The participants assembled in a line at the temple, and each pierced hole though his penis, across from side to side, and then passed a cord of considerable quantity—as much as they could stand—until all the participants were fastened and strung together. They then collected blood from each participant and anointed the statue of the devil [with the collected blood]. The more a man participated [in this ritual, and the more he] could endure, the more valiant he was considered. Their sons began to accustom themselves to this suffering from an early age; it is frightful to see how zealous they were into this practice.

Women engaged in no similar bloodletting ritual, although they were very devout [to their idols]. They would, however, use the blood of every kind of animal obtainable, from birds of the sky, animals of the earth, fishes of the sea, and would anoint the face of the demon [idols]; they also made offerings of whatever other thing they had [such as food and drink on altars]. They would remove the hearts of some animals and offer them [as sacrifices]; other [animals] were offered whole, some living, some dead, some raw, some cooked. They also made large offerings of bread [cooked maize] and wine [pulque] and of all the kinds of food and drink they prepared.

To make these sacrifices [and offerings], there were certain tall, decorated posts erected in the courtyards of the temples. Near the stairway of these temples there were broad, round pedestals, and in the

---

[23] Diego de Landa speaks of body modification, which remains a cult practice in our times, particularly among contemporary enthusiasts of the "modern primitive" movement.

middle of each [one there was] a stone, somewhat slender, four or five palms in height (approximately 16.5 inches or 425 millimeters), was set up. At the top of the temple stairs there was another similar such pedestal.

Apart from the festivals, which were solemnized by sacrificing animals, the priests or *chilanes* demanded the sacrifice of human beings during times of great tribulation or need. [It was custom] for all to contribute for this purpose, for the purchase of slaves [to be sacrificed]. Some, out of devotion, gave their young children. The [sacrificial] victims were feted [and indulged] until the day of the sacrifice, but [throughout this time, they were] carefully guarded to prevent their running away or defiling themselves through any carnal acts. Then, while they were taken from town to town [throughout the region and feted] with dances, the priests, the *chilanes* and the officials fasted.

When the day of the ceremony arrived, they gathered in the courtyard of the temple. If they were to be sacrificed with arrows, they were stripped naked and anointed with blue paint, with a cone-shaped cap placed on their heads. After a ceremony to cast out the devil, the community members, holding bows and arrows, performed a solemn dance with [the sacrificial victim] around a wooden pole. They tied the victim to the pole, still dancing, watching [him or her] as the victim was secured. The unholy priest ventured forward dressed in robes, approached the victim, and, whether it was a man or a woman, [used an arrow] to pierce the victim in the private parts with it. He then came down [from a stool] and anointed the face of the demon [idol] with the blood he had drawn. Then, making a sign to the dancers, they began, in an orderly fashion, to shoot an arrow aiming for the victim's heart, which was highlighted by a white mark, as they quickly passed, dancing. In this manner, the [victim's] chest soon resembled a single point, like a hedgehog of arrows.

If [the victim's sacrifice was to have his or her] heart removed, they brought him or her to the courtyard amid a great display and with a large company of people. They painted [the victim] blue and put a cone-shaped cap on his or her head, and then placed [the victim] on the rounded sacrificial stone altar. Then the priest and his assistants anointed the stone with blue paint and purified the temple by driving out the devil. The *chacs* then seized the poor victim and swiftly laid him or her on his or her back across the stone, and the four [*chacs*] secured the victim's arms and legs, spreading them out. Then the *nacón* executioner arrived and, with a flint knife in his hand, very skillfully made an incision between the ribs on the left side, below the nipple. He then plunged in his hand and, like a ravenous tiger, tore out the living heart, which he laid on a plate and gave to the priest. The priest then quickly went and anointed the faces of the idols with that fresh blood.

On occasion they performed this sacrifice on the stone pedestal located on the top step of the temple, and then they would let the dead body roll down the steps, where it was retrieved by attendants, and the corpse was flayed, except for the hands and feet. [If this was done,] the priest would then strip naked and would wrap himself in the skin [of the victim], and he would be joined by [the other attendants] and dance. This was a ceremony of solemnity for participants. The victims sacrificed in this manner were commonly buried in the courtyard of the temple itself. But on occasion [in times of famine] it happened that they ate the flesh, distributing portions to the community leaders and for others in attendance, should there be enough. The hands, feet, and head were [set aside] for the priests and officials. The victims sacrificed in this manner were considered as sainted [or sanctified]. In cases where the sacrificial victims were slaves seized in war, their masters were given the bones, and these would be displayed as insignia of victory during their dances. On occasion they threw the living victims into the well at Chichenitzá, believing that they would return on the third day, although they never appeared again [having drowned in the cenote, a natural sink hole].

XXIX
Arms of the Yucatecans. Military Leaders. Militia and Soldiers. Customs of War.

They had offensive and defensive weapons. The offensive ones consisted of bows and arrows carried in their quivers, tipped either with flints or very sharp fish teeth. They could shoot with great skill and force. The bows were made of a beautiful tawny wood, marvelously strong and more straight than curved. The strings consisted of [indigenous] hemp fibers. The length of the bow is always somewhat less than that of the person who carries it. The arrows are made of slender reeds that grow in tshe lagoons, and more than five palms long [approximately 21 inches or 525 millimeters]. They fasten a thin piece of very strong wood to the cane into which the flint is inserted. They do not know or use poisons [by dipping the tips of their arrows in it], although poison is available in abundance. They had hatchets of a certain metal and of this shape, fastened in a wood handle. These served them both as weapons in war and also for woodworking at home. The metal is soft, allowing them to sharpen it by pounding it with a stone. They had short spears, a man's height in length (5 feet 2 inches or 1.75 meters), topped with heads made of very hard flint. Apart from these they had no other weapons.

To defend themselves, they had round shields made of tightly woven split reeds, and covered with deerskin. They wore protective quilted cloaks [tunics] made of brine-soaked cotton; its padding was two layers thick, which were very strong. Some of the leaders and captains wore helmets constructed of wood, but this was not common. With these weapons, adorned with feathers and skins of tigers and lions [jaguars and ocelots], when they had them, they went to war. They always had two captains, one permanent whose position was inherited; the other was elected for three years with a great deal of ceremony. This latter captain was selected to celebrate the festivals of the month Pax, which corresponds to 12 May; or as commander of the men recruited for [a specific] war [or battle].

This captain was called *nacón* and during these three years he was forbidden to have relations with women, not even with his own wife, nor could he eat meat. They looked upon him with great respect and supplied him with fish and iguanas, which are a kind of edible lizard. He did not become intoxicated [with alcohol] during this time, and the vessels and household articles for his use were kept separate. No woman was placed in his service [as a servant]; he did not mingle much with the townsfolk.

After his three years of service, he returned to his regular [civilian] life.

These two captains handled matters for wars and organized everything [in launching a war or defending themselves when attacked]. [To accomplish this] were men chosen as soldiers, and when the need arose, they presented themselves with their arms. These [citizen soldiers] were called the *holcanes*, and if there were not enough of them, others were recruited. These drafted soldiers were then given orders and divided [between the two captains]. They would march off from their community, led by a lofty banner they carried, but in complete silence. They did [this in order] to take their enemies by surprise, [and when they came upon them] they attacked, with great war cries and without mercy.

Along the roads and trails, the enemy mounted defenses manned by archers, and barricades constructed of stakes and trees, and more often of stone [walls]. After a victory they cut off the jawbones from the dead, and, removing the flesh from them, they wore them on their arms. They made great offerings of the spoils in these wars. If they had captured a man of great renown, they promptly sacrificed him, not to leave alive those [educated or wealthy enough] who could later conspire against them. The rest became war captives and belonged to [the soldiers] who had captured them.

These *holcanes* received no salary except in time of war, and then when they were given any money it was from the captains. This was not much because it came from [the captains'] own funds; if they lacked enough money, then the townsfolk helped them. The community also supplied [the soldiers with] food, which the women prepared for them, and which they carried on their backs since they lacked pack animals. As a result, wars were of short duration. After the war, the battle spirit endured, and the soldiers, under this pretext, burdened the townsfolk, demanding to be serviced and regaled. If any had successfully killed some captain or leader he was greatly honored and feted [as a war hero].

XXX
Penalties and Punishments for Adulterers, Homicides, and Thieves. Education of the Young Men. Custom of Flattening the Heads of Children.

These people had the custom, inherited from the [traditions of] Mayapán, to punish adulterers in the following manner: when an investigation had been made and a man was convicted of adultery, the leading men assembled at the community leader's house. The adulterer, tied to a stake, was brought to him and then handed over to the husband of the woman. If he pardoned him he was set free; if not, he killed him by dropping, from a height, a large stone on his head. For the woman, infamy was a sufficient punishment, which was [considered] a great [shame]; husbands commonly abandoned wives for this [adultery].

The penalty for homicide, even when involuntary [manslaughter], was death imposed by the relatives [of the deceased], unless the murderer was able to compensate monetarily for the death. A thief had to reimburse the value [of what he stole] and was then enslaved, however small the theft. For this reason they had so many slaves, especially in times of hunger. Because of this [fact] we, the friars, exerted such effort to baptize them, that they might [forgive them] and grant them liberty. If the thief was one of the leaders or from an elite family, having seized [the delinquent], they assembled together. Then the culprit was scarified on both sides of his face from the chin to the forehead, which they considered a major dishonor.

Young men had great respect for their elders and took their advice. Elders boasted of being old and wished to pass [along their wisdom]. Elders told the young of what they had experienced [in life], which the young believed. If young men followed their counsel, the elder was even more respected [by the community]. Such was the respect bestowed on elder men that the youths did not socialize with them, but availed themselves of them in times of great importance, such as when they were about to enter into marriage. [Young men] also seldom socialized with married couples. [In consequence] it was the custom to have, in each town, a large building, whitewashed and open on all sides, where young men gathered for their pastimes. They played ball and a certain game similar to dice using knucklebones, and many others. They nearly always slept here [in this hall], together, until they married.

And although I have heard it said that in other parts of the Indies [young men who lived in communal housing] were guilty of unnatural offenses [homosexual acts] in these houses, I have not learned of their doing this in this country, nor do I believe they did so. [I say] this because they say that those addicted to this foul vice care nothing for women, and these people did. [In fact,] it was their habit to bring whores to these places and make use of [their services]. It is said that among them the miserable creatures who took up this mode of life [of prostitution], although they were paid [for their services by the young men], were so beset by the number of the youths [requesting their services] that they were harassed to [the point of] dying.[24]

Young men painted their bodies black before marriage and did not tattoo themselves, except slightly, until after [marriage]. [When not socializing among themselves] they were always accompanied their fathers, and in consequence they became as great idolaters as [their fathers]. [Young men also] helped [their fathers] carry out most of their labors [and work].

The [Maya] women raised their children both harshly and kept them entirely naked. Four or five days after the child was born they laid the infant on a small bed made of rods, facedown, and put the child's head between two pieces of board, one on the back [of the head] and the other on the forehead. They then tied [the boards] tightly and left the child suffering for several days until the head, squeezed [in such fashion], became permanently flattened, as is their custom. This, however, caused so much pain and [posed such] danger to the poor infants that they at times risked death. [This] writer witnessed [an instance in which] the head was pressed [so tightly the skull burst at the] back of the ears, which must have happened to many [other infants].

They were brought up completely naked until the age of four or five years, when they gave them a sleeping wrap [blanket] and strips of cloth to cover themselves as their fathers did; the little girls also began to cover themselves from the waist down. They were breastfed [for an extended period], for mothers gave them milk as long as they could, even if four or five years old. As a result [the Maya] counted among them so many robust people.

For the first two years they grew up wonderfully pretty and plump. After this time, because of their mother's constant bathing of them and the heat of the sun, they became tanned.[25] But throughout the whole of

---

[24] Long considered and exaggeration by Diego de Landa, recent research confirms the presence of certain chemicals in cacao that heighten human sexual response in both men and women, one reason the Maya have a reputation of being a randy ethnic group among the First Peoples of Mesoamerica.

[25] Diego de Landa describes the mistaken European belief that daily bathing washed off protective natural oils from the body, resulting in the darkening of the skin. Among the

their childhood they were attractive and mischievous, never ceasing to go about without bows and arrows and playing with each other. And so they grew up until adolescence and they began to behave as youths, taking on a more serious demeanor and leaving children's things [behind them].

Spaniards, heliophobia, fear of being darkened by the sun, endured until the first half of the twentieth century.

XXXI
Clothing and Ornaments of the Maya Women.

The Maya women of Yucatán are, in general, of better build than Spanish women, larger and better formed. They lack the wide hips of black women.[26] Those who are beautiful are quite proud of it, and indeed they are not unattractive. They are not fair-skinned, which is caused more by their constant bathing and by the sun than [by being] naturally [dark]. They do not powder their faces as our [own] women do, for they consider this immodest. They are in the habit of filing their teeth, leaving them like the teeth on a saw, which they consider elegant. This is done for them by the older women, who use certain stones and water.

They pierce the cartilage of the noses [nostrils], in order to place an amber stone for adornment. They also pierce their ears to wear ornaments, in the fashion of their husbands. They tattoo their bodies from the waist up, except for their breasts, out of concern for breastfeeding. The [tattoo] patterns are more delicate and beautiful than those of the men. They bathe frequently, like the men, in cold water, but with little modesty, [often] going stripped naked to the wells where they go for water. They also bathe in hot water, heated by an open fire. This is done, however, for health reasons rather than cleanliness.

Their custom is to rub themselves with a red ointment, not unlike their husbands. Those who can afford it use an odoriferous and very sticky gum that I take to be liquid amber [a genus of five species of flowering plants in the family *Altingiaceae*], which they call *istahté*. They apply this ointment to a sort of briquette-like soap, decorated with elegant designs, and apply it to their breasts, arms, and shoulders, until they are very elegant and sweet-smelling, or so they believe. If the ointment is of good quality, it lasts a long time without wearing off.

They wear the hair very long, which they used to and still do, and they arrange it in very fine braids, parted down the center, and the [resulting] coiffure is a very becoming fashion. When the young girls are to be married, their mothers go to such pains in arranging their hair and are so skilled that I have seen many with their coiffures as fine as those of the most fashionable Spanish women. The little girls, until they become adolescents, wear theirs in two or four braids that suit them well.

The [Maya] women of the coast, in the province of Bacalar and of Campeche, are more modest in their dress; for in addition to skirts that

---

[26] Diego de Landa uses the term "negress" which, like "negro," is now considered an archaic term.

they wear from the waist down, they cover the breasts with a double cloth fastened below the armpits. As for the others, their sole garment is a long, wide sack, open at the sides, reaching to the hips and fastened together at the ends. They had no other article of clothing, apart from the [nightgown] in which they always sleep. When they travel, they carry this folded and rolled up, and covered.

XXXII
Chastity and Education of the Female First People of Yucatán. Their Chief Qualities and Their Household Economy. Their Devotion and the Special Observances at the Time of Childbirth.

The women prided themselves on being chaste, and with reason, because before they knew our nation [of Spain], as their elders lament, they were extremely virtuous. I shall provide two instances [of what they mean]. Captain Alonso López de Ávila, father-in-law of the Admiral Montejo, captured a handsome and graceful [Maya] girl during the war at Bacalar. She, fearing that she would not be slain in the war, promised her husband that she would never surrender herself to another man. For this reason [of keeping her word to her husband] nothing, even the fear of death, could persuade her otherwise to consent [to surrender herself]. For this reason, he [Alonso López de Ávila] had her thrown to the dogs.

I once received complaints from a [Maya] woman I was about to baptize. She complained against a baptized man who followed her relentlessly for her beauty. After she had repeatedly rejected his overtures, to no avail, he came one night when her husband was away. He pleaded with her and offered gifts, all without success. When these overtures failed, he, being a big, strong man, attempted to force himself upon her, and for the entire night she fought him off. The only thing he gained was incurring her wrath to such a degree that she came to me to complain of this man's wickedness. This was her complaint.

The women were in the habit of turning their shoulders toward the men they encountered in passing [on the streets] and of turning to the side [away from them] on the roads. When they gave a man a beverage, they would [turn their backs to them], until he had finished [drinking] it. They taught their daughters the things they knew and raised them well in their traditions; they reprimanded them [when necessary] and taught them to work. When they misbehaved they punished them by pinching their ears or slapping their arms. If the mothers saw them roll their eyes, they reproved them severely and sprinkled pepper on them, which causes great pain. If they were immodest they whipped them and applied pepper on another part of their body as punishment and humiliation. It is also a serious reproach to accuse the young girls that they are [acting] like women brought up without mothers.

Women become very jealous to such a degree [that] at times they lay hands on those women who have aroused their suspicions. They are also quick to anger and resentful on this score, though in other ways they are very meek; so that they are inclined to pull their husband's hair for the least jealousy [such as flirting with another woman]. They are hard workers and capable homemakers, for on them rest most, and the more important, work in maintaining their homes: educating their children and paying tribute [taxes]. With all [these responsibilities] they bear disproportionate obligations, [which include] working the fields and harvesting the crops. They are great earners, working late into the night in the few moments left to them after their domestic labors [are complete], such as going to the markets to buy and sell their things.

They raise both native and [Spanish] fowls [turkeys and chickens, respectively] for sale and for eating. They also raise birds for their pleasure and for the feathers used to adorn their elegant clothes. They also raise other domestic animals; they even suckle the fawns, which they have to do in order to tame them so that they never run away into the forests, even when they take them there and back [to the woods] and raise them there.

They help one another in their working and weaving, repaying for this work in the same way as do their husbands on their farms. As they work [communally], they are in the habit of telling jokes and telling stories about their husbands, at times with a bit of complaining [about their husbands]. They consider it unbecoming to look at the men and laugh at them, so this fact alone is enough to cause trouble [making men think the women hold them in distain], and for no other grounds [than this, some] are held in disrepute.

They also perform most of their dances among themselves, although [on occasion] some dances are performed with the men; among these is the *naual* dance, one that is immodest. They are very fertile, and they bear the children [at a young age]; they are excellent nurses for two reasons. First, their hot morning beverage [consisting of maize and cacao] produces plenty of breast milk. Second, their constant grinding of the maize without tying up their breasts causes them to grow large and thus to hold a great deal of milk.

They also become drunk at their feasts, which they have among themselves, but [they do not drink as much] as do the men. They desire to bear many children, and a woman who has none avails herself of their idols, offering gifts and prayers. Now [having learned Christianity] they beg God for [children]. They are prudent and courteous, and affable with those who understand them [their friends and intimates]; they are also wonderfully generous. They cannot keep a secret; and they are very clean and proper in their persons and affairs as they should be, since they wash like ermines [the Old World weasel, renowned for its cleanliness] do.

They are very devout and pious, offering many devotions to their idols, burning incense before them and bringing gifts of cotton, food and drink. It was also their responsibility to prepare the offerings of food and drink made during their ceremonies. They did not, however, participate in the custom of drawing blood as an offering to their evil [idols], and never did so [at the time of the arrival of the Europeans]. Nor were they allowed to enter into the temples at times of the sacrifices, except at certain festivals when old women were admitted to enter and allowed to participate. At the time of childbirth they consulted their sorceresses, who made them believe all sorts of lies, and also to place a graven image of a demon called Ixchel, whom they called the goddess of childbirth, under their bed.[27]

When the children were born, they were bathed at once, and then when the torture of having their foreheads and heads was over, they took them to the priest that he might cast their fate, divine the occupation the child should have, and give the infant the name he or she was to retain during his childhood; they were accustomed to call the children by [these] different names until they were baptized or somewhat grown up. [After baptism, or when the children were older] they dropped these [names] and named them after their parents until they were married. Then they took the names of both father and mother.

---

[27] Diego de Landa dismisses the Mayas' beliefs as "lies of the devil" categorically. Ixchel is a deity associated with fertility and was much venerated among the Yucatec Maya.

XXXIII
Funerals. Burials of the Priests. Statues to Preserve the Ashes of the Community Leaders, and the Honors They Paid to Them. Their Belief Regarding a Future Life, with Rewards and Punishments.

These people had a great, excessive fear of death. They showed this in all their offerings rendered to their deities, for which they asked for nothing other than that they should be rewarded with health, life, and food. But when it came the time to die, it was a spectacle to see their grief and the lamentations they displayed for their deceased, the sadness they felt. They mourned in silence during the day, but at night their cries were loud and mournful [and these were such that it was] grievous to hear. They mourned deeply for many days. They observed abstinence and fasts for the deceased, especially a husband or wife. They declared it was the devil that had taken them off, because they believed all [of life's] ills came from him, especially death.

They wrapped the body of the dead in shrouds, filling the mouth with ground maize and a beverage they call *koyem*, and with this certain stones they used for currency. [They do this] so that he or she will not lack food in the afterlife. They buried them in their houses [beneath the dirt floors] or in the vicinity, tossing some of their idols into the grave. If he was a priest they also buried some of his books [with him]; if he was a sorcerer [they buried some of his] divining stones and other belongings of his occupation. They commonly abandoned the house after the funeral, except in cases where many people were living there: the presence of others would help them lose some of their fear of death.

They cremated the mortal remains of a community leader or high-ranking individual, placing the ashes in large urns. They built temples over [these urns], which was the custom in former times, as has been found to be the case in Izamal. Nowadays, it is [the custom] that they put the ashes of their great community leaders in hollow clay statues.

They made wooden statues, leaving the occiput hollow, for [their own] fathers and members of elite families. Then they cremated part of the body and placed a portion of the ashes there, sealing it. Then they removed the skin from the skull and fastened it there, burying the rest of the corpse in the usual fashion. They kept these statues [close to them], with much reverence, and [placed them] among their idols. When the community leader of the ancient House of the Cocom family died, they cut off the head from the corpse, boiled it to remove the flesh; and then they cut away the back part of the skull, leaving the front with the jaws and teeth. Having removed the flesh, the replaced the flesh with a sort of clay, with which they [molded and] reproduced, almost to perfection, the features of the person whose skull it was. These were kept together with the idols [containing] the ashes and were all placed in the shrines that housed their idols and were held with great reverence and affection. On all festivals and feast days they made offerings of food, so that they would not want of anything in the afterlife, where they believed the souls went to rest and receive their [appreciated] gifts.

These people have always believed in the immortality of the soul, more than many other First Peoples [in the New World], even though they have not so been civilized. They believed that after death there was another life better than this one, which the soul enjoyed after leaving the body. They said this future life was divided into good and bad, into sufferings and delights. The evil life of suffering, they said, was for the wicked; and the good and pleasurable one was for those who had led virtuous lives. They believed that if they were good they would be rewarded and enter a delightful place where there would be an abundance of food and delicious drinks, and a cool and shady tree they called yaxché, the ceiba tree. They would be able to rest and be in peace forever beneath the shade of [this tree's] branches.

The torments of an evil life which they said awaited the wicked lay in going to a place that was located below the other, and which they called mitnal, meaning Hell. There they would be tormented by demons, endure great pains of cold and hunger, and suffer exhaustion and sadness. They said there was in this place a prince demon who all there [had to] obey, whom in their language they called Hunhau. They said that these good and evil afterlives were without end, because the soul itself had [was eternal]. They also said, and with quiet certainty, that those who had hanged themselves went to this paradise. [In consequence], there were many who in times of lesser troubles, hardships, or sickness, hanged themselves in order to escape and go to that paradise, to which they believed they were carried off by the Deity of the Noose, whom they called Ixtab.[28] They had no knowledge of the resurrection of the body; neither could they offer an explanation of how they had come to believe these things, of their paradise and their hell.

[28] The Maya continue to believe in the virtues of suicide, one reason to this day Yucatán State has the highest suicide rate in Mexico.

XXXIV
Count of the Yucatecan Year. Characters of the Days. The Four Bacabs and Their Names. Deities of the "Unlucky" Days.

The sun in this land of Yucatán never goes away long enough for the nights to be longer than the days. [In consequence] at their full longest, from Saint Andrew's Day to Saint Lucia's Day [November 20 to December 13], they are of equal length. Then they begin to lengthen. To know the time during the night the First Peoples guided themselves by the evening star [Venus], the Pleiades, and the Twins [Castor and Pollux]. During the day the [reference point was] midday, and for different periods between sunrise to sunset [they had specific names], according to which they organized and arranged their hours for work.

They had a perfect year like ours, [comprised] of 365 days and six hours, which they divided into two kinds of months. The first [kind of] month consisted of 30 days, and they were called *U*, which means moon. The counted these from the new moon, until it disappeared.

The other kind of month consisted of 20 days and was called *Uinal Hunekeh*. The complete year consisted of 18 months, plus five days and six hours. With these six hours they made an additional day every four years, so that they had a 366-day year every fourth year.

For these 360 days they had 20 letters or symbols [glyphs] to name them, leaving the other supplementary days without names because they were considered inauspicious and unlucky. The letters are as follows, each with its [glyph] and its name written in our own [alphabet] so that they may be understood.

Kan

Manik

Chiccan

Lamat

Cimi

Muluc

Oc

Chuen

Eb

Been

Ix

Men

Cib

Caban

Ezanab

Cauac

Ahau

Ymix

Ik

Akbal

I have already mentioned that the First People's method of counting was in five to fives, and with four fives they reach 20. As such, from these 20 characters [glyphs], which represent 20, they take the first one from each of the four sets of five in the 20. Each of these serves for a year as do our dominical letters, being the first days of the various 20-day months.

Kan   Muluc   Ix   Cauac

Among the multitude of deities that these people worshipped were four they called Bacab. These were, they say, four brothers their deity placed at the four corners of the earth [the cardinal points] when he created the world, and who sustain the heavens lest they fall. They also say that these Bacabs escaped when the world was destroyed by the deluge.[29] To each of these they give different names, and they use them to indicate the four points of the world where their deity placed them holding up the sky. They also assigned one of the four dominical letters to name each, and to the position he occupies [North, South, East, and West]. They [finally] also understand what evil or good to expect in the year corresponding to each of these, and their accompanying letters.[30]

The Evil One [Satan], who has in this, as on many other occasions deceived them, told them what services and offerings they had to make in order to protect these from misfortunes.[31] [In consequence], if these [misfortunes] did not befall them, then they said it was because of the ceremonies they had performed. If, [on the other hand, misfortunes] did come to pass, the priests made the people believe that it was because of some error or failing in the ceremonies [on the part of those who performed them].

Kan

The first of these dominical letters, then, is Kan. The year indicated by this letter had as divination that Bacab, which was also called Hobnil, Kanalbacab, Kanpauahtun, Kanxibchac. He was assigned the [cardinal point of] South.

Muluc

The second letter, or Muluc, corresponded to the [cardinal point of] East, and this year had as its omen the Bacab, which was also called Canzicnal, Chacalbacab, Chacpauahtun, Chacxibchac.

---

[29] In Maya mythology the world has been destroyed on several occasions, including once by massive floods that were sent to drown the whole of humanity.

[30] The Maya believed there were auspicious and inauspicious years. The four cardinal points assigned to a specific year was one of the more important contributing factors that determined if a year was lucky or not.

[31] It is here that Diego de Landa reveals how, in this own mind, he struggles to reconcile the striking similarities between Maya beliefs and his own ideas. The "evil one," at times is just that: a malevolent spirit. On other occasions, it is a "demon," while in specific instances it is, without a doubt, the devil. Francisco Toral, on the other hand, never for a moment believed that Satan, as understood by Christians, Jews and Muslims, figured in the religions of the First Peoples. Toral was unconvinced that the Fallen Angel Lucifer worked his evil among the Maya.

Ix

The third letter is Ix, and the divination for this year in the Bacab called Zaczini, Zacalbacab, Zacpauahtun, Zacxibchac. [Its cardinal point] corresponded to North.

Cauac

The fourth letter is Cauac, its divination for that year corresponded in the Bacab as Hozanek, Ekelbacab, Ekpauahtun, Ekxibchac. This [one] corresponded to [the cardinal point of] West.

In any ceremony or feast these people celebrated for their deities, they always began by expelling the devil in order perform [the ceremony or feast] better.[32] This exorcism was, at times, carried out through prayers and benedictions they had for this purpose. On other occasions, [they performed] ceremonies, making offerings and sacrifices that they had for this purpose. In order to commemorate the solemnity of the New Year with the greatest of rejoicing and worthily, these people, consistent with their deluded ideas, did not work during the five supplementary days, which they regarded as unlucky, which preceded the first day of their New Year. [These days] were spent on a great ceremony [and feast], first and foremost for the Bacabs and the devil, to whom they gave four different names. These names were Kanuuayayab, Chacuuayayab, Zacuuayayab, Ekuuayayab. Once these ceremonies and feasts were concluded and the Evil was driven away, as we shall see, they began their New Year.[33]

---

[32] Diego de Landa came to believe these "purification" rituals were exorcisms to drive away Satan and his familiars.

[33] In the names enumerated, the words *chac, sac, ek, kan* mean respectively Red, White, Black and Yellow, which are the four colors assigned in this order to the East, North, West, and South. The Maya assigned a color with each of the cardinal points: Red with East, or sunrise; Black with West, or night; White with North, probably because of the association with the North Star; and Yellow with South, probably because of the lingering southern light during autumn.

XXXV
Festivals of the "Unlucky" Days. Sacrifices for the Beginning of the New Year Kan.

In all the towns of Yucatán it was customary to place, at each of the four entrances to the town, two piles of stones. [These were placed] opposite each other [in the cardinal points]; that is, at the East, West, North, and South entrances. It was here they celebrated the two festivals [devoted to] the unlucky days in this manner.

The year whose dominical letter was Kan was governed by Hobnil, and they say that both of these ruled the South. In this year, then, they created a [wooden] image or clay figure, with a hollow, of the demon they called Kanuuayayab. They carried it to the pile of dry stones they had erected at the South. They selected a leading figure in town, at whose house they would celebrate this feast during these days, and then they made a statue of a demon that they called Bolonzacab. They placed [this image] in the house of the master of ceremonies [for the feast], in a place [in his home] that was open to all.

Once this was done, the community leaders, the priest, and the men of the town, would assemble, having cleaned and prepared the road with arches and foliage all the way to the two piles of stones and where the statue were [located]. They gathered there, most devoutly. Then the priest would arrive and he would incense the statue with 49 grains of ground maize that were mixed with incense. Then the others tossed their [own] incense into the brazier of the demon idol to incense it [as well]. The ground maize alone was called *zacah*, and that of the community leaders was called *chabalté*. When the idol was well incensed, they cut off the head of a bird, and presented it as an offering.

When all had done this, they placed the idol on a wooden pole they called *kanté*, putting on its shoulders an angel as a sign of water, meaning that it would be a good year. They painted these angels to make them look frightening. Then they carried it with much rejoicing and dancing to the house of the master of ceremonies, where the other statue of Bolonzacab was located. From the home of the master of ceremonies they brought out to the road, for the community leaders and the priest, a beverage made of 415 grains of toasted maize, which they call *piculakakla*, for the men to drink.

On reaching the house, they placed the idol they were carrying opposite the statue of the demon they constructed there, and then they made several offerings of food and drink, and of meat and fish. These offerings were then distributed among any dignitaries who were present; and they gave a leg of venison to the priest.

Others drew blood by making incisions in their earlobes and anointing [with this blood] a stone image of the demon Kanalacantun they had there [for the occasion]. They fashioned a loaf of [maize] bread in the [shape of a human] heart and another of calabash seeds. These were offered to the image of the demon Kanuuayayab. They kept this statue and [graven] image through those fateful days, and scented them with their incense, which [consisted of] ground maize and incense. They believed that if they did not perform these rites, they were certain to suffer from disease in the unfolding year. When these ill-omened days were over they took the statue of Bolonzacab to their temple, and the [graven] image to the eastern entrance where it would remain until the following year. They left it there and returned to their homes to occupy themselves with what they had to do for the celebrations marking the New Year.

These ceremonies over, and the devil exorcised according to their deluded ideas, they believed the coming year would be a good one, because the bacab Hobnil [now] governed it under the letter Kan. They said of him [the bacab Hobnil] that he had not sinned as had his brothers, and because of this no evil would come upon them. But because misfortune so often befell them, [they believed] the evil deity also had established ceremonies that were performed in his honor, so that when they were afflicted, they could assign blame to the ceremonies or celebrants [for having not carried out the rites properly]; and thus they continued to remain deluded and blind.

[The Evil one] then commanded them to make an idol called Izamnakauil and place it in the temple. Then in the temple courtyard they burned three balls of a milk or resin they called *kik* [rubber] and sacrificed a dog or a man. They [performed this sacrifice] in keeping the same customs I have described [see Chapter XXVIII], except that in this case the method of the sacrifice was different for this festival. They erected a great pile of stones in the temple's courtyard and then placed the dog or the man to be sacrificed on something much higher. After throwing the bound victim [whether dog or man] upon the pile of stones below, attendants [seized] the victim and, with great swiftness, cut out his heart, raised it to the new idol, and offered it to the idol between two plates. They made additional gifts of food, and during this festival the town's older women danced; they had been specially selected to participate and wore specific dresses. They say that an angel descended and received this sacrifice.

XXXVI

Sacrifices for the New Year of the Character Muluc. Dances of the Stilt-Walkers. Dance of the Old Women with Terra-Cotta Dogs.

The year in which the dominical letter was Muluc then Canzienal governed. On this occasion the community leaders and the priest selected a master of ceremonies to host the feast. After the selection [of the host], they constructed an image of the demon as they had done in the previous year, and which they named Chacuuayayab. They carried this [statue] to the piles of stone at the East [entrance to the town], where they had left the other one the previous year. They also made a statue of the demon called Kinchahau, and placed it in the house of the master of ceremonies in a suitable place. The road having been cleaned and decorated [with plants and foliage], they all proceeded together for their accustomed devotions before the deity Chacuuayayab.

On arriving the priest perfumed the idol with 53 grains of the ground maize ground into the incense, which they call *zacah*. The priest gave this [incense] to the community leaders, who tossed additional incense into the brazier, the kind called *chabalté*. Then they cut off a fowl's head, just as they had before, and taking the image on a wooden pole called *chasté*, they carried it with great reverence, while performing certain war dances they call *holcanokot, batelokot*. During this performance, they lined the roads, and the community leaders and principal men were offered a beverage made from 380 grains of maize, toasted as before.

When they had arrived at the house of the master of ceremonies they placed this idol opposite the statue of Kinchahau and made all their offerings to it, which they distributed among those present as before. They offered the idol [maize] bread made with egg yolk, other pastries that contained deer hearts, and another that was made with the paste of native peppers. There were many participants who drew blood from their earlobes and with [this blood] anointed the [carved] stone they had of their deity Chacacantun. They seized boys and forcibly drew blood from their earlobes by making incisions. They kept this statue and the idol here until the fatal days were behind them, and during this time they burned incense. When the days were over, they carried the idol to [the gate entrance located in the] North, where [it would remain until] the following year when they retrieved it. The other [idol] they carried to the temple, and then went to their homes to attend to the preparations for the New Year. If they failed to do all these things, they feared [being victims] of an evil eye.[34]

This year, in which the dominical letter was Muluc, the Bacab Canzienal governed, and it was considered to be a favorable year. They said he was the best and greatest of the Bacab; for this [reason] they kept him in their prayers. Despite this, however, the devil required them to construct an idol called Yaxcocahmut, which they placed in the temple, and they removed the old idols. In the temple courtyard they raised a stone pile on which they burned their incense, and a ball of the resin or milk, called *kik*. They prayed there to the idol, asking protection from the misfortunes they feared for the coming year, which included a shortage of water [or drought], many weak offshoots [buds] of their maize [plantings], and things of this nature. To earn his protection, the demon required that they offer squirrels and an unembroidered cloth woven by the older women, whose duty was to dance in the temple to please Yaxcocahmut.

Although this was believed to be a good year, they still endured many hardships and evil omens should they not perform the ceremonies the [devil] demanded of them. These included performing dances on tall stilts, with offerings of heads of turkeys, [maize] bread, and maize beverages. They also had to offer clay dogs with [maize] bread on their backs, and the older women had to dance carrying [these terra-cotta dogs] in their hands. They also had to sacrifice a little dog that had a black back and was a virgin. The devout had to draw their blood and with it anoint the stone of Chacacantun. They believed this ceremony and sacrifice were pleasing to their deity Yaxcocahmut.

---

[34] The evil eye, a belief that dates back to antiquity, is the belief that a malevolent look or glance can cause injury or bring about bad luck to the person at whom it is directed usually for reasons of jealousy, envy or dislike.

XXXVII
Sacrifices for the New Year with the Sign Ix. Sinister Prognostics and Manner of Conjuring Their Effects.

In the year whose dominical letter was Ix and was governed by Zaczini, after the election of the master of ceremonies for the celebration of the festival, they constructed an image of the demon called Zacuuayayab. They carried it to the piles of stone at the North [entrance to the town], where they had left the other one the previous year. They then made a statue of the demon Ytzamná and set that in the master of ceremonies' house. Then all together, with the road prepared [and decorated with branches and foliage], they went devoutly to the idol of Zacuuayayab. On arrival they offered incense in their usual way. They [made a sacrifice by] cutting off the head of a fowl and placed the image on a pole stand called *zachia*, and then carried it away with much fanfare and performing a dance they called *alcabtan kamahau*.[35] They brought the usual beverages to the road [for the community leaders and dignitaries]. Upon arriving at the [master of ceremonies'] house they put this idol opposite the statue of Ytzamná. They made their offerings and distributed these [among participants]. To the idol of Zacuuayayab they offered the head of a turkey, [maize] pastries filled with quail and with other things, and their drink.

Others drew blood and with it anointed the stone of the demon Zacacantun. They then attended the idols as they had done the year before, scenting them with incense for the days remaining [until New Year]. Then they carried Ytzamná to the temple and Zacuuayayab to the place of the [entrance gates located in the] West, and left it there to be retrieved the following year.

The misfortunes the Maya feared for the ensuing year if they were careless in performing these ceremonies were loss of physical strength, fainting, and [being the victims of] evil eye. They considered this year as a bad one for [maize] bread and a good one for cotton. This year, bearing the dominical Ix, and the one over which the Bacab Zaczini governed, was believed to be ill-omened, with many hardships destined to occur: they said there would be great droughts and many heat waves that would wither the maize fields. They said [that in consequence] great famines would follow, and much theft of food, and from these thefts [many would be] enslaved as punishment for theft. Great disagreements and [civil]

---

[35] This phrase in Yucatec Maya can be translated as "Hasten to receive the Lord."

discord would arise, either among themselves or with neighboring towns as a result. They also said that this year would bring changes in their government as community leaders or priests would change as a consequence of warfare or [civil] disputes.

Another prophecy was that some men who aspired to become community leaders would not be successful. They also said that the locusts would come, and that many of their towns would be laid waste by famines. What the devil ordained that they should do to avert these misfortunes, some or all of which would befall them, was to create an idol of Cinchahau Ytzamná. They should place [the idol] in their temple, where they would burn incense and make many offerings and prayers to the deity. They were to draw of their blood for the anointing of the stone of the demon Zacacantun. They performed many dances, and the old women, as was their custom, danced. On this occasion, they would also build a new shrine for the demon, or else renovate the old [shrine], and they assembled there to make sacrifices and render offerings to him, and all became solemnly drunk, since this was a general and obligatory community feast [of debauchery]. There were some very devout participants who, of their own volition, made another idol like the above and placed it in other temples, where they rendered offerings and heavy drinking took place. These drunken debaucheries and sacrifices were believed to be very pleasing to the idols, and a way to free themselves from the miseries the prophecies foretold.

XXXVIII
Sacrifices of the New Year of the Letter Cuac. The Evils Prophesized and Their Remedy in the Dance of the Fire.

In the year when the dominical letter was Cauac and the governing deity was Hozanek, after the selection of a sponsor for the celebrations had been completed, the made a graven image of the demon named Ekuuayayab. They carried this [idol] to the piles of stone to the West [entrance to their town], where they had left the other [idol they had carved] the year before. They also carved a statue of a demon called Uacmitunahau, which they put in the sponsor's house in an appropriate place. Then they set out all together on a road that had been properly prepared for the pilgrimage to where the image of Ekuuayayab stood. Upon arriving, the priest and the leaders offered incense, as was their custom, and cut off the head of a [sacrificial] fowl. After this they carried the idol on a standard called *yax-ek*, putting on its back the image a skull and a corpse, and on top a carnivorous bird called *kuch* [vulture] as a sign of a great death toll [feared], since they regarded this as a very ominous year.

Afterward they carried it with much respect and devotion, amid performing various dances, one of which was one like the *cazcarientas* [sic], which they called the *xibalbaokot*, meaning the Dance of the Devil. The stewards came out to the road offering the community leaders beverages, which they drank. They arrived at the place of the idol Uacmitunahau, and then they placed their offerings in front of the image they carried. Then they presented their offerings, lit incense, and offered prayers; many drew blood from various parts of their bodies. They anointed the stone of the demon called Ekelacantun with this blood. The fatal days passed in this manner, at the end of which they carried Uacmitunahau to the temple and EkuUayayab to the place of the South, to retrieve it the following year.

This year, whose sign was Cauac and which was ruled over by the bacab Hozanek, was held as one of mortality and very portentous, according to the omens. They said there would be fierce heat that would wither the maize fields, while the multitudes of ants and birds would devour the seeds that had been sown. This, however, would not be the case everywhere. In some areas they would have famine, but in others [there would be enough], although with great difficulty. To avoid this calamity they had to make four idols, Chichacchob, Ekbalamchac,

89

Ahcanuolcab, Ahbulucbalam, and place them in the temple where they would offer fragrant incense, burn two balls of the milk or resin called *kik*, along with certain iguanas and bread [made of corn], a miter headdress, a bunch of flowers, and one of their precious stones. After this, to celebrate the festival, they built a great wooden vault in the courtyard and stacked its tops and sides with firewood, leaving the doors open [in order] to enter and leave. Then most of the men took two bundles each of very dry and long sticks, tied together, and had a singer who stood on top of the wood pyre. While he sang and beat one of their drums, those below danced in perfect time and devotion, entering and leaving the doors of that wooden vault. They danced until dusk, and then each one left, taking his bundle of sticks. They went home to rest and eat.

At nightfall, they returned. They were accompanied by a great crowd, because they held this ceremony in great regard. Each then took his bundle of sticks, lit it with a torch, and one by one they set fire to the pyre; it blazed high and quickly. When only the embers remained, they leveled them and spread them evenly. Those who had danced, joined by others, began to walk barefoot and naked from one side to the other across the ashes and embers; some of these crossed without being harmed whatsoever, others were seriously burned, and others only slightly. They believed that in [this ritual] was the solution against misfortunes and ill omens, and that this was the most pleasing offering to their deities. When this [ceremony] was concluded, they went off to drink and get drunk, for this was called, by custom [and tradition], the Festival of Heat and of Fire.

XXXIX
An Explanation of Their Calendar.

Together with the characters [glyphs] of the First Peoples already mentioned [see Chapter XXXIV], they named the days of their months, and with all the months together they had a kind of calendar. They used [this calendar] to regulate their festivals, accounts, trading and business, just as we do with ours. They did not begin the first of their year on the first day of their calendar; New Year came much later. I shall provide here [an explanation that this] was the result of the complicated fashion with which they counted the days of the months all together, as will be seen in the calendar itself. Although the signs and names of the days of their months are 20, they were used to count them from one to 13; after the 13 they began counting from one again. [In consequence], they divide the days of the year into 27 [months] plus 13 [days], or plus 11 days, without counting the "unlucky" days.[36]

With this cumbersome count and periodic juggling, it is a marvel to see the ease with which they know how to count and understand [their calendar]. It is notable that the dominical letter always falls on the first day of their year, without fail or error, and that no other of the 20 days ever falls in that position. They also used this method of counting to provide another method of reckoning time from the symbols [glyphs] they used for other things that, although they were important to them, do not concern us much here. [In consequence, for the time being] I shall be content with saying that the character or letter with which they began their count of the days or calendar is called Hun Imix, which is this:

And which has no fixed or assigned day on which it must fall because each symbol [glyph] changes the count itself. As such, the dominical letter never fails to fall on the first day of the following year.

The first day of the year for these people always fell on our 16 July and was the first of their month Pop. It is to be wondered that this people, otherwise simple as we have found them in many of their ways, also had ability in these matters and ideas such as other peoples: in Ezekiel's

---

[36] This account of the Maya calendar is mistaken. It is probable that various copyists simply transposed sections of the Maya calendar, resulting in obvious errors and omissions.

commentaries we find that according to the Romans, January began the year; according to the Hebrews it was April; according to the Greeks, it was March; and according to the Asians [the year began in] October. But although they began their year in July, I shall place their calendar here in the order of ours, and parallel [to it], so that our letters and theirs will coincide, our months and theirs, together with their above-mentioned count of the 13s, placed in the order of their numerical progression.

Since there is no need to deal with the calendar in one place and the festivals in another, I shall include in each of the months the feasts, ceremonies and celebrations with which they observed it. Thus I shall fulfill what I have promised: I will [now] set out their calendar and write of the feasts and ceremonies they observed when constructing their wooden idols, and other things. All of these things, and the other things I have told of these people serve no other purpose than to praise the divine Almighty who has permitted this [to coexist] and has seen well to remedy it in our times [through the spread of Christianity]. As such, with deeply felt Christianity, we pray to Him for their preservation and progress in true Christianity; and that those charged [with its spread] may promote and aid this end, so that neither to this people for their sins, nor to ourselves, may there be lacking help; nor may they fail in what has commenced and so return to their misery and sinful errors, so that worse things than before would befall them, returning the devil [and demons] we have been able to drive out of their souls, where we [Franciscan missionaries have, with] laborious care been able to drive out of them, cleansing them and sweeping out their vices and evil customs of the past. And this is not a vain fear [or apprehension], when we see the perdition which, after so many years, is to be seen in great and most Christian Asia; in the good, Catholic and most august Africa; and the miseries and calamities which today our own Europe suffers, both in our country and homes. I might say that the evangelical prophecies about Jerusalem have been fulfilled, [specifically] where her enemies would encircle her, weaken her, and bring her to the ground [and to her knees]. All of this God must have permitted [to come to pass] as we are, but we, His Church cannot fail and neither can [we forget] what He said: *Nisi Dominus reliquisset semen, sicut Sodoma fuissemus.*

XL
The Roman and Yucatecan Calendar.

January

According to what they said, they created [idols] of their deities with much fear [reverence]. When the [idols] were done to perfection, the owner made an offering, as best as he was able to afford. These [offerings] consisted of birds, game, and money [cacao beans or stone beads], to pay the person who had made the idols. They would take them from their homes and place them in another structure, a thatch-roof hut, which stood in the courtyard. The priest would bless the idols with much solemnity and a large number of prayers. The owner and officials first cleaned themselves of dirt, because they had fasted while the idols were being created. The idol was anointed to expel the devil, as was their custom, and then these [idols] were wrapped in cloths, placed in a woven basket, and handed over to the owner. He received it with great devotion. The priest would then preach on the merits of the occupation of making idols of their deities, and the danger the artisan risked [from the devil] should he break his abstinences and fasts [during the creation of the idols]. Afterward, they feasted very well, and drank to the point of drunkenness.

Yax

In whichever of the months Chen or Yax was designated by the priest, and on the day selected by him, they celebrated a feast they called Ocná, which means "renovation of the temple." This feast was in honor of the Chacs, who were the deities of maize fields. During this festival they consulted the prophecies of the Bacabs, as has been explained [in Chapters XXXV to XXXVIII]. They celebrated this feast each year, and it was a time when they refurbished the terra-cotta idols and their braziers, since it was the custom for each idol to have his own little brazier for the burning of incense. If it was necessary, they built a new shrine, or repaired the old one, placing on the walls the record of these things with their characters.

February

It is here that the Mayas' calendar begins, which in their language is Hun Imix.

Zac

The priest selected one day in the month of Zac to commemorate the festival, and he instructed the hunters, who had celebrated a similar feast in the month of Zip, to appease the anger the deities had [against humanity] and their sown fields [of maize]. [This anger arose from the] blood the hunters spilled in hunting; the deities regarded with abhorrence the shedding of blood, except in sacrifices made to [honor them]. For this reason, whenever they went to the hunt, the hunters invoked the devil and burned incense to him; and if they could they anointed the faces [of the idols] with blood from the heart of the game [provided the animal was large enough].

On whichever day of the year 7 Ahau fell they held a very great festival that lasted three days, and they lit incense and made offerings, and with moderate drinking. Since this was a movable feast, the priest was careful to announce it with sufficient lead time, so that they might fast beforehand in due manner.

Ceh

Mac

March

On any day during the month of Mac, the oldest people [in the community] celebrated a festival to the Chacs, the deities of sustenance, and Ytzamná. One or two days prior to this they performed the following ceremony, which they called *tuppkak*, meaning "fire-quenching." They caught as many animals and creatures in the fields and the countryside as they could. With these they assembled in the temple courtyard, where the priest had placed the chacs in the [cardinal] corners to exorcise the devil as was their practice. Each [participant] carried a pitcher of water, which was brought over to him. They erected a bundle of dry sticks, tied together, at the center. First lighting the incense in the braziers, they then set fire to the sticks, and as the pyre burned they tore out the hearts of the birds and animals and liberally tossed them into the flames. If they had been unable to get any of the larger animals, such as tigers, lions, or caimans, [jaguars, ocelots, and alligators, respectively], they molded hearts out of incense instead. If they had killed any [of these larger animals], they brought their hearts for the fire. Then when the hearts were all consumed, the chacs extinguished the fire with their pitchers of water. The celebration of this [ritual] and the following feast were offered to secure a good season of rains for their maize crops during the ensuing year.

They celebrated the feast once the fire was extinguished. This celebration differed from the others in that fasting was not required, except that the sponsor of the feast did [the customary] fast. When the time arrived [for the feast], all the townspeople, the priest, and the dignitaries assembled in the temple courtyard, where they had constructed a mound of stones, with stairways, all clean and dressed with green branches. The priest then offered the prepared incense to the feast's sponsor, and he burned it in the brazier: they said the devil was thus exorcised. This [rite] being done with their accustomed reverence, they spread the lower step of the mound of stones with mud from the well, and the other steps with blue pitch. They burned a great deal of incense and invoked the Chacs and Ytzamná with prayers and devotionals, and made their offerings [of presents]. When this had been done they took consolation in eating and drinking what had been offered [to their deities], confident that their service and invocations would bring about a prosperous new year.

Muan

During the month Muan those who owned cacao groves made a festival for the deities Ekchuah, Chac, and Hobnil, who were their protectors.[37] To do this they went to the property of one of the [cacao grove owners], where they sacrificed a dog marked with the colors of the cacao, burned incense to their idols, and offered iguanas of the blue kind, with certain birds' feathers and other game. Then they gave to each one

---

[37] Diego de Landa uses the word "cacahuate," which today means "peanuts," but it is generally understood he probably used it to mean "cacao" because of description of the color of the pods. That cacao groves were so common during his time throughout Yucatán is a point of contention. Although many believe the conditions necessary for extensive cacao cultivations in Yucatán were unfavorable, current cacao production of the superior Criollo cacao.

of the dignitaries a present consisting of a pod of the cacao beans [currency]. When the sacrifice and the prayers were over, they feasted on the offerings [of foods] and drank, but (as they tell) no more than three draughts of the wine [pulque], no more than they had brought [for this celebration]. After this, they went to the house of master of ceremonies who had hosted the feast, for various dances and diversions.

Pax

In this month of Pax they commemorated a feast called Pacumchac, for which the community leaders and priests of the smaller villages assembled in the larger towns. For five nights they all kept vigil in the temple of Citchaccoh, saying prayers, making offerings, and burning incense, as has been stated of the feast to Kukulkán during the month Xul, in November. Before these days were over, they all went to the house of their war captain, the nacón, of whom I wrote [in Chapter XXX]. Amid great pomp they carried him to the temple, offering incense to him as if he were [one of their] idols. Then, seating him and burning incense as they do to their deities, he, and they, remained for five days. During [these days] they ate and drank of the offerings [of food] that had been brought to the temple, and they performed a great dance in the style of war games, called in their language Holcanokot, or the Dance of the Warriors. After these five days were concluded they went on to celebrate their feast which, since it was for matters of war and victory over their enemies, was very solemn.

First they conducted the ceremony and sacrifices of the Fire-Quenching, as I described, during the month of Mac. Then as was their custom they drove out the devil with great solemnity. After this came prayers and the offering of gifts [of food] and incense. While they did this, the community leaders, and those who had before assisted, again carried the nacón on their shoulders around the temple, with incense burning. When they returned with him, the priests sacrificed a dog, removed its heart, and offered it between two platters to the devil, while the chacs each broke large jars full of drink [pulque], and with this ended the ritual. When it was over they ate and drank the offerings that had been brought and then took the nacón back to his home, with great solemnity but without perfumes.

There they held a great feast in which the community leaders and the priests and leading men drank to the point of intoxication, and the rest of the people returned to their towns; but the nacón did not join in the drunkenness. On the next day, when the effects of the wine [pulque] had worn off, all the community leaders and priests of the towns who had remained at the host community leader's residence and taken part in this last act received a great quantity of incense prepared for the purpose from him [their host]. This [incense] had been blessed by the unholy priests. He then joined them and delivered a long speech in which, with much emphasis, he commended them on the feasts they should, in their own towns, celebrate for the deities during the coming year in order to enjoy abundant harvests. After the address, they took their leave with expressions of affection and merry-making, each returning to his town and his home.

There they busied themselves with the celebrations, depending on their [financial] circumstances, which continued until the month Pop. These feasts were called Zabacilthan, and were performed as follows. They looked through the town for the wealthiest man able to afford the costs of the feast, and then they settled on the [most auspicious] day for entertainment during the remaining three months before their New Year. They assembled at the house of the host, went through the ceremonies of driving away the devil, burning copal, made offerings of merriment and dances, and helped themselves to wine kegs [caskets of pulque]. Such was the excess in these feasts during these three months that it was pitiful to see them. They went about scratched and with head wounds and red-eyed in their wanton drunkenness; their love of the wine [pulque] was such that they became lost over it.

June

Kayab
Cumku

July

It has been stated in the previous chapters how the First Peoples began their year following these "unnamed days" by preparing for the celebration of the New Year festival. During the same interval they commemorated the festival of the demon Uuayayab, for which they left their homes as little as possible. They offered, apart from gifts [of food] for the general feast, beads for their deities and the other [idols] in the temples. They did not take back the beads offered for their own use, nor did they take anything that was offered to the devil, but they brought incense for burning with them. During these days neither the men nor women combed their hair nor did they bathe, nor otherwise cared for themselves. They likewise did not perform any humble or difficult work, fearing evil would befall them if they did.

Pop

The first day of Pop, which is the first month of their calendar, was the Mayas' New Year. [It was] celebrated with a great festival because it was a general holiday and for all. [In consequence] the entire community assembled together to celebrate and fete all their idols. To do this with the most solemnity, on this day they replaced all the household articles they used, such as plates, vessels, benches, mats, and old garments, and the shrouds in which they kept their idols. They swept out their houses and threw the sweepings and all these old utensils outside their town in a trash heap; no one dared touch an article, even if he was in need of it.

For this festival the community leaders, the priest and the leading men, and those who wished to show their devotion, fasted and abstained from sexual relations with their wives according to however many days seemed appropriate to them. As such, some began three months prior, others two, and the rest as they wished, but no one fasted and remained celibate for fewer than 13 days. During these 13 days, in addition to remaining celibate, they gave up salt or pepper in their food; they considered this to be a great act of penance. During this time they chose the chacs; [others to act as] officials who assisted the priest, whose task was to prepare a great number of fresh incense pellets in small molds the priests provided. This was the incense burned for the idols by those who were fasting and remaining celibate. Those who undertook these fasts did not dare to break them; they believed that to do so would bring evil upon them or their households.

When the New Year arrived, all the men assembled in the temple courtyard, alone; women were not present during any of the temple ceremonies, with the exception of the old women who performed dances. Women were allowed at the festivals held in other places. The men assembled, clean and elegantly painted with red-colored ointments; they had washed the black soot from their backs that they smeared on themselves while fasting. When all were gathered, with the many offerings of food and drink they brought and much wine [pulque] they had made, the priest proceeded to purify the temple. He was seated, in ceremonial garments, in the middle of the courtyard, at his side a brazier and the incense pellets. The chacs seated themselves in the four [cardinal] corners and stretched a new rope from one to the other. They allowed those who had fasted to enter the enclosure in order to drive out the devil. When the devil had been exorcised, all began reciting their devout prayers, and the chacs made new fire, and lit the brazier. In festivals celebrated by the entire community they always lit a new fire, which was lighted with the brazier. The priest began to throw his incense into the brazier, and all came in an orderly fashion, beginning with the community leaders, to receive incense from the hands of the priest. He gave it to them with much gravity as if he were handing them holy relics. They then threw it a little at a time into the brazier, waiting until it finished burning. After this burning of the incense, all ate the offerings and gifts, and the wine [pulque] flowed until they became very drunk. This was the festival of the New Year, a ceremony most pleasing to their idols. Afterward there were others who, out of devotion, celebrated this festival during this month of Pop, [privately and at their own expense] among their friends, with the community leaders and the priests; these latter were always the most important participants in their feasts and drinking.

Uo

In the month Uo the priests, and the physicians and sorcerers, who were all the same, began to prepare themselves for the festivals with fasting and the rest. Hunters and fishermen began to celebrate on the seventh day of Zip, each group celebrating on their own day, different from the other groups. First the priests celebrated their own fete, which was called Pocam [meaning "'the washing"]. They gathered, in all their finery, at the house of the community leader. They first cast out the devil in their customary way; after that they brought out their books and spread them upon a bed of fresh leaves they had prepared for [this purpose]. Then, reciting many prayers and very devoutly, they invoked an idol they called Cinchahau Ytzamná, who they said was the first priest. They offered him their gifts and burned the pellets of incense in a new fire. Meanwhile, they dissolved a little verdigris in virgin water, as they called it, in a vessel that they say was brought from the forests where no woman ever went. They anointed the wooden covers of their books to purify them. After this had been completed, the most learned of the priests would open a book and look for the predictions for that year. He announced his prophecies and then preached to them a little, prescribing the proper observances [for them to follow], and then he assigned which priest or community leader was responsible for the festival for the coming year. Should the appointed person die within the course of the year, then his sons were under obligation to carry out the feast on behalf of the deceased. After this they ate the gifts and food that they had brought, and drank until they were drunk; thus they ended this ceremony, during which, on occasion, they performed a dance called *okotuil*.

Zip

September

The following day the physicians and sorcerers assembled at one of their homes, together with their wives. The priest exorcised the devil. After this, they unwrapped their medicines. They [also] brought trifles, including, each of them, small idols of the principal deity of medicine whom they called Ixchel; this festival was called Ihcil Ixchel. They also had certain small stones, called *am*, [they used] for casting fortune. Then with great devotion they invoked the deities of medicine with their prayers; these [deities] were named Ytzamná, Citbolontun and Ahauchamahez. The priests offering them incense, burned in braziers with new fire. Meanwhile the chacs anointed the idols and the small stones with a blue ointment, similar [to the blue paste] used to anoint the books the priests used. After this, each one wrapped up the instruments of his trade, and placing the bundle on his back, performed a dance they called Chantuniah. After the dance, the men sat by themselves and the women by themselves. After drawing lots to determine [the details for] the festival for the following year, they ate the offerings [of food], and drank themselves senseless; except for the priests, who as they say abstained from the wine [pulque], since [they prefer] to drink it when alone and at their leisure.

The following day the hunters gathered in the house of one of their companions, bringing their wives, like the others. Then the priests arrived and exorcised the devil in their [customary] manner. Afterward, in the center [of the courtyard], they placed materials prepared for the sacrifice of the incense and the new fire, and the blue ointment. The hunters then invoked their deities of the chase [hunt], Acanum, Zuhuysib, Zipitabai, and others. They distributed incense, which they then threw in the brazier. While it burned, each one took an arrow and the skull of a deer, which the chacs anointed with the blue ointment, holding them in their hands. Some danced with these [deer skulls] while others [drew blood] by piercing their ears; others pierced their tongues, and passed through these incisions seven leaves of a broad plant called *ac*. After this was done, first the priest and then the officials of the feast at once made their offerings, and proceeded to dance. They were then served wine [pulque] and became senseless drunk.

On the following day it was the fishermen who celebrated their festival in the same manner as the others [had], except that this time they anointed their fishing tackles. They did not pierce the ears but flayed them on the sides. They performed a dance called *chohom*, and when all this was done they blessed a tall, thick pole [tree trunk] and set it up [in the courtyard of the host's residence]. After these festivals had been commemorated in the towns, it was the custom for the community leaders to go with many of the townsfolk to the coast, where they had great fishing and sport [on holiday], taking with them a great number of [fishing] nets, hooks, and other fishing equipment. The deities who were the patrons of this festival were Ahkaknexoi, Ahpua, Ahcitzamalcum.

Zodz

In the month Zodz beekeepers prepared themselves to celebrate their festival in Tzec, and although the master of ceremonies for these preparations fasted, there was no obligation for anyone else, apart from the priest and his assistants to fast. [Sexual abstinence and fasting] were voluntary on the part of the others.

Tzec

When the day of the festival arrived, they all assembled in the appointed house and did all that was done in other ceremonies, except that there was no drawing of blood, since the patrons were the Bacabs, especially Hobnil. They made many offerings, especially to the four chacs to whom they gave four plates with balls of incense in the middle of each, and the rims [of these plates were] decorated with figures of honey, because the purpose of the ceremony was for abundance of the same. They ended it with wine [pulque] as customary, in plentiful quantities, because the beehive owners had contributed large amounts of honey [to make the pulque].

Xul

November

It has already been related of the departure of Kukulkán from Yucatán, after which some of the First Peoples [of greater Yucatán] said he had ascended to heaven with the deities. As such, they regarded him as a deity and appointed a temple [for his worship], as well as a time of year when they should celebrate a feast for him. This was observed throughout the entire country until the destruction of [the city-state of] Mayapán. After [the fall of Mayapán] only the province of Maní continued this practice, while the other provinces, in recognition of what they owed to Kukulkán, made presents, [taking turns] once each year, of four or sometimes five magnificent feather banners, which were sent to Maní. They celebrated this festival in this fashion, and not in the previous ways.

On the sixteenth of Xul all the community leaders and priests assembled at Maní, and with them great multitudes from the villages, all of them having fasted and abstained as part of their preparations. In the evening of that day they set forth in a great procession from the community leader's home at which they had assembled, with many farce players [and comics] in tow, and marched in solemn silence to the temple of Kukulkán, which had been duly decorated. Upon arriving, having recited their prayers, they stood their banners on the top of the temple, and below, in the courtyard, each pilgrim laid out each of his idols on leaves of trees brought for this purpose. After kindling a new fire they began to burn their incense in many places; they made offerings of dishes that had been cooked without salt or pepper; and prepared beverages from their beans and calabash seeds. There the community leaders and those celebrants who had fasted remained for five days and nights, always burning copal and making their offerings. They did not return to their homes, but continued in prayers and performed certain sacred dances. Until the first day of Yaxkin these farce players and comics went about the business [of visiting] the principal houses, performing their plays and receiving the offerings bestowed on them. They brought these offerings to the temple.

After the five days had passed, they divided the gifts among the community leaders, priests, and performers, collected their banners and idols, gathered them at the residence of Maní's civic leader, and from there they set out to return to their home [villages]. They said, and believed, that Kukulkán descended from heaven and received these ceremonies, abstinences, and offerings. This festival they called Chicckabán.

Yaxkin

In this month of Yaxkin they began to prepare, as usual, for the general feast they would celebrate in Mol, on the day appointed by the priest to honor all their deities. They called it Olobzab Kamyax. After they assembled in the temple they conducted the familiar ceremonies and the burning of incense as in the previous festivals. They anointed with their blue ointment all the tools of all their various occupations, from that of the priest to the spindles of the women, and even the posts of their houses. For this festival they gathered together all the boys and girls, and instead of the painting and the ceremonies they gave to each child nine slight blows on the outside of their knuckles. For the girls this was done by an old woman, dressed in a robe of feathers, who had been brought there [to the festival], and for this reason she was called Ixmol, meaning "the gatherer." These blows were administered so that they might grow up expert artisans in their fathers' and mothers' occupations. The conclusion [of the festival consisted] of a fine drinking debauchery, with the eating of the offerings, except that it is possible that the devout old woman was not allowed to take [alcoholic drink to prevent her becoming] so drunk as to lose the feathers of her robe on the road [home].

Mol

December

In this month the beekeepers held another festival as they had done in the month Tzec, so that the deities would provide flowers for the bees.

One of the most arduous and difficult things that these poor people had to do was the carving of wooden idols, which they called the deities. They had a specific month designated for this work, and this was the month Mol, or another if the priest said it was opportune. Those who wished to make them first had to consult their priest, and after taking his counsel went to the artisans. They say that the artisans always tried to excuse themselves, fearing that either they or someone in their household would die or would suffer a fatal illness [as a consequence of these commissioned jobs]. When, however, they did accept, the chacs whom they had chosen to assist in the matter, together with the priest and the artisan, began their fasts. While they were fasting, he who commissioned the idols went himself, or else sent someone, into the forests for the wood, which was always cedar. When the wood arrived they built a small, fenced-in, thatch hut, in which they placed the wood and a large urn in which they placed the idols. They did this to keep them covered up [and dry] while they were working. They placed incense to burn as an offering to the four deities called the Acantuns, which they brought out and placed at the four cardinal points. They also brought the tools with for scarification, [which consisted of drawing blood from their earlobes]; and which were also the tools used for carving their sinister deities. When all these preparations were ready in the hut, the priest, the chacs, and the artisan shut themselves in the hut. They began carving their deities, from time to time cutting their earlobes and anointing the statues [with this blood] and burning incense. In this manner they continued until they were finished, their families bringing them their food and [attending to their] needs. During the time they abstained [from sexual relations with] their wives, even in thought; nor could anyone enter that place [the hut] where they labored.

An Overview of the Maya Calendar

Nos. of the months.	1	2	3	4	5	6	7	8	9	10	11	12	13	14	15	16	17	18
Cauac	1	8	2	9	3	10	4	11	5	12	6	13	7	1	8	2	9	3
Ahau	2	9	3	10	4	11	5	12	6	13	7	1	8	2	9	3	10	4
Ymix	3	10	4	11	5	12	6	13	7	1	8	2	9	3	10	4	11	5
Ik	4	11	5	12	6	13	7	1	8	2	9	3	10	4	11	5	12	6
Akbal	5	12	6	13	7	1	8	2	9	3	10	4	11	5	12	6	13	7
Kan	6	13	7	1	8	2	9	3	10	4	11	5	12	6	13	7	1	8
Chicchan	7	1	8	2	9	3	10	4	11	5	12	6	13	7	1	8	2	9
Cimi	8	2	9	3	10	4	11	5	12	6	13	7	1	8	2	9	3	10
Manik	9	3	10	4	11	5	12	6	13	7	1	8	2	9	3	10	4	11
Lamat	10	4	11	5	12	6	13	7	1	8	2	9	3	10	4	11	5	12
Muluc	11	5	12	6	13	7	1	8	2	9	3	10	4	11	5	12	6	13
Oc	12	6	13	7	1	8	2	9	3	10	4	11	5	12	6	13	7	1
Chuen	13	7	1	8	2	9	3	10	4	11	5	12	6	13	7	1	8	2
Eb	1	8	2	9	3	10	4	11	5	12	6	13	7	1	8	2	9	3
Been	2	9	3	10	4	11	5	12	6	13	7	1	8	2	9	3	10	4
Ix	3	10	4	11	5	12	6	13	7	1	8	2	9	3	10	4	11	5
Men	4	11	5	12	6	13	7	1	8	2	9	3	10	4	11	5	12	6
Cib	5	12	6	13	7	1	8	2	9	3	10	4	11	5	12	6	13	7
Caban	6	13	7	1	8	2	9	3	10	4	11	5	12	6	13	7	1	8
Ezanab	7	1	8	2	9	3	10	4	11	5	12	6	13	7	1	8	2	9

XLI
Cycle of the Mayas. Their Writings.

Not only did the First Peoples keep a count for the years and months, as has been stated and described earlier, but they also had a certain methodology for counting time and their affairs by ages. They counted by 20-year periods, counting 13 twenties, with one of the 20 signs in their months, which they call Ahau, not in order, but going backward as appears in the following circular design:

They call these periods *katuns* in their language, and with them they kept a reckoning of their ages that is wonderfully accurate. [In consequence] it was easy for the old man of whom I spoke in the first chapter to recall events that he said had taken place 300 years before.[38] If I did not know of these [calendar] reckonings, I would not have believed it possible to recall so many ages [history].

As to who it was who devised this count of *katuns*, if it was the devil [then] it was so done, as is his custom, to draw up honor on his behalf. If it was a man, he must have been a great idolater, because to these *katuns* he added all the deceptions, omens, and fallacies by which these people

_____

[38] Diego de Landa does not mention an old man in Chapter I. It is possible that this is a clerical error of a person who subsequently copied the original text.

went about [their lives] in their misery, completely deluded in error.[39] This [calendar system] was the science to which they gave most credence, held in highest regard, and which not even all their priests were able to explain [and use to count the ages]. The way they had for keeping an account of their affairs and making divinations by this system [required] that they keep two idols in their temples dedicated to these two characters [glyphs]. To the first [glyph], corresponding to the cross above the circular design, they offered prayers, with ceremonies and sacrifices [designed] to avert diseases [plagues and pestilences] during 20 years [one cycle]; and for ten years of the first 20[-year cycle] had passed, they only burned incense to the idol with reverence. When the 20 years of the first [cycle] had passed, they began to be guided by the fates of the second. They removed the first idol and set up another idol to venerate for the following ten years, offering their sacrifices.

Verbi gratia [For example]: The First Peoples say that the Spaniards finally reached the city of Mérida in the year of Our Lord's birth 1541, which was exactly at the first year of the era of Buluc-Ahau, which is in the section where the cross stands. They arrived in the month Pop, which is the first month of their year. Had the Spaniards not arrived, they would have worshipped the image of Buluc-Ahau [until the year 1551 in the European calendar], or for ten years. They would have set up another idol for Boloc-Ahau [to worship] up to the year 1561 [in the European calendar]. They would have then removed it from the temple and replaced it with the idol for Uuc-Ahau, then following the predictions of Bolon Ahau for another ten years, in due course. [In such fashion] they venerated each *katun* for 20 years, and during ten years they were governed by their superstitions and false beliefs, all of which were so many and such as to deceive these simple people, that one would have to marvel over it, for those [Europeans who had arrived and] knew the things of Nature and the devil's experience is using [ignorance to deceive humanity].

They also used certain characters or letters [glyphs], with which they wrote in their books about their lore [histories] and their sciences. With these [glyphs] and with figures, and with certain signs in the figures, they understood their affairs. [They were able] to make them known, and taught them [to others]. We found a great number of books in these letters,[40] and since they contained nothing but superstitions and

---

[39] Diego de Landa laments that, in his opinion, the Maya lived in fear of demons and misfortunes, from which they tried to protect themselves through pagan rituals which included human sacrifice. He sought to liberate them from these "deluded" and "demonic" beliefs through the evangelization of Christianity.

[40] Diego de Landa scourged the land and located 27 hieroglyphic rolls, or books.

falsehoods of the devil we burned them all, which they took most grievously, and which gave them great pain.[41]

I give here an *a*, *b*, *c* [alphabet] of their letters. Their cumbersome nature does not permit any more, because they use them for all the sounds of the letters they use in one character, and then add to the parts another, going on in this manner ad infinitum. [Consider] the following example. *Le* means a "lasso" and "to hunt with one." To write *le* using their letters, they wrote them with three, although we taught them that it was two letters, the *l* and the vowel *e*. They would place the *e* in front of the *l*, although they use the *e* if they wish to do so for the sake of precision. Example:

e l e lé

Afterward they join the syllable:

Há means "water," because the name of the letter *aitch* has an *a* sound at the beginning, *h*, before it, they place at the beginning with *a*, [and an *a ha* at the end] in this fashion:

a   ha

They can also write in syllables, but only in one and the other style: I only put it here in order to give a complete account of the customs of these people.

Ma in Kati means "I do not wish," and they write it in syllables in this manner:

ma   i n   ka ti

Here begins their *a, b, c:*

The letters that do not appear are lacking in this language; and there are others in addition to ours, for other sounds where they are needed.

---

[41] This action enraged Francisco Toral, who promptly denounced Diego de Landa before the Council of the Indies.

Nowadays they no longer use any of the characters, especially the young people who have learned ours.[42]

[Here is a detail of the "alphabet" Diego de Landa describes:]

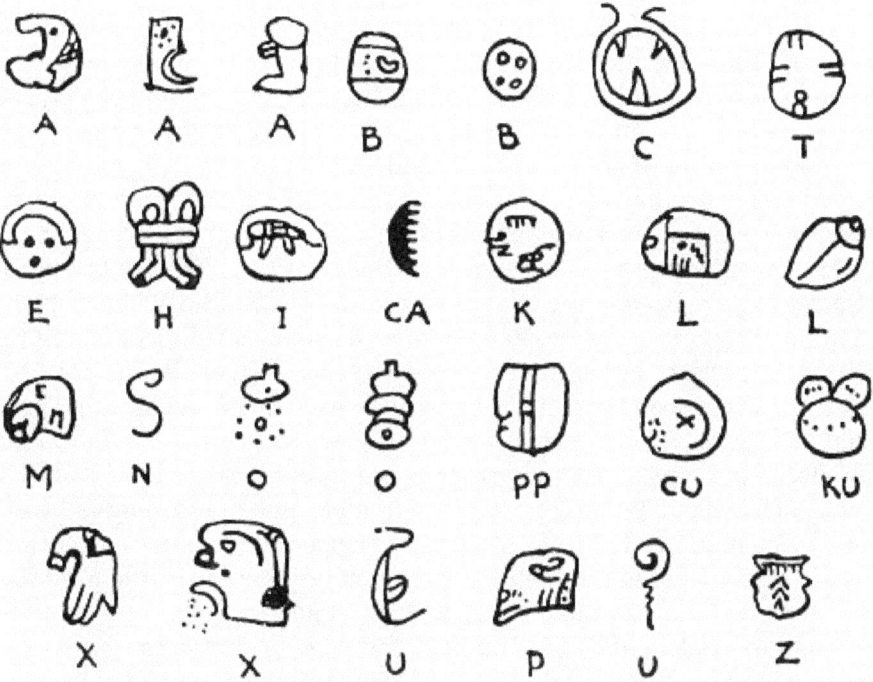

---

[42] It is apparent that Landa mentions this to explain why the "alphabet" that he provides was more imaginary than real; the glyphs he cites do not correspond to an "alphabet" at all.

XLII
Multitude of Buildings in Yucatán. Those of Izamal, of Mérida, and of [Chichén Itzá].

Yucatán would have become as famous as Perú and New Spain if the number, grandeur, and beauty of its buildings were to count toward the attainment of renown and reputation in the same way as gold, silver, and riches have done for other parts of the Indies. [It is so rich in its buildings] and there are so many, in so many places, and so well built of carved stone are they, it is a marvel. The buildings themselves, and their number, are the most remarkable things that have been discovered in the Indies. Considering that this country, as good land as it is, is not today as it seems to have been at the time of its prosperous apogee, when so many great buildings were constructed without the aid of any kind of metals for their construction, I shall offer here the reasons I have heard given by those who have seen these buildings. These are that the people must have been the governed by princes who wished to keep them busy and therefore kept them occupied [carrying out] these tasks; or else that they were such devout worshippers of their idols that these temples were built by community work; or else that because the [ceremonial centers] were abandoned [and new settlements founded] there was [the need for] new temples and sanctuaries, as well as houses for the use of their [community leaders and elite families], these being always constructed of wood and thatch. Another reason offered is the plentiful supply of limestone rocks and white earth [lime and limestone], which is excellent for construction, throughout the land, so that it would seem an imaginary tale [or a hoax], except for people who have seen them [with their own eyes].

It may also be that this country holds a secret that up to the present moment has not been revealed, or which the natives of today themselves cannot divulge.[43] To say that other nations [peoples] compelled these [Maya] to build these structures is not correct, because of the evidence that they were built by the Maya [native to Yucatán] themselves. This is evident to the eyes, for in one out of the many and great buildings that stand, on the walls of the bastions there still remain [painted or carved]

---

[43] The collapse of the Classic Maya civilization was so complete that the Maya people the Spanish encountered in the sixteenth century had become illiterate, unable to read their own writing. They had lost their history, apart from folk tales. When asked who had built the vast ceremonial centers, pyramids and marvelous residential compounds of their elite, the Maya almost always answered uniformly with two words: "Who knows?"

figures of men naked save for the long girdles over the loins called in their language *ex*, together with other apparel the Maya of today still wear, fashioned in very hard mortar.[44]

While I was living there, a large jar with three handles, adorned with figures applied on the outside, was found in a building we were demolishing. Inside, among the ashes of a cremated body, we found three beads of fine stone, such as the Maya today use as money. All [the images] depict people who were Maya. It is also clear that if [the Maya] were the builders, then they were of better physiques than those of today, and greater in bodies and strength.[45] This can be seen more clearly here in Izamal than elsewhere, since there are, as I say, today on the bastions figures [depicted] in semi-relief, made of mortar, showing men of great height. The extremities of the arms and legs of the man whose ashes we found in the jar I have referred to were also very thick, and their unburned state a marvel.

There is here in Izamal a building, among the others, of an amazing height and beauty, which can be seen in the drawing and its explanation [for its construction]. It has 20 steps, each more than two handspans in height and in breadth [a handspan is 9 inches or 2 handspans would be 18 inches or about 45.5 centimeters], and it runs over a hundred feet in length (approximately 30 meters). These steps are constructed of very large carved stones, although they are now much worn and eroded by time and [the effects of centuries of] rainfalls. Surrounding them, as is shown by the curved line, is very strong stone wall. At about one and a half times the height of a man there is a cornice made of beautiful stone that runs all the way around. From this [point,] the structure rises to the height that is level with the platform and the plaza [as seen in the drawing].

From this plaza there another stairway that rises like the first, but this one is not so broad nor with so many steps. Again, a wall encircles it. At the top of these steps there is another fine courtyard, and close to the surrounding wall one finds a very high mound with steps facing the south side like the other great stairs. On top of this a handsome chapel of finely

---

[44] Diego de Landa correctly identifies the contemporary Maya as being the descendants of the people who built the vast cities, ceremonial centers, pyramids and other architectural structures throughout the whole of Yucatán, and not as the work of other peoples.

[45] Diego de Landa correctly notes that the Maya of centuries before his time were better-nourished, taller and stronger than those living in the sixteenth century. Chemical analysis of human remains from Classic Maya tombs indicates that the diets were superior to that of many Maya living today. Diego de Landa identifies that previous generations were not subject to the malnutrition that characterizes the lives of the Maya both in the sixteenth century, and which continues into our own times.

carved stone. I climbed to the top of this chapel, and since Yucatán is a flat country I could see as far as the eye could reach, an amazing distance, as far as the sea. There were 11 or 12 of these buildings at Izamal, but this one was the largest, and all near one another. No one today remembers who the builders were, but they appear to have been [Izamal's] first inhabitants. It is eight leagues (about 24 miles or 36 kilometers) from the sea, built at a beautiful site in a good, well-populated country. For this reason, in 1549, at their insistence, [we acquiesced] to the Maya and built a monastery to Saint Anthony atop one of these structures. Here and in all the surrounding district assistance has been given for [the Maya which has] been of great benefit in the matters of the Christianization [of the Maya]. As such, two good communities have been established in this place, separate from each other.

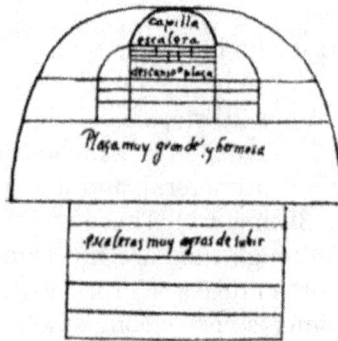

The second of the principal ancient structures in this land—so ancient that there is no record of who constructed them—are those at T'ho, located 13 leagues (39 miles or 59 kilometers) from those at Izamal, and, like them, eight leagues from the sea (24 miles or 36 kilometers). There are signs of there having been a fine paved road from one [city] to the other [linking Izamal and T'ho]. The Spaniards established a city here [at T'ho], and named it Mérida, from the strangeness and grandeur of the buildings [which reminded them of the ancient Roman ruins located in Mérida, Spain]. The principal structure I shall describe here as well as I can, as I did that at Izamal, so that it may be better seen for what it was like.

This is the drawing I have made, and to understand it, it must be noted that it is a square plaza of great size, more than two runs of a horse (800 yards or 800 meters).[46] The stairway rises on the eastern section at the ground level, with seven steps as high as those at Izamal. The other

---

[46] One horse run is roughly 1,200 feet or about 400 meters.

three sides, the south, west, and north, rise from a strong, thick wall. The entire base of the platform is square and made of dry stone, and the flat part of the eastern stairway is, in my judgment, between 28 and 30 feet (about 10 meters) longer than the other stairway, and the steps are equally large. It is likewise set back the same distance, with two strong walls that run until they meet those on the western side, on the north and south sides, but not on the west. These walls form a great central building of dry stone, built by hand, of a wonderful greatness to behold.

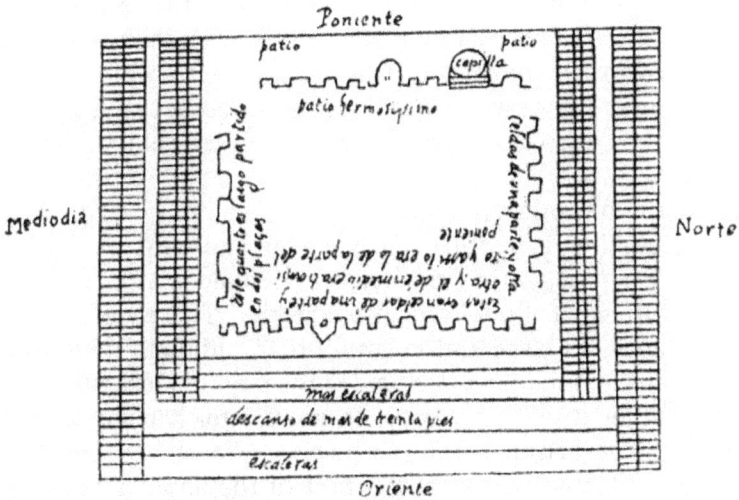

There are buildings on the top level in the following manner: on the east side, set back six feet (2 meters), is a wing that does not reach the ends. It is built of fine stone measuring 12 feet long by eight feet long (4 meters by 2.6 meters, respectively). The doorways, in the center of each of them, have no jambs or pivots that would permit their being closed, but they are flat and of elaborately worked stone. It is all wonderfully constructed, and the tops of the doorways are capped by single large stones. In the center is a passageway arched like a bridge. There are protective reliefs of worked stone running the entire length of the structure above the entrances to the cells [chambers]. There is a line of small pillars above this. Half of them are rounded and half engaged in the walls. These pillars reach to the top of the vaults that comprise the roof and cover the chambers. There is another pillar that extends the entire length of the wing above these pillars. The ceilings are flat and constructed of very hard stucco made with the water from the bark of a certain tree.

On the north was another series with chambers, the same as the others, but running only about as long. There was another line of the chambers on the west side, punctuated, every fourth or fifth vault there was one [vault] across similar to the one in the center of the eastern section. There was a round, quite tall building, then another arch, and the rest consisted of chambers like the others. This wing crosses the entire courtyard, forming two courts, one at the back in the west, the other to the east, surrounded by four wings as described. The last of these wings, however, located in the south, is quite different. It is comprised of two sections and has two arches along the front like the rest. The first part of these chambers has a corridor with very thick columns topped by very beautifully worked whole stones. In the middle is a wall upon which rests the vault of both rooms. There are two passageways into the other chamber; the entire chamber is enclosed [with a ceiling] and serves as a retreat.

About two good stone-throws distant (about 36 yards or 36 meters) from this building is another one, very tall and with a beautiful court. It contains three elegantly ornamented pyramids. Atop one is a chapel [temple] with vaults built in the usual fashion. There was a pyramid a fair distance away, so large and beautiful that, although they used the [cut stones from it] to build a large part of the city [of Mérida] they founded, I doubt whether it will ever come to an end [of it being a source of cut stone for the new city].[47]

Admiral Montejo gave us the first of the above buildings, with the four wings. It was all covered with large trees, which we cleared before we could build ourselves a proper all-stone monastery and a fine church. We christened it after the Mother of God. There was so much stone left over from the southern wing, and part of the other wings that we gave much stone to the Spanish settlers so they could [construct their own] houses; the stones were particularly suited for [constructing] doorframes and window frames; such was the abundance [of this stone].

The buildings at the town of Tikoch are neither as abundant nor as sumptuous as many of these others, although they were good and noteworthy. I only mention them here because there must have been a large population [at some previous time], as I have mentioned before and have [no need to mention again here]. These buildings are three leagues (9 miles or 13.5 kilometers) from Izamal toward the east, and seven leagues (21 miles or 31.5 kilometers) from Chicheniźá.

---

[47] Building atop existing structures to build grander ones was a common practice among the Maya. Many pyramids are built atop smaller pyramids, resulting in structures that resemble Russian dolls with one pyramid one inside another.

Chicheniza, then, is a splendid site, ten leagues (30 miles or 45 kilometers) from Izamal and 11 (33 miles or 50 kilometers) from Valladolid. The elder First Peoples tell that three lords reigned here. They were, according to what they say their forefathers told them, brothers who arrived here from the Land of the West [Mexico] assembled and then raised a great settlement and [adjacent] communities.[48] They ruled for years in peace and with justice. They revered their deities and built many magnificent buildings; one especially, the greatest [of all], whose design I will describe, using a sketch I made while standing atop of it, so that it may be better understood.

They say that these lords lived as celibates and most uprightly, being held in high esteem and obeyed by all throughout their [rule]. In the course of time, however, one of them vanished—he must have died. [Some oral traditions of] the First Peoples tell, however, [contradict this], saying that he abandoned [the peninsula] through the port of Bacalar. However his absence came about, the result was [not in dispute]: it affected those who ruled after him, and partisan dissensions arose throughout the realm. They became so [vain] and immodest, they became dissolute in their ways, and [acted] without restraint. Such was [their excess] that the people came to hate them so intensely that they killed them, and overthrew their rule. They abandoned the site, leaving behind the buildings and the [ceremonial center], both beautiful, and only ten leagues (30 miles or 45 kilometers) from the sea, with fertile lands and all the districts around it, which were [also] deserted. The design of the principal building follows:

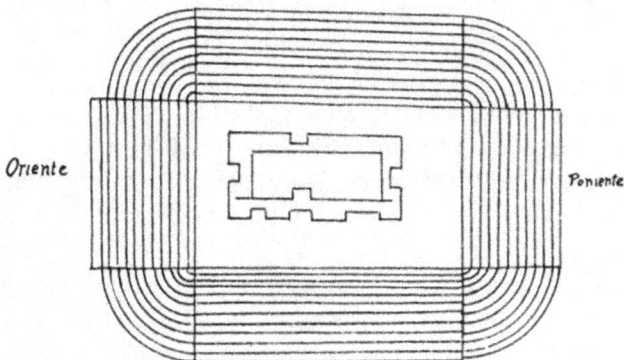

Oriente   Poniente

---

[48] The oral traditions related by the Maya and other First Peoples in Yucatán are consistent with the historical record documenting the arrival of the Itzá nation, which raised Chichén Itzá, introducing architectural elements from the Valley of Mexico to the Yucatán during the Late Classic (600-900 C.E.) period.

This structure has four stairways placed to the four [cardinal points], 32 feet wide (9.75 meters), with 91 steps to each that are laborious to climb. The steps have the same rise and width as we give to ours. Each staircase has two low ramps level with the steps, two feet broad (0.6 meters) and of well-dressed stonework, like all the rest of the [pyramid itself]. The structure has no sharp corners because, starting from the ground up, it narrows in, as shown, away from the ramps of the stairs, with round-cut blocks [of stone] rising by stages and tapering in a very graceful manner.

When I saw it there was [a sculpture of] the fierce jaw of a serpent at the foot of each side of the stairway; it was curiously carved from a single stone. The staircase ends in this manner: at the summit there is a small flat platform, on which there is a building with four rooms, each having an entrance in the middle [of the facade] and roofed with a vaulted arch. The north chamber [however] stands by itself with a corridor of thick columns. The chamber in the center has a sort of interior room court and follows the lines of the outside of the building. [It has] a door opening into the corridor at the north and has a ceiling [comprised] of wooden beams; this was where incense was burned. At the entrance of this doorway, or of the corridor [hallway], there is a sort of arms carved on a stone, which I could not discern very well.

There were, and there still are today, many other well-built and large structures around this [pyramid]. All the ground around them was formerly paved, traces being still visible, so strong was the cement of which the [roads] were constructed. There were two small theaters of masonry, with four staircases located in front of the north stairway, standing at some distance. It is said that they performed plays and comedies to entertain the townspeople.

A beautiful broad paved causeway runs from there and leads to a well two stone-throws (about 36 yards or 36 meters) across from the court in front of these theaters. They are still accustomed to throwing into this well living men and women as sacrifices to their deities during times of drought. They maintain that [these sacrificial victims] did not die, even though none were ever seen again. They also threw in many other offerings of precious stones and things they valued greatly; as such, if there were gold in this country, this well would [be where one would most likely find] most of it, seeing the devotion the First Peoples had [for this sacred well].

This well is seven long fathoms (about 13 yards, 13 meters) deep to the surface of the water, more than a hundred feet wide (30.5 meters) round, of natural rock [sinkhole] wonderfully smooth down to the water.

The water looks very green, and I think it is caused by the trees that surround it; it is very deep. There is a small building where I found idols made in honor of all the principal deities throughout the land, like the Pantheon at Rome. It is located at the top, near the mouth [of the well]. I do not know whether this is an ancient invention or one of the modern ones, [but it is clear that the purpose was to find] their idols when they [arrived] with offerings to [throw into] the well. I found sculptured lions [jaguars], pitchers, and other things, so that I do not understand how anyone can say that these people had no [metal] tools. I also found two immense statues of men, carved of a single stone block, naked save for the waist-covering the First Peoples use [throughout the peninsula]. The heads were separate pieces, with rings like the ones the First Peoples use in their ears, and a tang that rested in a depression made in the neck for it, which made the sculpture complete.

XLIII
For What Other Things the First Peoples Made Sacrifices.

The feasts on these peoples' calendar that have been described earlier show us what and how many they were, and how and why these were celebrated. But because their feasts were only to secure the goodwill or favor of their deities, when [their deities] were angered, they made [these ceremonies] neither more nor less bloody [than deemed necessary]. Whenever they were visited by pestilences, discord, droughts, or similar misfortunes, they believed [their deities] were angry, and [it was] then they did not undertake to appease the demons by sacrificing animals, nor making offerings only of their food and drink, or shedding their own blood and enduring vigils, fasts, and abstinences. Rather, forgetful of all natural mercy and all the law of reason, they made sacrifices of human beings as easily as they did of birds, and as often as their malevolent priests, or the *chilanes*, said it was necessary or as it was the fancy or will of their community leaders. [Considering] the number of people [in Yucatán] was much smaller than the great population in Mexico, and that after the fall of Mayapán they were governed not by one leader but by many, they did not slaughter [great numbers] of people together. Nevertheless many still died miserably, since each town had the authority to sacrifice whomever the priest, or the *chilán*, or the community leader saw fit. They had in their temples and public places areas where they carried out [these human sacrifices], which they undertook as if these were the most important things in the world for the preservation of the state. In addition to the sacrifices [carried out] in their towns, they had those wicked sanctuaries of Chichénitzá and Cuzmil where they sent an innumerable number of poor wretches to be sacrificed, one to be hurled from a height, another to have his heart torn out. May the merciful Lord, He who saw fit to sacrifice himself to the Father on the cross for all mankind, see fit to free us from such miserable errors forever more.

O Lord my God, light, being, and life of my soul, holy guide and safe road for my daily course, solace in my grief, inner joy of my suffering, comfort and rest of my labors: Why, O Lord, dost thou command me to undertake tasks that I cannot perform, rather than rest? Why dost thou ask of me tasks that I cannot carry through? Lord, dost thou not know the measure of thy vassal and the strength of my limbs, and the nature of my strengths? Dost thou perchance fail me, Lord, in my labors? Art thou not the loving Father of whom the holy prophet spoke in the psalm: "And call upon me in the day of trouble: I will deliver thee, and thou shalt glorify me?"[49]

Lord, if thou art, and thou art He of whom the prophet spoke when full of thy Holy Spirit, that makes a burden of thy command, and thus it is, Lord, that those who have not enjoyed the sweetness of thy service and the fulfilling of thy commands, find a burden in them; but Lord, it is a false burden, a task feared, a burden to the weak of spirit, and they fear it who never put the hand to the plow to accomplish it. Those [in contrast] who give themselves to thy services find them sweet, they seek after the odor of their salves, their sweetness comforts them at every step; many more pleasures do they find daily that the others cannot know, as in another Queen of Saba.

Thus, Lord, do I implore thee, that thou give me grace in thy example to leave the house of my sensuality and the kingdom of my vices and sins behind, making of all the occasion to serve thee and keep thy commandments, so that in observing them my [obedience] may instruct me more, that by reading and becoming familiar with them I may find the good of thy grace for my soul; and thus as I believe thy yoke to be pleasant and light, I may render thee thanks that I find myself under thy protection, and free from the errors into which thou seest that so many multitudes of people walk and have walked, traveling on the road to Hell.

It is such agony that I do not know whose heart would not be torn apart, witnessing the suffering and intolerable grief with which these idol worshippers are led by the devil, and are continued to be led away, to the [confines of] Hell. And if this on the devil's part, who attempts to secure this, is a great cruelty, it is justly permitted, on God's part, in order that, since men will not let themselves be governed by the light of the reason He has given them, they may begin to be tormented in this life and to endure part of the Hell they deserve for the difficult rituals they continuously perform for the devil, with long fasts, and vigils, and abstinences; with unbelievable offerings and presents of their effects and property, constant pouring out of their own blood, severe pains and wounds to their bodies, and what is worse and graver, with the lives of their fellows and brothers. Yet, with all this, the devil is never satiated or satisfied with their torments and toils, nor with carrying them off to Hell where he torments them eternally. Truly, it is that God is more easily appeased and with less of torments and deaths; did He not cry unto the great patriarch Abraham and bid him to stay his hand from taking of his

---

[49] There are various translations to the psalm Diego de Landa quotes in this passage, but the consensus is that it is Psalm 50:15. The King James Bible is quoted here.

son's life, because his Majesty had determined to send his own son into the world and let Him lose His life on the cross, that humanity might see that for the son of the eternal God the command of the Father is heavy, and yet very sweet is it to Him, and for humanity only an apparent burden.

Therefore, let those cast out the faintness of their hearts, and the fear of a burden in this blessed work of God; for the weight is illusionary, and becomes a balm to the body and soul, beyond all which it is worthy that God be served well. This we owe to Him as a just debt and payment; it is all for our benefit, not only for eternity but also temporal. Therefore let all us Christians, and especially the priests, behold what shame and disgrace there is in this world, and yet more in that [which is] to come, to see the devil finds [men and women] who serve him with unbelievable labors only to be repaid for by it going to Hell, but that God can hardly find anyone who, by keeping His so sweet commandments, serves Him faithfully that he may go to eternal glory.

Therefore do you, priest of God, tell me if you have taken heed of the office of these unhappy priests of the devil, and of all those that in the Holy Scriptures we find in times past, how much more laborious were their fasts than yours, and how long and many; how much longer were their vigils and their miserable prayers than those you offer, how much more careful and painstaking they were of the duties of their office than you are of yours; with how much more zeal than you they understood how to teach [their] foul doctrines. And should you find yourself in any error, correct it, and see that you are a priest of the Lord above, who solely by your office obliges you to seek to live in purity and righteousness, the purity of an angel rather than of humanity.[50]

---

[50] This chapter becomes a meditation in which Diego de Landa justifies the actions for which he was accused before the Council of the Indies. He maintained that, because the devil had arrived in Yucatán and was undermining the work of the Church, he was justified to act in a decisive way against the satanic spell under which the Maya had fallen.

XLIV
The Soil and Its Products.

Yucatán is a land with the least soil I have seen, being all flat living sandstone [lowlands] with very little earth.[51] [As such] there are, curiously, few places where one can dig down a fathom (2 yards or 2 meters) without encountering great banks of very large rocks. This stone is not very good for fine carving, because it is hard and coarse. Nevertheless, such as it is, it has served in the construction of the great number of buildings that there are in the country. The country is excellent for lime, of which there is much. It is a marvel to behold the fertility of the soil atop or between the [layers of] stones. All that grows throughout the country grows more plentiful and robust among the rocks [and stones] than in [open] fields. The First Peoples do not sow [in the fields] where no trees grow, [and as such] there is nothing [there] but only grass. But where they do sow [among] the rocky areas they harvest crops, and all the trees flourish; some of them marvelously large and beautiful to behold. The reason this is so, I think, is that there is more moisture, and it is retained better [in these microclimates] than in the open fields.

Until now, no kind of native metal has so far been found in this country, and it is astonishing that without it they have been able to build so many buildings. The First Peoples cannot provide any information [regarding] what tools were used [in the construction of the vast ceremonial centers throughout the peninsula]. But since they lack metals, [it is evident] God provided them with ranges nearby where they secured flints where the sierra crosses the country, which I described [in Chapter I]. From this [flint] they fashioned points for their war spears, and also made knives used in sacrifice (of which the priests have a great supply). They used to make, and still make, arrow tips from [flint], which serves them as metal [tools]. They had a certain malleable brass that, when melded with a light mixture of gold [when cast] provided them with hatchets and the little rattling bells they used in their dances, as well as a sort of chisel that they used in making the idols and hollowed-out blowpipes. They use the blowpipe a great deal and shoot very well with

---

[51] Diego de Landa uses the expression "es una viva laja," of a "living stone" or "living sandstone" to denote a rock limestone flat landmass capable of harboring a wide variety of ecosystems, from mangroves to scrub forests, tropical vegetation to tropical rain forests. In anthropological terms, the Yucatán peninsula is known as the northern Maya lowlands.

it. This brass and other plaques of sheets or harder metal were secured from the First Peoples from Tabasco [to the west of Yucatán], and which they used in making their idols. There is no other kind of [native] metal among [the First Peoples of Yucatán].

According to the wise, one of the things most necessary for humans to live is water, without which the earth cannot yield its fruits or mankind live. Yucatán lacks the abundance of rivers that are found in neighboring lands; it has only two. One of these is Río Lagartos, which flows into the sea at a headland, and the other is the Champotón; which is both brackish and with poor water. God [however] provided many sources of fine water, some natural and others created by [the First People's] industry. Nature has in this respect worked so differently in this country [than it has in] the rest of the world, where the rivers and springs flow aboveground. Here, [in contrast] all [water currents] run in hidden channels underground. As I have been shown, the entire coast is full of springs of fresh water, rising in the sea, and from many of which one can take water, as I myself have done, when the shore is left dry by the ebb tide.

Inland, God has provided various hollows in the natural rock [natural sinkholes in the limestone flatbed], which the First Peoples call cenotes. [These formations] drop with sheer sides reaching down to the water. At times there are furious currents that have been known to carry off cattle that fall into them. All these currents flow out into the sea and create the springs that have been mentioned. These cenotes contain very fine fresh water and are a great sight to behold, for some of them are of cut sheer rock clear down to the water; others have mouths that God created or were caused by lightning strikes (which occur with frequently) or in other manners. Inside there are handsome vaults of the living rock [which are caverns of stalagmites and stalactites, collectively known as dripstone]. Atop [there are] trees, so that above and beneath [the cenotes there are] forests. [Some cenotes are large enough so that] a boat may be sailed; others are larger or smaller. The people who could [availed themselves] of these cenotes [as a water source] and drank of them. [Those who had no cenotes] dug their own wells, but these were very poor ones because they lacked tools [to construct proper wells].[52] Now, however, we have provided them [technology] for constructing good wells, as well as most excellent [technology to] pump wells from which fresh water can be taken as from a spring [and stored in proper tanks]. There are also lagoons to be found, but all of these are of brackish water,

---

[52] In consequence, a general observation is that most settlements in Yucatán, dating from pre-Hispanic times, are located near cenotes, or other naturally-occurring sources of fresh water.

are too foul to drink, and without the flowing currents found in the cenotes.

There is one thing in this country, in all this [discussion of its] marvelous matter of the wells, and it is this: wherever the ground is dug [and excavated] a fine spring gushes forth. Some [of these springs are] so beautiful that a spear can be sunk down into them. Also, in all the places where wells have been excavated, at about half a man's height above the water level, one finds a layer of seashells and conches in many different kinds and colors, large and small, similar to those found on the seashore, with the sand already turned into hard white rock. At Maní, [now decreed to be a] royal town, we dug a great shaft well to construct [a bucket well] for the First Peoples to use and, after having dug seven to eight fathoms (about 14 yards or 14 meters), in the solid rock we discovered a grave [located] a good seven feet long (2.1 meters). It was filled with very fresh bright-red earth and with human bones, which when removed were found to be almost turned to stone. This was still two to three fathoms (about 4.5 yards or 4.5 meters) before hitting the water and before reaching what we found to be a hollow arch created by God in such a way that the tomb was enclosed within the rock. [It was possible] to walk underground to reach the water. We could not understand how this could have been possible, unless we might surmise that the grave was placed there on the inside, and afterward through the moisture of the cave and with the lapse of time the rock hardened, [thus] sealing up the tomb.

In addition to the two rivers that I have said are in the country, there is a spring three leagues (9 miles or 14 kilometers) from the sea, near Campeche, that is brackish; in the whole land there is no [source of above-ground] water. The First Peoples living near the sierra, who need to dig very deep wells, are accustomed to collect rainwater for their homes [during the] rainy season in great cavities in the rocks. [The reason for this being that] very heavy [tropical] downpours occur then, with much thunder and lightning at times. All the wells, especially those near the sea, rise and fall with the low and high tides every day, which demonstrates clearly that the underground rivers run into the sea.

XLV
The Waters and the Fishes Found in Them.

There is a marsh in Yucatán worthy of mention. It is 70 leagues (210 miles or 320 kilometers) in length and entirely saline. It begins on the coast of Ekab, which is near the Isla de Mugeres, and continues very close to the seashore between the coast and the marshy woodlands [scrub forests], until it almost reaches Campeche. It is not deep, [the terrain] lacking soil, but it is [cumbersome] to cross when traveling from the towns to the coast or vice versa because of the trees and the great quantity of mud. This marsh, created by God, is saline and it has the finest salt I have seen in my life. When ground up it is very white, and those who know [about salt] claim that a half peck of it salts more than a [full] peck from [salt of] other places. Our Lord created the salt in this marsh from the rainwater, not from the sea, for the [sea] does not enter [the swamps] because of a strip of land [that runs parallel along the shore for] the whole distance, between the marsh and the sea.

During the rainy season these marshes become swollen [with rainwater], and the salt coagulates in large and small lumps that resemble nothing less than sugar candy. Four or five months after the rains have ceased and the lagoon somewhat dried [through evaporation], the First Peoples, in the earlier times, had the custom of going to gather the salt, taking the lumps from the water and carrying them off to dry. They had identified the specific places in the lagoon that were where the salt was richest and there was less mud and water. It was their custom not to harvest this salt without the permission of nearby community leaders, who had [by default] control [over the salt deposits]. Those who [journeyed] to collect salt offered some tribute to these leaders, either of the salt itself or of things from their own region. A leading man named Francisco Euan, [born in the] the town of Caucel, offered proof of this and demonstrated that his forebears on the coast had received from the authorities of Mayapán the responsibility of managing the matter [of salt harvesting] and of the distribution of the salt. [In consequence] the Audiencia of Guatemala ordered those who went to collect salt [to pay him] the same tribute [his forebears had traditionally received]. [To this day] a great deal [of salt] is gathered to be taken to Mexico [City], Honduras, and Havana. In some places this marsh harbors some very fine fish that, although not large in size, are of an excellent flavor.

There are fish not only in the lagoon but also along the coast, and in such abundance, that the First Peoples care little for those of the lagoon, except those of them who do not have nets; these fish along the many shallow waters with their arrows [spearing them]. Other [fishermen] catch great quantities of fish, which they either eat or sell throughout the entire region. It is their custom to salt and cook [the fish] or to dry them in the sun without salt, depending [on which is appropriate to the species of fish caught]. The [fish] that are sun-dried they keep for days, and carry 20 to 30 leagues (60 to 90 miles or 90 to 135 kilometers) to sell. To eat it, they then season and cook the fish again, and is it both savory and wholesome.

The fish they kill [along the coast] are skates, very plump and good; a fish similar to trout more or less in color, speckles and taste but fatter and savory to eat, which in [the Maya language] they call *izcay*. [They also catch] very fine sea bass [*róbalos*], and sardines; also [Spanish] flounders, sawfish [*sierras*], horse mackerel, *mojarras*; and an infinite variety of other small fish. On the Campeche coast there are very good octopus [and squid], three or four kinds of pike (*sollos*) that are good and wholesome, especially one variety with a different head from the others, for these have a round head, remarkably flat, with the mouth underside and the eyes on the edges of the round part. They call these *alipechpol*. They also catch some very large fish that look like mantas, which they slice up and salt; it dies [and subsequently floats] around the edges of the lagoons and is very excellent. I do not know whether it is a ray fish [or skate].

There are many manatees on the coast between Campeche and La Desconocida, which apart from the amount of flesh they provide [they] also yield a great deal of fat useful for cooking [frying] food. Wonderful things are said of the manatees. [Indeed,] the author of the *General History of the Indies* tells that on the Island of Hispaniola [shared by the nations of Haiti and the Dominican Republic today], a leader of the First Peoples there raised one in a lake that was so well trained that it came to the shore when called by the name he had given to it, which was Matu.

What I can say about them is that they are so large as to provide much more meat than a large calf, and much fat. They breed their young like [land] animals [mammals], having their male and female sexual organs. The females give birth to two young, and neither more nor less; they do not lay eggs as do other fish. They have two fins like strong arms for swimming. Their face much resembles that of an ox, and they thrust it out of the water to eat shore plants [and other vegetation]. Bats often bite them on their round flat snouts, and they die from these bites, for they bleed to death in the water from any cut. The flesh is good, especially when it is fresh, and when [accompanied] with mustard it tastes like good beef.

The First Peoples [along the coasts of Yucatán] kill them with harpoons in the following manner: they hunt for them in the streams and shallow waters (for it is not a fish that swims in deep [open] waters), tying their harpoons to lines with floats on the ends. When they find them, they shoot their spears [harpoons] at them and then release the line and floats. The fish [manatees] try to escape from the pain of the wounds and seek shelter, swimming into shallows, never going into the depths of the sea, since they do not know how to [navigate open waters]. [Because of their] large size, they stir up mud and leave a trail of blood, [often] bleeding to death. The First Peoples then follow in their boats [and canoes] the trail of stirred mud [and blood] until they capture them with the floating line. It is a fish of great value and highly appreciated, since it is all flesh and fat.

There is another fish on this coast that they call *ba*, broad and round, and it makes [for a] good meal, but it is dangerous to kill or to encounter. It also does not go into deep waters but inhabits the shoals [and shallow fresh waters], where the First Peoples hunt it with bow and arrow. But if they are careless walking near it, or if they step on it in the [shallow] water, it attacks at once with its long, thin tail, and it inflicts such a wound with a saw [stinger] that it [has at the end of its tail] that it cannot be removed without greatly enlarging the cut, since the teeth are set backward. The First Peoples use these small stingers to cut themselves when they make [blood] sacrifices to the [devil], and it was the responsibility of the priest to have them [on hand for use in bloodletting ceremonies]. As such, they had many very fine ones, for the bone is white and curiously formed like a saw, so sharp and pointed that it cuts like a knife blade.

There is a small fish that is so poisonous that no one who eats it fails to swell up and die quickly. Although it is known [that this fish is poisonous], it deceives people on many occasions, since, when out of the water, it takes time [for the victim] to die [despite the fact that] the entire body swells greatly [and many fail to make the connection between being poisoned by the fish and the sudden onset of death]. There are also very fine oysters in the Champotón River, and there are many sharks all along the coast.

XLVI
Iguanas and Alligators.

In addition to the fish that live in the waters, there are other creatures they also use, living both in the water and on the land. Such as the many iguanas, which are like the lizards of Spain in shape and size, although they are not as green in color. These lay many eggs, and are always found near the sea or where there is water, living in either element [salt or fresh water sources]. [In consequence] the Spaniards eat them during the periods of [religious] fasting, and find them to be an exceptional and wholesome food.[53] There are so many of them that they provide [nourishment] for everybody during Lent. The First Peoples hunt them with lassos as they rest high on trees or in the holes [of trees]. It is incredible how long they can go without food; after they have been captured, they can go for even for 20 or 30 days without eating a mouthful and without growing lean. I have also heard, as a fact, that if their underbellies are rubbed with sand, they fatten up. Their excrement is an excellent medicine for curing clouds over the eyes, when applied to them while fresh.

There are turtles of wonderful size, some of which are much larger than immense shields, and they are excellent eating, and yield satisfying [meat]. They lay eggs as large as a hen's, in numbers up to 150 and 200 [at a time]. They scoop out a great hole in the beach sand, away from the water, lay [their eggs], then cover them up and leave; there the turtle hatchlings are born. There are other kinds of turtles on the land, in the [tropical] forests, and in the lagoons.

Several times I saw a fish on the coast, which being completely in a shell, I left to mention here. It is, then, about the size of a small turtle, covered above with a delicate, round shell of beautiful shape and a very pale green [color]. It has a tail covered in the same shell and is very slender like a gimlet, and some six inches in length. On the underside it has many legs, and it is filled with eggs, which are the only edible part. The First Peoples eat [this roe] in large quantities, and in their language call this fish *mex*.

There are many fierce alligators which, although they live in the water, come out and stay for long time on land. They eat either while on land or with their heads out of the water, since they lack gills and are unable to chew under water. It is a heavy animal and does not stray far

---

[53] In his log, Christopher Columbus described the taste of iguanas as being similar to chicken.

from water. [It is] able to move fiercely quick when it attacks or when it flees. It will devour anything, and strange [stories] are told of it. To my own knowledge one killed one of our Maya [pupils] while he was bathing in a lagoon near a monastery. Then one of the friars quickly went with some Maya to kill it. To do this they took along a small dog, running a pointed hard stake through its body from snout to tail and then, fastening a very strong rope to it inside, they threw it in the lagoon. The alligator came out at once and seized [the dog] with its teeth, and swallowed it. When [the dog] had been swallowed, the men who had gone with the friar tugged hard, while the stake turned crosswise in the alligator's body. Upon opening the underbelly [of the alligator] they found inside the half of the man's [body], as well as the little dog.

These alligators breed like [other] animals, but lay eggs for which they dig a large hole in the sand near the water's edge. They lay 300 or more eggs, and [these are] larger than birds' eggs. They leave them until the time when nature has taught them they are to hatch. Then [the adults] return and wait until the young hatch. These [hatchlings] are the size of the palm of the hand, and they wait for a wave to break close to them. When they feel it, they leap into the water; those [newborns that] do not reach the water and remain on the sand quickly die, since they are so tender and the sun is as hot as it is; they burn up and die at once. Those that reach the water all begin to swim immediately, and survive. They remain there until their parents return, and they follow the adults. In this manner, very few survive, in spite of the number of eggs that are laid; it is by the favor of the Divine Providence that there should be more of the things that are beneficial to us than for those that injure us, and could do harm as would these beasts if they were all to live.

XLVII
How There Are Serpents and Other Poisonous Animals.

The diversity of snakes or serpents is tremendous, and these are of many colors and not dangerous, except for two kinds which very poisonous ones, much larger than those we have here in Spain. They call these [snakes] *taxinchan*. There are also others, these being very long and very poisonous, with rattles on their tails. There are others so large that they can swallow a hare, or two, but are not dangerous [to people]. It has to be said that some of the First People can easily handle both of these kinds [of snakes] without being harmed.

There is a sort of lizard, larger than those here [in Spain]. It is surprising [to witness] the great fear the First Peoples have of them; they claim that merely touching them gives a person a sweat that is a deadly poison. There are many scorpions among the rocks, but they are not as poisonous as those here in Spain.

There is a kind of large ant whose bite is much worse; the pains and inflammation are [more painful] than that of the scorpions, and last twice as long. I know this from experience. There are two sorts of spiders, one small and foul-smelling, and the other very large and completely covered with very fine black spines that look like hair, and which is poisonous. The First Peoples are, as a result, most careful not to touch them. There is a small reddish grub from which they make a yellow ointment that is very good for swellings and sores, and it requires little more than to crush or knead [the grubs] together [to extract the ointment]. It also is useful as an ointment [emulsion] for painting vases and thickening the paint.

XLVIII
Of the Bees and Their Honey and Wax.

There are two kinds of bees, and both are much smaller than ours [found in Spain]. The larger of them are raised in very small hives. They do not build honeycombs as do ours, but instead construct small sacs about the size of walnuts, all close together and full of honey. To collect the honey the First Peoples simply open the beehive and break the sacs with a stick, for the honey runs out, and then they gather the wax as they wish.[54]

The others live in the forests, in the hollows of trees and rocks, where one must search them out for their wax. The country abounds with this honey. The honey is most excellent except for the fact that it is somewhat watery because the plants on which the bees feed are luxuriant, the honey is thin and watery. In consequence, it is necessary to [reduce the honey over] fire, which [thickens it] and makes it very good and very firm. The wax is very good, except that it is smoky. I have not been able to discover the reason for this. In some districts [throughout Yucatán] it is more yellow [in hue] as a result of the flowers [on which the bees feed]. These bees do not sting, even when the honey is gathered.

---

[54] The Maya honey bee (*Melipona beecheii*) is stingless.

XLIX
Of the Plants, Flowers, and Trees; Of the Fruits and Other Edibles.

The variety of plants and flowers that adorn Yucatán in their seasons is great and remarkable, both among the trees and on the plants. Many of them are wonderfully delicate and beautiful, of many colors, and fragrant. These flora, apart from dressing the woods and fields in beauty, also afford the greatest abundance of food for the bees for their honey and wax. I shall mention a number here, both for their exquisite perfume and beauty and for the benefits derived from them by those who inhabit these lands.

There are sages much leafier and more aromatic than those here [in Spain], and with longer and slenderer leaves. The First Peoples [of Yucatán] cultivate them for their fragrance and for their pleasure. I have noted that they grow better when the Maya women put ashes around their stems.

There is one plant with broad leaves and tall, thick branches, and it is of a singular freshness and fertile. It grows easily from cuttings, with the same profusion as do osiers, although they cannot be compared to these in any way. If the leaf is rubbed a little between the hands it has a real odor of clover, although it loses this scent when it is dry; it is very good for keeping the temples fresh during festivals and it is used for this purpose.

There is also sweet basil found in the woods and fields, which are full of it in some places. It grows among the rocks and is very fresh, beautiful, and scented, though it is not comparable to what is grown in the gardens, imported from here [Spain], and which now grows and spreads in a wonderful fashion.

There is a flower they call *tixzula*, of the most delicate scents I have ever known, much more so than the jasmine.[55] It is white, or light mauve in some cases, and [because it grows] from bulbs, it could be brought here to Spain. It is cultivated in this way: the bulbs put forth tall, thick, and very fresh spires that last year-round, and once a year in the center they bear a green stem as broad as three fingers and as long as the spires. At the top of these stems the flowers sprout in a bunch, each being some six inches (15 centimeters) long with its stem. When they bloom they have five long petals, open and connected at the base by a delicate white

---

[55] *Hymenocallis americana.*

membrane in the center, yellow and white. They are wonderfully beautiful. When this stalk is cut and put in a jar of water, it holds the soft perfume for many days, because the joined flowers open only a little at a time.

There are certain small lilies that are very white and fragrant, which last long in water and would be easy to bring here [to Spain], since they also grow from bulbs and are quite like our Easter lilies, except that the odor is more delicate and does not give headaches. These flowers also lack the yellow center of our lilies.

There is a tree [laurel] they call *ixlaul*, which I have been told is of much beauty, and fragrant. There is also a kind of tree they call *nicte* that bears many white roses; others are half yellow, and yet others are half purplish. These [nightshades and yerba buenas] are fresh and fragrant, and of them they fashion elegant posies, and they can also be used in confections.

There is a flower they call *kom*, which is very fragrant and gives a strong scent that burns [and irritates the nostrils] when inhaled [deeply]. It could easily be brought here [to Spain]. Its leaves are broad and marvelously fresh.

Besides these sweet-smelling flowers and plants there are many others most beneficial and medicinal, among them two varieties of nightshade, fresh and very fine. There is much scale fern [*doradilal*], and also maiden's hair; also a plant whose leaves, when boiled, are a wonderful remedy for swollen feet and legs.

There is another especially good for curing sores, which they call *yaxpahalché*. Another one has the odor of fennel both when eaten raw or boiled. It is also applied to cure sores. At Bacalar, sarsaparilla is found.

They have a certain plant that grows in wells and other places, three-cornered like the sedge, but much thicker. They make their baskets from its leaves, staining them beautifully with colors. They also have a plant that grows both wild and is cultivated near their houses, where it flourishes. It is a kind of hemp fiber that they use for making an innumerable quantity of useful articles. Also, there is a certain plant that grows wild on certain trees. It bears fruit like small cucumbers from which they make [sticky] gums or glues for sticking things together when needed.

The crops they have for human consumption are very good [varieties of corn, or] maize. Their corn is of many different sorts and colors. They harvest it in great quantities and store it in cribs and grain silos for lean years. There are two kinds of small beans, one black and the other of various colors. They [now] have others, small and white, that were introduced from Spain.

Their peppers have many different pods.[56] They have many [varieties of squash and pumpkins], the seeds of which are used for seasoning. Others are prepared roasted or boiled, and still others are used for [gourd] vessels for household use. They have very good melons, and [now] also Spanish calabashes. They [also now] harvest millet, which yields abundantly and is good food.

They have a yellow fruit that is refreshing and delicious. It is cultivated, and its fruit grows at the root; it resembles a short, fat, round turnip.[57] They eat it either raw or salted.

There is another cultivated root that grows under the earth. It is very nutritious, has many varieties, and comes in several colors, purple, yellow, and white. They eat it boiled or roasted. It is good eating and tastes somewhat like chestnuts. They also serve it roasted for a drink.[58]

There are two other kinds of good roots they cultivate as food.[59] There are also others that grow wild and are salty in flavor. I have described these, and the First Peoples eat them in times of hunger; otherwise they pay no mind to them.

They have a small tree with soft branches containing much sap. They eat its leaves after boiling them; it tastes like cabbage [or kale] and is good with plenty of fat bacon. The First Peoples plant it as soon as they make their homes anywhere, and then they can harvest its leaves [throughout] the entire year. There is much fresh endive grown in the gardens, but they never think of eating it.

It is a reason to praise God together with the prophet who has said, "O LORD our Lord, how excellent *is* thy name in all the earth!"[60] because of the great number of trees Thy Majesty has created in this country, and all so different from ours, so unlike what I have seen elsewhere (I speak of Yucatán, for I have been elsewhere), and both the First Peoples and the Spaniards have great use and benefit from them.

One tree bears a fruit [shaped] like round gourds. The First Peoples make their vessels [*jícaras*] from them. They are very handsome, and they paint them elaborately and beautifully. There is also gourd of the same species, only smaller and very hard, from which they make small containers for ointments and other purposes.[61]

---

[56] *Capsicum* in the nightshade family *Solanaceae*.

[57] *Pachyrhizus erosus* is commonly known as *jícama*.

[58] Diego de Landa, perhaps, is describing cacao, which grows in these colors and when toasted is prepared as a beverage.

[59] Yam and sweet potato.

[60] Diego de Landa quotes Psalm 8:9. The King James bible is quoted here.

[61] *Lagenaria siceraria* or calabash.

There is another kind that bears a fruit similar to hazelnuts. They use its pits to make fine beads, and its bark is used for to make a soap, with a fine lather, with which they wash their clothes.

They take great care of the tree [copal] from which they harvest the incense used [in ceremonies to honor] their demons. They extract the bark with a stone [flint], letting the sap run out. This tree is shady, tall, and with fine leafage and foliage, but its flower turns beeswax black wherever it grows.

There is a very handsome tree that grows near the wells, tall and with fresh green leaves; it spreads its branches in a marvelous manner, growing in groups of three or more at regular intervals from the trunk, and it continues to extend and the trunk grows [thicker].[62]

There are also cedars, but not of the finer kind.[63] There is a sort of yellowish tree, with veins similar to an oak. It is marvelously strong and very hard, and so stout that we have seen it used in the doorways of the buildings in Izamal; they are [capable of] supporting the entire weight of the building. There is another wood, of the hardest kind, with a tawny color, from which they make bows and lances [sapote, or *Sapotaceae* tree]. There is [yet] another [wood], the color of an orange, from which they make staffs. It is very strong. I think it is called brazilwood.

There are many trees that they say are good for the affliction of blisters, which they call *zon*. There is a tree whose sap causes sores if it is touched, and even its shade is noxious, if one sleeps under it.[64] There is another with [sets of] double thorns, long and very hard and thick, in which the birds never rest; these thorns are all hollow inside, and always filled with ants.[65] There is another tree of great height and size, which bears a fruit similar to carob beans. It is filled with certain black seed-nuts that they eat in time of famine; from its roots they make buckets for drawing water from the wells. The First Peoples make small cups for collecting water from the bark of certain trees. They make ropes from others; yet the bark of others they crush and smash to use for polishing plastered walls [of their homes] and hardening the walls. There are beautiful mulberry trees that yield fine wood; also so many other beneficial and beautiful trees as to astonish one.

In the fields and woods there are many kinds of long osiers or willows, [different from] the kind of which they make baskets, which they

---

[62] *Ceiba pentandra.*

[63] *Cedrela mexicana* or Spanish cedar.

[64] *Metopium brownei* (more commonly known as Chechem or Black Poisonwood) is a species of plant in the *Anacardiaceae* family.

[65] Diego de Landa is describing the *Acacia cornigera*, commonly known as the *Bullhorn acacia*, which figures prominently in the mythology and art of the Maya.

use for lashing together their houses, or for whatever else they need them.[66] The use they make of these [tree and plant materials] is very great indeed. Another tree gives a sap that is a fine remedy to strengthen the gums [and set loose teeth]. There is another that bears a certain large fruit that is filled with [downy] floss that is used for pillows and is superior to the tow of the Alcarria plateau in Spain.[67]

Fearing to do less than justice to the fruit of their trees, I have felt best to write of them on their own. I will first speak of the wine [pulque] that the First Peoples esteem so highly, and in consequence they plant [this leguminous tree] in all their plots [fields] or around their houses.[68] It is an ugly tree, producing nothing but its roots, from which [they ferment] its wine using honey and water. In the country there are certain wild vines that bear edible grapes; many of these are found on the Cupul coast.[69] There are plum trees of many kinds, some of them very tasty and wholesome.[70] They are very different from ours, having but little meat and a large stone [pit], contrary to the ones found here [in Spain]. The tree produces its fruit before the leaves; it has no blossom.

There are many bananas, which the Spaniards introduced, since there were none before then.[71] There is an enormous tree that bears a large, longish, fat fruit that has red flesh, and it is very fine to eat.[72] It does not produce a flower, but only the fruit itself [sprouting from the branches]. At first it is very small and grows gradually.

There is another very leafy and beautiful tree, which never loses its leaves. This one also bears no flowers, but a fruit as sweet if not sweeter than the one [mentioned] above. It is small, delicate, and delicious to eat. Some of these [tropical fruits] are better than others, and the best would be much appreciated if they were introduced over here [in Spain]; they call them *ya* in their language.[73]

There is another fresh and beautiful tree that also keeps its leaves [year round], and it bears a small fig they call *ox*.[74] Another wonderfully beautiful and fresh tree bears a fruit the size of large eggs; the First

---

[66] *Hibiscus tiliaceus* is a species of flowering tree in the mallow family *Malvaceae*.

[67] *Ceiba aesculifolia*.

[68] *Lonchocarpus* is a plant genus in the legume family *Fabaceae* from which balche pulque, an alcoholic beverage, is made.

[69] *Coccoloba uvifera* is a species of flowering plant in the buckwheat family *Polygonaceae*. It is common throughout the tropics.

[70] *Spondias mombin* is a species of flowering plant in the family *Anacardiaceae*.

[71] *Musa paradisiaca.*

[72] *Calocarpum mammosum.*

[73] Sapodilla, or *Manilkara zapota.*

[74] *Brosimum alicastrum*, the breadnut or Maya nut or *ramón* tree, is widespread throughout Yucatán.

Peoples gather them while green and they ripen them in the ashes. When ripe it lasts well; it is sweet and tastes like the yolk of an egg.[75] Another tree bears a yellow fruit, not as large as the one [described] above, but softer and sweeter. This fruit, when eaten, has a kernel like a small, soft burr that is curious to see. Another fresh and beautiful tree bears a fruit similar to hazelnuts with its shell. Inside these husks is fruit similar to a cherry, with a large [pit the size of a] kernel. The First Peoples call these *vayam*, and the Spaniards call them *guayas*.[76] There is another good and wholesome fruit the Spaniards introduced, which they call *guayabas*.

In the sierras there are two kinds of trees. One bears fruit as large as a good-size pear and is very green, with a thick skin. These [the Maya] ripen by pounding them on a stone, and their flesh has a special flavor. The other bears fruit similar in shape to pineapples; they are good to eat, juicy and acidic. It has many small pits, but these are not [edible]. There is another tree that grows only in open spaces, never among other trees, but alone. Its bark is good for tanning hides, serving like [a native] sumac. It bears a small, tasty yellow fruit, of which women are very fond. There is a very large and leafy tree that the First Peoples call *on*. It bears a fruit similar to a fair-size calabash gourd. Its [flesh is] soft and tastes like butter; it is oily but very nourishing and satisfying. It has a large pit, a thin skin, and is eaten cut in slices like a melon, and with salt.[77]

There are [fruits that resemble] artichokes. They are very spiny and ugly, always found on stems attached to other trees, and growing mixed in with them. The [*pitayah*, or dragonfruit] is red-skinned, shaped like an artichoke, soft to open, and without spines. The flesh inside is white, with many small black seeds. It is sweet, most delicious, and watery and melts in the mouth. It is eaten like an orange in sections around, and with salt; the Maya cannot satisfy the Spaniards' demand for this fruit, [however many they collect] in the forests.

There is a tree that is spongy, ugly but large, and it bears a sort of large fruit full of very savory yellow meat, with pits like hemp seeds but larger. This fruit [is said to be] good for urine [flow and the health of kidneys]. They make an excellent preserve from this fruit. The tree sheds its leaves after the fruit [is no longer in season].

There is a small, rather spiny tree that bears a fruit shaped like a slender cucumber, somewhat long.[78] It is similar to the artichoke in taste,

---

[75] Diego de Landa refers to the papaya fruit. *Carica papaya* is the sole species in the genus *Carica* of the plant family *Caricaceae*.

[76] *Talisia oliviformis* (*Sapindaceae*).

[77] The avocado (*Persea americana*) is associated with fertility and is indigenous to Mexico.

[78] *Bromelia karatas*.

and is eaten in the same fashion, with salt and in slices. Its seeds are like those of the small cucumbers, numerous and tender. If by chance a hole is made in the fruit while still on the tree, a gum collects in it smelling like fine civet. There is another tree whose blossom is full of a soft aroma, and whose fruit is like what we here in Spain call *blanc mange* ["white-flesh fruit"]. There are many different varieties of this tree, and it [bears] fruit that is good or excellent. There is a tree that the First Peoples cultivate near their homes. It bears spiny pods like chestnuts, but neither as large nor as prickly. They open when ripe and contain small seeds that both the Maya and Spanish settlers use to color their condiments, as one does with saffron; the color is refined, and [the achiote spice] stains a great deal.[79]

I am sure that there must be other fruits I omitted, but I shall, however, [now] speak of the palms, of which there are two kinds.[80] The fronds of one kind [of huano] serve as thatch for their houses. It is very tall and slender. These palms bear great bunches of a black fruit similar to chickpeas, of which the Maya women are very fond. The other kind is a low, very spiny palm plant whose leaves are very short and thin. It serves no [useful] purpose. This palm bears great bunches of a round green fruit, the size of pigeon eggs. When the skin is removed there is a very hard kernel inside of which is a pit about the size of a hazelnut. It is very tasty and useful in times of poor harvests. They make hot nourishment from it that they consume in the mornings, and on occasion its milk is used to flavor any dish, since it resembles almond milk.

They harvest an amazing amount of cotton, which grows [wild] in all parts of the country. There are two kinds [of cotton trees]. The first is sown every year and does not last more than a [season]. This [cotton] tree is small. The bush of the other kind lasts five or six years and [it produces fruit throughout]. The fruit of both trees is in the forms of pods similar to walnuts [but] with a green husk that opens when ripe, yielding the cotton within.

They are accustomed to collect cochineal, which [many claim] to be the finest in the Indies because the country is [exceptionally] dry. The First Peoples [of the peninsula] still gather a little here and there.

There are colors of many kinds made from the dyes of certain trees and flowers, but because the First Peoples do not know how to refine them with gums to temper [their color] so as not to change, [the colors] fade [with time]. But those who gather the fiber [claim to] have already

---

[79] Achiote (*Bixa orellana*) is also called anato.
[80] The two palms Diego de Landa refers to are: *Acrocomia Mexicana* and *Gossypium barbadense*.

found remedies, and say that they give as perfect a result as the best found anywhere.

L
Of the Birds.

This country possesses an abundant number of birds. They are of such great variety that He who gave them as a blessing is much to be praised. They have domestic poultry which they raise in their backyards. They have hens and cocks in great number, although they are troublesome to raise. They have begun to raise Spanish fowl, in great numbers, so that throughout the entire year they have chickens. They raise tame pigeons similar to ours, which breed much. They raise a certain sort of large white duck for their plumage, [originating] I believe in Perú. They pluck the breasts [of these ducks] often, and frequently use these feathers for embroidering their garments.

There are many kinds of birds, and many of them are very handsome. Among these there are two kinds of pretty turtle doves, one being quite small and tame that they raise in their homes. There is a little bird like the nightingale, whose singing is melodious [and sweet], which they call *ixyalchamil*. It frequents the walls of the houses that have gardens, or trees [nearby]. There is another large and very beautiful bird, of very dark green plumage. [It has] only two long feathers in the tail, and no others, but at the tips they have down on them. It lives in buildings and goes out only in the mornings. There are other birds that are similar in looks and are as mischievous as [our] magpies. These always cry at the passersby and do not allow them to pass [in peace]. There are many swifts or swallows, though I think they are swifts [martins] since they do not breed in dwellings as do the swallows.

There is another large [bird], of many colors and of great beauty, with a large, strong beak. It always frequents the dry, rotting trees, holding to the bark with its claws and hammering so loudly with the beak that it can be heard a good distance away. It extracts the worms on which it feeds from the decayed wood. These birds carry on [making so many holes] that trees harboring the worms are riddled from top to bottom like a sieve.

There are many field birds that make excellent eating, including three kinds of handsome little pigeons. There are birds similar to Spanish partridges in every way except that their legs are long and red; they are very poor eating. They are[, however,] very tame if raised [in a domesticated setting]. There are many fine quail, somewhat larger than ours, and they make fine meals. They fly but little, and the Maya use dogs to catch them as they perch in the trees, [using] lassos they throw around their necks. It makes for quite delightful sport.

There are many grayish-brown, speckled pheasants, of a fair size, but they are not as good to eat as those from Italy. There is one very large bird as big as the turkey, which they call the *kambul*. It is very beautiful and very bold, and good to eat. Another one, which they call *cox*, is equally large, walks in a furious [manner], and stirs up things. The males are jet-black all over, with fine crests of little curled feathers, and yellow eyelids, [and very pleasing] to admire. There are many turkeys, which although not of as fine plumage as those here in Spain, are still very attractive. The birds are handsome; they are as large as the [indigenous] birds, and just as good to eat.

The First Peoples hunt all the large ones found in the trees with arrows. They steal their eggs [to have] their hens [hatch the eggs], and they raise [the chicks] in a domesticated [fashion]. There are three or four kinds of large and small parrots, in such flocks that they do much damage to the crops.

There are other nocturnal birds, such as [barn] owls, the red owl [or *mochuelo*], and nightjars; it is amusing to travel at night with great stretches of the road filled with them taking [to flight as people approach]. They trouble the First Peoples greatly, for they believe these birds are of ill omen, which [is true of] certain other [birds].

There are carnivorous birds that the Spaniards call *auras*, and the First Peoples call *kuch*. These are black, with head and breast like the native poultry, and [have] long-hooked beaks. They are very squalid, since they always go among the stables and latrines eating and hunting carrion. It is a known fact that, so far, [none of their] nests have been found, [and it is not known] how they breed. [In consequence] some say they live 200 years or more, and others believe them to be in fact crows. They can smell the dead so that when the First Peoples have shot a deer [with an arrow or spear] and the wounded [animal flees into the forest], one way to locate it is by climbing a tree and looking where these birds are gathering. [Vultures] are sure to find the [dying animal].

There is a great variety of birds of prey: there are small eagles, most handsome goshawks, a great number of hunting birds, and also very fine sparrow hawks, larger than the ones here in Spain. There are lanner falcons, and gerfalcons, and others whose names I do not recall since I am not a falconer. On the sea there is a wonderful multitude of birds of infinite variety, and each is also beautiful in its own way. There are large birds the size of brown ostriches, but they have larger beaks. They keep near the water [where they] hunt fish, and when one is seen they rise in the air and swoop themselves with great force upon the fish. [Pelicans] never strike in vain, and on making the dive continue swimming and swallowing the fish without [chewing it] in any way. There are certain large, lean birds that fly at great height and have forked tails; their fat is an excellent remedy for scars, and for numbness caused from cuts [and wounds].

There are some large ducks that remain under water for a long time catching fish to eat; they are very quick, and have a hook on the beak that they use [when hunting] fish. There are other beautiful little ducks [that are] raised at their homes; these are very tame [and domesticated]; and they are called *maxix*.

There are many sorts of large and small herons, some white and others brown. In the Laguna de Términos, there are many [birds that] are of a very bright scarlet, [and they look] like powdered cochineal. There are so many sorts of small birds, as well as large, that their numbers and variety are a source of wonderment. It is still more to see them so busy hunting their food along the shore, some entering the incoming waves only to retreat from them [as the waves lap ashore]. Others hunt [for their] food on the beaches or [by stealing it] away [from other birds]. What is most admirable is [to witness] how God has provided for all with His blessing.

LI
Of the Larger Animals, and of the Smaller Ones.

The First Peoples [of Yucatán] are in need of many animals, especially those that are most useful to humanity. They do have others, however, most of which they make use of for nourishment. None of these are domesticated, with the exception of domestic dogs. These [dogs] do not bark or harm either people or game, although they aid in trapping quail, other birds, and in deer hunting; some of them are fine trackers. They are small, and the First Peoples eat them at festivals, though I understand they are ashamed of it, and consider it a sign of poverty to resort to [eating dogs]. They are said to taste very good.

There are tapirs, but only in the region beyond the Campeche hills among the dogwood trees, where many are found. The First Peoples have told me that they are of many colors, gray, dappled, bay, and chestnut. Some are very white, and others black. They keep in this part of the [peninsula] more than in any other areas, for it is an animal very fond of water, and there are many lakes among those woods and hills. They are as large as ordinary mules, very agile, with cloven hoofs like oxen, and a short trunk in which they hold water. The First Peoples regard it a great feat to kill them, and they preserve the skins [as trophies] that are [handed down to] their great-grandchildren, as I myself have seen. They call them *tzimin*, and they have given this name to horses.

There are small lions and tigers, which the First Peoples kill with bows as they rest in the trees. There is also a certain kind of bear that is very fond of taking honey from beehives. It is brown with black spots, with a long body, short legs, and a round head. There is a sort of wild goats. These are small, very light-footed, and rather dark in color.

There are certain small pigs, very different from ours, since they have the navel on their backs, and stink badly. There is an amazing number of small deer; the meat is excellent. There is an infinite number of rabbits, like ours in all respects except that the nose is long and not blunt, [but rather] resembles that of a sheep; they are large and very good to eat.

There is a small animal of sad [disposition] since it inhabits caverns and other dark places, and [is only active] at night. It is similar to hares, moving by leaps, and bunches up; the First Peoples hunt it by setting a kind of trap to catch them. The front teeth are very long and thin; the tail is still shorter than that of a rabbit, and it is of a dark goldish hue in color. [The agouti, a rodent] is exceedingly tame and friendly, and is called *sub*.

There is another little animal whose paws and snout resemble a newborn pig, and it has a large rooter [snout for digging], but is all covered with graceful scales so that it looks just like an armored horse. Only its ears and paws stick out, and even its neck and head are covered with scales. [The armadillo] is tender and very good to eat.

There are other animals similar to little dogs, with a head shaped like a pig's and a long tail. They are a smoky color, and so slow-moving that the First Peoples often catch them by the tail. They are predators and [nocturnal], moving about the houses at night, so that no domestic fowl eventually escapes their slow approach. The female gives birth to litters of 14 to 18 young at once; these are completely hairless and very slow-moving, [resembling] weasels. God[, however,] has provided the mother with a curious sort of pocket in the belly for their protection. They have a flap of skin that covers the pocket that extends the entire length of the belly and covers the nipples, concealing them when it is closed. When [the female opossum] wishes it so, she opens so that each of the little ones can get a teat into its mouth. When the young are all inside she presses the flanks of the skin up and closes it so tightly that none of them can fall out. Then thus laden she goes about in search of food. She cares for them in this way until they have fur and can move about independently.

There are foxes in every way like ours here, except that they are not as large and do not have such long tails. There is an animal the First Peoples call *chic* that is very mischievous. [The badger is] as large as a small dog, but with a snout similar to a suckling pig's. Women raise them, and there is not a thing they do not get into and turn upside down. It is quite a sight to see how fond they are of playing with the women, and how they track down fleas. But they have a mortal fear of men. There are many of these, and they always go about in single file, in a line with the snout of one tucked under the tail of the other. They [cause much] damage in the maize fields [if] they [trail] through them.

There is a small animal similar to a white squirrel, with dark yellow stripes around its body, which [the Maya] call *pay*. This [creature] defends itself against those who follow it or hurt it by letting loose a stream of urine, which has such a horrible smell that nobody can tolerate it, nor can anything it touches be used again. They tell me that it is not actually the urine, but a substance, [a kind of sweat] that it secretes from a pouch under its tail. Be that as it may, its weapon protects it so well that only as by a miracle do the First Peoples ever kill [a skunk].

There are many very beautiful squirrels, moles, and weasels; and many rats like those of Spain, except that their snouts are [generally] longer.

LII
Conclusion.

The First Peoples have not lost, but rather have gained much with the coming of the Spaniards. Even in small matters [they have benefited] and many things that, with the passage of time, they will enjoy are increasing. [Although introduced] at first by force, they are now beginning to enjoy and use [many things from Europe]. There are many and fine horses, and mules, both male and female. Asses do not do well, and I believe their introduction has not been good, for it is, without doubt, a hardy beast and comfort [ill suits] them. There are many and fine cows, pigs, rams, ewes, goats, and those of our dogs that [work] to earn their keep. All of these [animals] have come to be regarded as beneficial to [the First Peoples] of the Indies. Cats are very useful and necessary, and the First Peoples are fond of them.

Hens and pigeons; and oranges, limes, citrons, grapes, pomegranates, figs, guavas, dates; bananas, melons, and most legumes [and vegetables] have been brought here. Of these only melons and calabashes [pumpkins and squashes] grow from their own seeds; for the rest one must bring fresh seeds from Mexico [City]. Silk is now produced and it is very good. They have been given [metal] tools, and the use of mechanical devices has been introduced, [both innovations] being welcomed [by the Maya]. There is also the use of coin [currency] and many other things that have come to them from Spain. Although they had done without these, and could have continued on without them, they [now] live, beyond question, more as [civilized] men and women by [virtue of] having them to aid in their everyday commercial activities, and the lightening of their [labor]. In the words of the philosopher, Art aids Nature.

God, through our nation of Spain, has given the First Peoples not only the benefit of these things that are so necessary for humanity's service, and for which alone whatever they give or will be able to give to the Spaniards in return is no payment, but also they have received [something that] has come to them without compensation that can neither be bought or deserved, which is this: Christian justice, and the peace in which they live.

For these they owe more to Spain and to the Spaniards, and chiefly to their very Catholic monarchs, who with such continuous care and such great Christianity have provided and do continue to provide them with these two things, than they do to their first forebears, evil parents who begat them in sin and as sons of wrath, while Christianity re-creates them in birth and grace and for the enjoyment of life eternal. Their first founders did not know how to give them [Christian] guidance that they might avoid the so many and so great errors in which they have lived [human sacrifice and idolatry the most egregious sins]. Justice has delivered them out from these errors through preaching, and it must keep them from returning [to their old ways]; or if they revert, it must be pulled out of them [once more through instruction in catechism].

It is with reason then, that Spain can glorify God since He has selected her among the nations to be the salvation for so many First Peoples, and for which they owe her much more than they do to their founders or progenitors. For as the blessed Saint Gregory said, little benefit would it be to us to be born had we not come to be redeemed through Christ our Lord. We can also say with [Saint] Anselm [of Canterbury], *What profit to us is it to be redeemed if we do not attain the fruit of redemption, which is our salvation?* Thus, those who say that because the First Peoples have suffered wrongs, ill-treatment, and bad examples [suffered at the hands of] the Spaniards [through colonialization], that it had been better for them not to have been discovered [are mistaken]. [And they err] because [the First Peoples] were still subjected to greater wrongs and ill-treatment to which they perpetually [suffered at the hands of their own leaders] through the killing, enslaving, and sacrificing of themselves to demons. As to the bad example [and the vices the Spaniards have introduced], if they have had such [uncivil examples], or today [are subjected to bad examples] from some [Spanish settlers], the king has remedied it, and daily does [in fact] remedy it through his Justices, and by the constant preaching and persevering opposition of the monastic orders to those who set such examples, or have set them. It is for the evangelical instruction [that the First Peoples can better understand that human failings result in] offenses and bad examples [of human sinning that] are necessary things. I believe that for the First Peoples [exposure to human sins] is [necessary], that they might understand [virtue], [learning to] separate the gold from the clay and the grain from the chaff; how to esteem virtue as they have done by seeing, like the philosopher, how virtues outshines vices; and the virtuous [outshine] among the wicked. [Whomever lives a life of] bad examples and offenses has, invariably, terrible punishment [in store] if he or she does not atone for them with that which is good.

And so you, beloved reader, on your part, pray to God that it might be so, and receive [this work] my small effort, pardoning its shortcomings, and remembering when you encounter them that not only do I not defend them (as Saint Augustine said of Tully that he declared he had never had spoken a word he wished to revoke, a statement of which the saint disapproved because it is human to err). But first, before you encounter [my errors], you will find them revoked or confessed in my introductions or prologues. And thus you will judge, as did the blessed [Saint] Augustine in his letter to Marcella, the difference between the individual who confesses his or her error or fault and the individual who defends it. It is you who will pardon mine as, according to the prophet, God does pardon both mine and yours, saying: "Lord, I said I will confess my ill deeds and injustice, and thou dost quickly give pardon."

The historian of the things of the Indies, to whom much is due for his work and the light he shed on them, in writing of the things of Yucatán, says that they used slings and spears hardened by fire in [carrying out] warfare. I have related of the things they used in war, and I am not surprised that Francisco Hernández de Cordova and Juan de Grijalva thought that the stones launched at them by the First Peoples at Champotón were discharged from slings, since they retreated [from Champotón]. But they neither throw with a sling nor knew of them, although they do throw stones with great accuracy and force, aiming with the left arm and index finger as they do it.

[The historian] says that there are hares, and about that you will find [a description in Chapter LI]. He says that there are partridges, and of what sorts, and about that you will find in the [fourth] paragraph of [Chapter L].

Our historian further reports that at Cape Cotoch they found crosses among the dead and idols, and he does not believe this to be true because if these items were taken from Spaniards who sailed [from Spain and] who [subsequently] perished, they would certainly have reached other lands first, of which [islands] there are many. I do not believe this [to be true;] this reasoning does not convince me. I do not believe it because I do not know any other places they could have sighted [west of Cuba] where they could have landed before reaching Yucatán, or whether they did reach land or not before arriving in Yucatán. But the reason I do not believe it, is because when Francisco Hernández and [Juan de] Grijalva reached at Cotoch, they did not go about digging up the dead, but searched for gold among the living. I also believe so much in the virtue of the cross and the malice of the devil, that [I believe the devil] could not endure seeing a cross amongst the [Maya] idols, because of the [devil's] fear that one day miraculously the virtue [of the cross] would shatter [the idols], and confound him [the devil] as the ark of the covenant did with Dagon, although it had not been sanctified by the blood of the Son of God and dignified by his holy limbs, as was done on the sacred cross.

In addition to all this, I will say what I was told by an elder [Maya leader], a man of fine understanding and great repute among them.

Speaking with him on this matter one day, I asked him whether he had at any time heard reports of Christ our Lord, or of the Cross. He replied that he had never heard anything about either Christ or the Cross from his forebears, except that once while tearing down a small building on a certain part of the coast, he and others found some graves [and that] on the corpses and bones of the dead, [there were] some small metal crosses. They had not given any thought to the cross until now when they became Christians and saw it worshipped and venerated. They now believe those dead men that had been buried there were also Christian. If that is so, it is possible that some small party had reached this land from Spain and quickly perished, with no memory of them left.

The End

Relación de las cosas de Yucatán

Relación de las cosas de Yucatán

Diego de Landa

Introducción

En un entonces la mayoría de la gente del mundo creía que el diablo caminaba entre nosotros. En un entonces la gente aceptaba la propuesta que nuestras almas eran tan valiosas que el diablo era capaz de hacer cualquier cosa para engañarnos con el fin de privar a Dios de la preciosa belleza de nuestras almas. En un entonces las personas, basándose en estas premisas, vivían sus vidas cotidianas siempre conscientes de la posibilidad de que el diablo mismo pudiera aparecer entre nosotros en cualquier momento.

Estas creencias, principalmente cristianas y basadas en las enseñanzas bíblicas, las compartían también judíos y musulmanes. Tanto en el Judaísmo como en el Islam existen ángeles y demonios, quienes compiten desbordadamente poniendo en nuestros caminos tentaciones y peligros que acechan en el mundo que nos rodea.

En Salem, Massachusetts, por ejemplo, entre febrero de 1692 y mayo de 1693, varias personas fueron acusadas de brujería y de asociarse con el diablo, y estos acusados fueron sometidos a juicio. Diecinueve personas fueron ejecutadas durante estos eventos que hoy son recordados como uno de los primeros episodios de histeria colectiva entre los colonos de Nueva Inglaterra.

Un siglo antes de Salem se cree que el diablo visitó a Yucatán, en ese entonces una remota provincia de la Nueva España.

Durante la restauración del gran monasterio franciscano de Izamal, llevada a cabo en la primera década de este siglo, se descubrieron varios frescos que representan a fieles luchando contra el demonio. Los murales muestran a los frailes franciscanos, junto con mayas convertidos al Cristianismo, luchando contra el diablo y sus secuaces. Estos frescos, perdidos por mucho tiempo en la historia y en la memoria pero ahora recuperados, iluminan uno de los episodios coloniales más convincentes de Yucatán. Al mismo tiempo, los frescos documentan como los europeos interpretaban el mundo a su alrededor en tierras de las Américas.

En el siglo XVI Francisco Toral, quien sería el primer obispo residente de Yucatán, estuvo en completo desacuerdo con Diego de Landa, quien se convertiría en el segundo obispo de esta provincia, sobre el tema de la presencia del diablo en la región. Los murales de Izamal, que muestran una batalla épica entre las fuerzas del bien y del mal, confirman que las opiniones de Landa finalmente prevalecieron.

Hoy en día, por supuesto, con nuestra sensibilidad moderna, la creencia de que el diablo encarnado camina entre nosotros ha disminuído enormemente. Actualmente preferimos invocar el concepto o la idea del "mal". Sin embargo, es necesario entender el concepto ampliamente: a fin de cuentas existe un consenso universal de que, en el hsiglo pasado, Adolf Hitler era un hombre poseído por el "mal" sea como fuere que alcanzara esa condición de malvado. En este siglo fue George W. Bush, presidente de los Estados Unidos de Norteamérica, quien ofreció un discurso desde la Oficina Oval de la Casa Blanca la noche del 11 de septiembre del 2001 declarando que la nación "vio la maldad hoy". Asimismo se declaró "presidente en tiempo de guerra" y lanzó una campaña militar contra el "terrorismo" por el mundo entero.

La representación del diablo en los frescos de Izamal ha generado una gran revaluación de nuestro entendimiento de la época colonial yucateca. También, de las grandes discusiones teológicas que consumían a los misioneros franciscanos de esta aislada provincia de la Nueva España.

¿De hecho, visitó el diablo Yucatán?

La pregunta conduce a una revisión clave sobre la interpretación de "Relación de las cosas de Yucatán" escrita por Diego de Landa, y esta nueva traducción publicada por primera vez en una edición bilingüe ofrece al lector del idioma inglés una prosa contemporánea y accesible. Al igual que en toda Europa, en la Nueva Inglaterra colonial el tema de la brujería ofrecía una clara distinción entre la llamada "magia blanca" y su contrapartida la "magia negra". Asimismo, protocolos rigurosos eran aplicados con el fin de establecer la "prueba" de presencias demoníacas. Los acontecimientos suscitados en Yucatán deben ser examinados en el mismo contexto.

¿Qué evidencias llevaron a Diego de Landa a concluir con certeza que el demonio estaba presente en Yucatán? ¿Por qué estas mismas pruebas resultaron insuficientes para convencer a Francisco Toral? ¿Cómo surgió el conflicto entre estos dos hombres, al grado de llevar a Toral a denunciar a Diego de Landa ante el Consejo de Indias?

Es importante recordar que, en ese momento histórico, tanto en Europa como en sus posesiones coloniales en las Américas los tribunales aceptaban "evidencia espectral" en los procedimientos judiciales. La "evidencia espectral" quiere decir el testimonio basado en sueños y visiones: si dos testigos tenían el mismo sueño o había presenciado la misma visión, estos hechos podían someterse como prueba legal ante un juez. Aunque el concepto fue inventado por los católicos, también fue ampliamente aceptado por los protestantes. El ejemplo más famoso de "evidencia espectral" en el mundo de habla inglesa se encuentra en los juicios conocidos como "Bury St. Edmunds", celebrados en Inglaterra entre los años 1599 y 1694 en contra de las brujas.

Diego de Landa creía en la "evidencia espectral" pero Francisco Toral no.

Finalmente, ¿qué papel desempeñaron los propios mayas en este episodio? ¿Cómo fueron esos mayas recién convertidos al Cristianismo impugnados por otros mayas que rechazaban la Cristiandad? ¿Cómo fue que los españoles y los mayas se entendían unos a los otros, y cómo llegaron a un consenso en conjunto, si así fue, sobre las normas para determinar si se debía o no juzgar quienes eran verdaderamente fieles al Cristianismo?

¿Cómo se reconoce al diablo? ¿Cómo se reconoce al mal?

Estas preguntas trascienden el paso de los siglos, de Izamal en Yucatán a Salem en Massachusetts, desde la casa del lector hasta la Casa Blanca.

Louis E.V. Nevaer.
Mérida, Yucatán

Relación de las cosas de Yucatán

I
Descripción de Yucatán— Variedad de las estaciones.

Que Yucatán no es isla ni punta que entra en la mar como algunos pensaron, sino tierra firme, y que se engañaron por la punta de Cotoch que hace la mar entrando por la bahía de la Ascensión hacia Golfo Dulce, y por la punta que por esta otra parte, hacia México, hace la Desconocida antes de llegar a Campeche, o por el extendimiento de las lagunas que hace la mar entrando por Puerto Real y Dos Bocas.

Que es tierra muy llana y limpia de sierras, y que por esto no se descubre desde los navíos hasta muy cerca salvo entre Campeche y Champotón donde se miran unas serrezetas y un Morro de ellas que llaman de los diablos.

Que viniendo de Veracruz por parte de la punta de Cotoch, está en menos de 20 grados, y por la boca de Puerto Real en más de 23, y que bien tiene de un cabo al otro 130 leguas de largo camino derecho.

Que su costa es baja, y por esto los navíos grandes van algo apartados de tierra.

Que la costa es muy sucia de peñas y pizarrales ásperos que gastan mucho los cables de los navíos, y que tienen mucha lama, por lo cual aunque los navíos den a la costa, se pierde poca gente.

Que es tan grande la menguante de la mar, en especial en la bahía de Campeche, que muchas veces queda media legua en seco por algunas partes.

Que con estas grandes menguantes se quedan en las ovas, y lama y charcos, muchos pescados pequeños de que se mantiene mucha gente.

Que atraviesa a Yucatán de esquina a esquina una sierra pequeña que comienza cerca de Champotón y va hasta la villa de Salamanca que es el cornijal contrario al de Champotón.

Que esta sierra divide a Yucatán en dos partes, y que la parte de mediodía, hacia Lacandón y Taiza, está despoblada por falta de agua, que no la hay sino cuando llueve. La otra que es al norte, está poblada.

Que esta tierra es muy caliente y el sol quema mucho aunque no faltan aires frescos como brisa o solano que allí reina mucho, y por las tardes la virazón de la mar.

Que en esta tierra vive mucho la gente, y que se ha hallado hombre de ciento cuarenta años.

Que comienza el invierno desde San Francisco y dura hasta fin de marzo, porque en este tiempo corren los nortes y causan catarros recios y calenturas por estar la gente mal vestida.

Que por fin de enero y febrero hay un veranillo de recios soles y no llueve en ese tiempo sino a las entradas de las lunas.

Que las aguas comienzan desde abril hasta fin de septiembre, y que en este tiempo siembran todas sus cosas y vienen a maduración aunque siempre llueva; y que siembran cierto género de maíz por San Francisco que se coge brevemente.

II
Etimología del nombre de esta provincia. Situación de ella.

Que esta provincia se llama en lengua de [los indígenas] Ulumil cutz yetelceh que quiere decir tierra de pavos y venados, y que también la llamaron Petén que quiere decir isla, engañados por las ensenadas y bahías dichas.

Que cuando Francisco Hernández de Córdoba llegó a esta tierra saltando en la punta que él llamó cabo de Cotoch, halló ciertos pescadores [indígenas] y les preguntó qué tierra era aquella y que le respondieron Cotoch, que quiere decir nuestras casas y nuestra patria, y que por esto se puso este nombre a aquella punta, y que preguntándoles más por señas que cómo era suya aquella tierra, respondieron ciuthan que quiere decir, dícenlo; y que los españoles la llamaron Yucatán, y que esto se entendió de uno de los conquistadores viejos llamado Blas Hernández que fue con el Adelantado la primera vez.

Que Yucatán, a la parte del mediodía, tiene los ríos de Taiza y las sierras de Lacandón, y que entre mediodía y poniente cae la provincia de Chiapas, y que para pasar a ella se habían de atravesar los cuatro ríos que descienden de las sierras que con otros se viene a hacer San Pedro y San Pablo, río que descubrió en Tabasco Grijalva; que al poniente está Xicalango y Tabasco, que son una misma provincia.

Que entre esta provincia de Tabasco y Yucatán están las dos bocas que rompe la mar, y que la mayor de éstas tiene una legua grande de abertura y que la otra no es muy grande.

Que entra la mar por estas bocas con tanta furia que se hace una gran laguna abundante de todos pescados y tan llena de isletas, que [los indígenas] ponen señales en los árboles para acertar el camino para ir o venir navegando de Tabasco a Yucatán; y que estas islas y sus playas y arenales están llenos de tanta diversidad de aves marinas que es cosa de admiración y hermosura; y que también hay infinita caza de venados, conejos, puercos de los de aquella tierra, y monos, que no los hay en Yucatán.

Que hay muchas iguanas que espanta, y en una de (las isletas) está un pueblo que llaman Tixchel.

Que al norte tiene la isla de Cuba, y a 60 leguas muy enfrente la Habana, y algo adelante una islilla de Cuba, que dicen de Pinos.

Que al oriente tiene a Honduras y que entre Honduras y Yucatán se hace una muy gran ensenada de mar la cual llamó Grijalva Bahía de la

Ascensión, y que está tan llena de isletas y que se pierden en ellas navíos, principalmente los de la contratación de Yucatán a Honduras; y que hará 15 años que se perdió una barca con mucha gente y ropa, y al zozobrar el navío se ahogaron todos salvo un (tal) Majuelas y otros cuatro que se abrazaron a un gran pedazo de árbol del navío y anduvieron así tres o cuatro días sin poder llegar a ninguna de las islillas, y que se ahogaron faltándoles las fuerzas, menos Majuelas que salió medio muerto y tornó en sí comiendo caracolejos y almejas; y que desde la islilla pasó a tierra en una balsa que hizo de ramas como mejor pudo; y pasado a tierra firme, buscando de comer en la ribera, topó con un cangrejo que le cortó el dedo pulgar por la primera coyuntura con gravísimo dolor. Y tomó a tiento la derrota por un áspero monte para la villa de Salamanca, y que anochecido se subió a un árbol y que desde allí vió un gran tigre que se puso en acechanza de una cierva, y se la vio matar y que la mañana (siguiente) él comió de lo que había quedado.

Que Yucatán tiene algo más abajo y enfrente de la Punta de Cotoch a Cuzmil, 5 leguas de una canal de muy grande corriente, que hace la mar entre ella y la Isla.

Que Cuzmil es isla de quince leguas de largo y cinco de ancho, en que hay pocos [indígenas] y son de la lengua y costumbres de los de Yucatán, y está en 20 grados a esta parte de la equinoccial.

Que la isla de las Mujeres está a trece leguas abajo de la punta de Cotoch y a dos leguas de tierra enfrente de Ekab.

III
Cautiverio de Gerónimo de Aguilar.— Expedición de Hernández de Córdoba y Grijalva a Yucatán.

Que los primeros españoles que llegaron a Yucatán, según se dice, fueron Gerónimo de Aguilar, natural de Écija, y sus compañeros, los cuales, el año de 1511, en el desbarato del Darien por las revueltas entre Diego de Nicuesa y Vasco Núñez de Balboa, siguieron a Valdivia que venía en una carabela a Santo Domingo, a dar cuenta al Almirante y al Gobernador de lo que pasaba, y a traer 20 mil ducados del rey; y que esta carabela, llegando a Jamaica, dio en los bajos que llaman de Víboras donde se perdió, no escapando sino 20 hombres que con Valdivia entraron en un batel sin velas y con unos ruines remos y sin mantenimiento alguno anduvieron trece días por la mar. Después de muertos de hambre casi la mitad, llegaron a la costa de Yucatán, a una provincia que llaman de la Maya, de la cual la lengua de Yucatán se llama mayathan, que quiere decir lengua de maya.

Que esta pobre gente vino a manos de un mal cacique, el cual sacrificó a Valdivia y a otros cuatro a sus ídolos y después hizo banquetes (con la carne) de ellos a la gente, y que dejó para engordar a Aguilar y a Guerrero y a otros cinco o seis, los cuales quebrantaron la prisión y huyeron por unos montes. Y que dieron con otro señor enemigo del primero y más piadoso, el cual se sirvió de ellos como de esclavos; y que el que sucedió a este señor los trató con buena gracia, pero que ellos, de dolencia, murieron quedando solos Gerónimo de Aguilar y Gonzalo Guerrero, de los cuales Aguilar era buen cristiano y tenía unas horas por las cuales sabía las fiestas. Y que éste se salvó con la ida del marqués Hernán Cortés, el año de 1519, que Guerrero, como entendía la lengua, se fue a Chectemal, que es la Salamanca de Yucatán, y que allí le recibió un señor llamado Nachancán, el cual le dio a cargo las cosas de la guerra en que (est)uvo muy bien, venciendo muchas veces a los enemigos de su señor, y que enseñó a [los indígenas] pelear mostrándoles (la manera de) hacer fuertes y bastiones, y que con esto y con tratarse como indio, ganó mucha reputación y le casaron con una muy principal mujer en que hubo hijos; y que por esto nunca procuró salvarse como hizo Aguilar, antes bien labraba su cuerpo, criaba cabello y harpaba las orejas para traer zarcillos como [los indígenas] y es creíble que fuese idólatra como ellos.

Que el año de 1517, por cuaresma, salió de Santiago de Cuba Francisco Hernández de Córdoba con tres navíos a rescatar esclavos para las minas, ya que en Cuba se iba apocando la gente. Otros dicen que salió a descubrir tierra y que llevó por piloto a Alaminos y que llegó a la Isla de Mujeres, que él puso este nombre por los ídolos que allí halló de las diosas de aquella tierra como Aixchel, Ixchebeliax, Ixbunic, Ixbunieta, y que estaban vestidas de la cintura abajo y cubiertos los pechos como usan las [mujeres indígenas]; y que el edificio era de piedra, de que se espantaron, y que hallaron algunas cosas de oro y las tomaron. Y que llegaron a la punta de Cotoch y que de allí dieron vuelta hasta la bahía de Campeche donde desembarcaron (el) domingo de Lázaro, y que por esto la llamaron Lázaro. Y que fueron bien recibidos por el señor, y que [los indígenas] se espantaban de ver los españoles y les tocaban las barbas y personas.

Que en Campeche hallaron un edificio dentro de la mar, cerca de tierra, cuadrado y gradado todo, y que en lo alto estaba un ídolo con dos fieros animales que le comían las ijadas, y una sierpe larga y gorda de piedra que se tragaba un león; y que los animales estaban llenos de sangre de los sacrificios.

Que desde Campeche entendieron que había cerca un pueblo grande que era Champotón, donde llegados hallaron que el señor se llamaba Mochcouoh, hombre belicoso que lanzó a su gente contra los españoles, lo cual pesó a Francisco Hernández viendo en lo que había de parar; y que por no mostrar poco ánimo, puso también su gente en orden e hizo soltar artillería de los navíos; y que aunque a [los indígenas] les fue nuevo el sonido, humo y fuego de los tiros, no dejaron de acometer con gran alarido; y los españoles resistieron dando muy fieras heridas y matando a muchos. Pero que el señor animó tanto (a [los indígenas]) que hicieron retirar a los españoles y que mataron a veinte, hirieron a cincuenta y prendieron dos vivos que después sacrificaron. Y que Francisco Hernández salió con treinta y tres heridas y que así volvió triste a Cuba, donde público que la tierra era muy buena y rica por el oro que halló en la Isla de Mujeres.

Que estas nuevas movieron a Diego Velázquez, gobernador de Cuba, y a otros muchos, y que envió a su sobrino Juan de Grijalva con cuatro navíos y doscientos hombres; y que fue con él Francisco de Montejo cuyo era uno de los navíos, y que partieron el primero de mayo de 1518.

Que llevaron consigo al mismo piloto Alaminos, y llegaron a la isla de Cuzmil, desde la cual el piloto vio Yucatán; y como la otra vez, con Francisco Hernández, la había corrido a la mano derecha, quiso bojarla, (para comprobar) si fuere isla, y echó a mano izquierda siguiendo por la bahía que llamaron de la Ascensión porque en tal día entraron en ella; y que dieron la vuelta a toda la costa hasta llegar otra vez a Champotón donde sobre tomar agua les mataron un hombre y les hirieron cincuenta, entre ellos a Grijalva, de dos flechas, y le quebraron diente y medio. Y que así se fueron y nombraron a este puerto el Puerto de la Mala Pelea; y en este viaje descubrieron la Nueva España, y Pánuco y Tabasco, y que con esto gastaron cinco meses, y quisieron saltar a tierra en Champotón, lo cual les estorbaron [los indígenas] con tanto coraje que en sus canoas entraban hasta cerca de las carabelas a flecharlos, y que así se hicieron a la vela y los dejaron.

Que cuando Grijalva tornó a su descubrimiento y rescate de Tabasco y Ulúa, estaba en Cuba el gran capitán Hernán Cortés y que oyendo la nueva de tanta tierra y tantas riquezas deseó verlas y aun ganarlas para Dios y para su rey, para sí y para sus amigos.

Que Hernán Cortés salió de Cuba con once navíos de los cuales el mayor era de cien toneladas y que puso en ellos once capitanes siendo él uno de ellos; y que llevaba quinientos hombres y algunos caballos, y mercancías para rescatar, y a Francisco de Montejo por capitán y al dicho piloto Alaminos, piloto mayor de la armada; y que puso en su nao capitana una bandera de fuegos blancos y azules en reverencia a Nuestra Señora, cuya imagen, con la cruz, ponía siempre donde quitaba ídolos; y que en la bandera había una cruz colorada con un letrero en torno que decía: *amici sequamur crucem, & si nos habuerimus fidem in hoc signo vincemus.*

Que con esta flota y no más aparato partió y que llegó a Cuzmil con diez navíos porque el otro se le apartó con una refriega, y que después le recobró en la costa. Que la llegada a Cuzmil fue por la parte del norte y halló buenos edificios de piedra para los ídolos y un buen pueblo, y que la gente viendo tanto navío y salir los soldados a tierra, huyó a los montes.

Que llegados los españoles al pueblo lo saquearon y se aposentaron en él, y que buscando gente por el monte toparon con la mujer del señor y con sus hijos, de los cuales, con Melchor, intérprete indio que había ido con Francisco Hernández y con Grijalva entendieron que era la mujer del señor, a la cual y a sus hijos regaló mucho Cortés e hizo enviasen a llamar al señor, al cual venido trató muy bien y le dió algunos donecillos y le entregó su mujer e hijos y todas las cosas que por el pueblo se habían tomado; y que le rogó que hiciese venir [los indígenas] a sus casas, y que venidos les hizo restituir a cada uno lo que era suyo; y que después de asegurados les predicó la vanidad de los ídolos y les persuadió que adorasen la cruz, y que la puso en sus templos con una imagen de Nuestra Señora, y que con esto cesaba la idolatría pública.

Que Cortés supo allí que unos hombres barbados estaban camino de seis soles en poder de un señor y que persuadió a [los indígenas] que los fuesen a llamar, y que halló quien fuese, aunque con dificultad, porque tenían miedo al señor de los barbados. Y escribioles esta carta:

> Nobles señores: yo partí de Cuba con once navíos de armada y quinientos españoles, y llegué aquí, a Cuzmil, de donde os escribo esta carta. Los de esta isla me han certificado que hay en esa tierra cinco o seis hombres barbados y en todo

a nosotros muy semejables. No me saben decir otras señas, mas por éstas conjeturo y tengo por cierto que sois españoles. Yo y estos hidalgos que conmigo vienen a poblar y descubrir estas tierras, os rogamos mucho que dentro de seis días que recibiereis ésta, os vengáis para nosotros sin poner otra dilación ni excusa. Si viniereis, conoceremos y gratificaremos la buena obra que de vosotros recibirá esta armada. Un bergantín envío para que vengais en él, y dos naos para seguridad.

Que [los indígenas] llevaron esta carta envuelta en el cabello y la dieron a Aguilar, y que los navíos, porque tardaban [los indígenas] más del tiempo del plazo, creyeron que los habrían muerto y se volvieron al puerto de Cuzmil; y que Cortés, sabiendo que ni [los indígenas] ni los barbados tornaban, se hizo al otro día a la vela. Mas aquel día se les abrió un navío y les fue necesario tornar al puerto; y que estando aderezando (el navío), Aguilar, recibida la carta, atravesó en una canoa el canal entre Yucatán y Cuzmil y que viéndole los de la armada fueron a ver quién era; y que Aguilar les preguntó si eran cristianos y respondiéndole que sí, y españoles, lloró de placer y puestas las rodillas en tierra dió gracias a Dios y preguntó a los españoles si era miércoles.

Que los españoles lo llevaron a Cortés así desnudo como venía, el cual le vistió y mostró mucho amor; y que Aguilar contó allí su pérdida y trabajos y la muerte de sus compañeros y cómo fue imposible avisar a Guerrero, en tan poco tiempo por estar más de ochenta leguas de allí.

Que con este Aguilar que era muy buen intérprete, tornó Cortés a predicar la adoración de la cruz y quitó los ídolos de los templos y dicen que hizo esta predicación de Cortés tanta impresión en los de Cuzmil, que salían a la playa diciendo a los españoles que por allí pasaban: María, María; Cortés, Cortés.

Que partió Cortés de allí y que tocó de paso en Campeche y no paró hasta Tabasco, donde entre otras cosas y indias que le presentaron los de Tabasco, le dieron una india que después se llamó Marina, la cual era de Xalisco, hija de padres nobles y hurtada de pequeña y vendida en Tabasco; y que de ahí la vendieron también en Xicalango y Champotón donde aprendió la lengua de Yucatán, con la cual se vino a entender Aguilar, y que así proveyó Dios a Cortés de buenos y fieles intérpretes, por donde vino a tener noticia y entrada en las cosas de México, de las cuales la Marina sabía mucho por haber tratado con mercaderes [indígenas] y gente principal que hablaban de esto cada día.

V
Provincias de Yucatán.— Los principales edificios antiguos.

Que algunos viejos de Yucatán dicen haber oído a sus pasados que pobló aquella tierra cierta gente que entró por levante, a la cual había Dios librado abriéndoles doce caminos por la mar, lo cual, si fuese verdad, era necesario que viniesen (de) judíos todos los de las Indias, porque pasado el estrecho de Magallanes se habían de ir extendiendo más de dos mil leguas de tierra que hoy gobierna España.

Que la lengua de esta tierra es toda una, y que esto aprovechó mucho para su conversión aunque en las costas hay alguna diferencia en vocablos y en el tono de hablar; y que así los de la costa son más pulidos en su trato y lengua; y que las mujeres cubren los pechos, y las de más adentro no.

Que esta tierra está partida en provincias sujetas a los pueblos de españoles más cercanos. Que la provincia de Chectemal y Bachalal, está sujeta a Salamanca; las provincias de Ekab y Cochuah y la de Kupul, están sujetas a Valladolid; la de Ah kin Chel e Izamal, la de Zotuta, la de Hocabai Humun, la de Tutul Xiú, la de Cehpech y la de Chakan, están sujetas a la ciudad de Mérida; la de Camol, Campech, Champutun y Tixchel, acuden a San Francisco de Campeche.

Que en Yucatán hay muchos edificios de gran hermosura que es la cosa más señalada que se ha descubierto en las Indias, todos de cantería muy bien labrada sin haber ningún género de metal en ella con que se pudiesen labrar.

Que están estos edificios muy cerca unos de otros y que son templos, y que la razón de haber tantos es por mudarse las poblaciones muchas veces; y que en cada pueblo labraban un templo por el gran aparejo que hay de piedra y cal y cierta tierra blanca excelente para edificios. Que estos edificios no son hechos por otras naciones sino por [indígenas], lo cual se ve por hombres de piedra desnudos y honestados de unos largos listones que llaman en su lengua ex y de otras divisas que [los indígenas] traen.

Que estando este religioso, autor de esta obra, en aquella tierra, se halló en un edificio que desbarataron, un cántaro, grande con tres asas, pintado de unos fuegos plateados por de fuera, y dentro ceniza de cuerpo quemado y algunos huesos de los brazos y piernas, muy gruesos a maravilla, y tres cuentas de piedra buenas de las que usaban [los indígenas] por moneda.

Que estos edificios de Yzamal eran once o doce por todos sin haber memoria de los fundadores; y que en uno de ellos, a instancia de [los indígenas], se pobló un monasterio el año de 1549, que se llamó San Antonio.

Que los segundos edificios más principales son los de Tikoch y Chichenizá, los cuales se pintarán después.

Que Chichenizá es un asiento muy bueno a diez leguas de Izamal y once de Valladolid, donde dicen que reinaron tres señores hermanos que vinieron a aquella tierra de la parte de poniente, los cuales eran muy religiosos y que así edificaron muy lindos templos. Y que vivieron sin mujeres muy honestamente, y que el uno de éstos se murió o se fue, por lo cual los otros se hicieron parciales y deshonestos, y que por ello los mataron.

La pintura del edificio mayor pintaremos después, y (d)escribiremos la manera del pozo donde echaban hombres vivos en sacrificio y otras cosas preciosas. (El pozo) tiene más de siete estados de hondo hasta el agua y mucho más de cien pies, hecho redondo en una peña tajada que es maravilla y el agua parece verde: dicen que lo causa la arboleda de que está cercado.

VI
Kukulcán.— Fundación de Mayapán.

Que es opinión entre [los indígenas] que con los Yzaes que poblaron Chichenizá, reino un gran señor llamado Kukulkán, y que muestra ser esto verdad el edificio principal que se llama Kukulkán; y dicen que entró por la parte de poniente y que difieren en si entró antes o después de los Yzaes o con ellos, y dicen que fue bien dispuesto y que no tenía mujer ni hijos; y que después de su vuelta fue tenido en México por uno de sus dioses y llamado Cezalcuati y que en Yucatán también lo tuvieron por dios por ser gran republicano, y que esto se vio en el asiento que puso en Yucatán después de la muerte de los señores para mitigar la disensión que sus muertes causaron en la tierra.

Que este Kukulkán tornó a poblar otra ciudad tratando con los señores naturales de la tierra que él y ellos viniesen (a la ciudad) y que allí viniesen todas las cosas y negocios; y que para esto eligieron un asiento muy bueno a ocho aguas más adentro en la tierra que donde ahora está Mérida, y quince o dieciséis de la mar; y que allí cercaron de una muy ancha pared de piedra seca como medio cuarto de legua dejando sólo dos puertas angostas y la pared no muy alta, y en el medio de esta cerca hicieron sus templos; y que el mayor, que es como el de Chichenizá, llamaron Kukulkán; y que hicieron otro redondo y con cuatro puertas, diferente a cuantos hay en aquella tierra, y otros muchos a la redonda, juntos unos de otros; y que dentro de este cercado hicieron casas para los señores solos, entre los cuales repartieron la tierra dando pueblos a cada uno conforme a la antigüedad de su linaje y ser de su persona. Y que Kukulkán puso nombre a la ciudad, no el suyo, como hicieron los Ahizaes en Chichenizá, que quiere decir pozo de los aizaes, mas llamola Mayapán que quiere decir el pendón de la Maya, porque a la lengua de la tierra llaman maya; y [los indígenas] llaman Ychpa (a la ciudad), que quiere decir dentro de las cercas.

Que este Kukulkán vivió con los señores algunos años en aquella ciudad, y que dejándolos en mucha paz y amistad se tornó por el mismo camino a México, y que de pasada se detuvo en Champotón, y que para memoria suya y de su partida, hizo dentro de la mar un buen edificio al modo del de Chichenizá, a un gran tiro de piedra de la ribera, y que así dejó Kukulkán perpetua memoria en Yucatán.

VII
Gobierno, sacerdocio, ciencias, letras y libros de Yucatán.

Que partido Kukulkán, acordaron los señores, para que la república durase, que el mando principal lo tuviese la casa de los Cocomes por ser la más antigua y más rica y por ser el que la regía entonces hombre de más valor; y que hecho esto ordenaron que pues en el cercado no había sino templos y casas para los señores y gran sacerdote, que se hiciesen casas fuera de la cerca donde cada uno de ellos pusiese alguna gente de servicio y donde los de sus pueblos acudiesen cuando viniesen a la ciudad con negocios; y que en estas casas puso cada uno su mayordomo, el cual traía por señal una vara gorda y corta y que le llamaban Caluac y que este mayordomo tenía cuenta de los pueblos y de quienes los regían y que ellos se enviaban aviso de lo que era menester en casa del señor, como aves, maíz, miel, sal, pesca, caza, ropas y otras cosas, y que el Caluac acudía siempre a la casa del señor y veía lo que era menester en ella y lo proveía luego, porque su casa era como oficina de su señor.

Que acostumbraban buscar en los pueblos los mancos y ciegos y les daban lo necesario.

Que los señores proveían (a los pueblos) de gobernadores y si les eran adeptos confirmaban en sus hijos los oficios; y que les encomendaban el buen tratamiento de la gente menuda y la paz del pueblo y el ocuparse en trabajar para que se sustentasen ellos y los señores.

Que todos los señores tenían cuenta con respetar, visitar y alegrar a Cocom acompañándole y festejándole y acudiendo a él con los negocios arduos, y que entre sí vivían muy en paz y en mucho pasatiempo como ellos lo usan tomar, en bailes, convites y caza.

Que los de Yucatán fueron tan curiosos en las cosas de la religión como en las del gobierno y que tenían un gran sacerdote que llamaban Ah Kin May, y por nombre Ahau Can May, que quiere decir el (gran) sacerdote May, que era muy reverenciado de los señores, el cual no tenía repartimiento de [indígenas], y que además de las ofrendas los señores le hacían presentes y que todos los sacerdotes de los pueblos le contribuían; y que a éste le sucedían en la dignidad sus hijos o parientes más cercanos y que en éste estaba la llave de sus ciencias, y que en éstas trataban lo más, y que daban consejo a los señores y respuestas a sus preguntas, y que cosas de los sacrificios pocas veces las trataban si no en fiestas muy principales o en negocios muy importantes; y que éstos proveían de sacerdotes a los pueblos cuando faltaban, examinándolos en sus ciencias y ceremonias y que les encargaban de las cosas de sus oficios y el buen ejemplo del pueblo, y proveían de sus libros; y que éstos atendían al servicio de los templos y a enseñar sus ciencias y escribir libros de ellas.

Que enseñaban a los hijos de los otros sacerdotes y a los hijos segundos de los señores que les llevaban para esto desde niños, si veían que se inclinaban a este oficio.

Que las ciencias que enseñaban eran la cuenta de los años, meses y días, las fiestas y ceremonias, la administración de sus sacramentos, los días y tiempos fatales, sus maneras de adivinar, remedios para los males, las antigüedades, leer y escribir con sus letras y caracteres en los cuales escribían con figuras que representaban las escrituras.

Que escribían sus libros en una hoja larga doblada con pliegues que se venía a cerrar toda entre dos tablas que hacían muy galanas, y que escribían de una parte y de otra a columnas, según eran los pliegues; y que este papel lo hacían de las raíces de un árbol y que le daban un lustre blanco en que se podía escribir bien, y que algunos señores principales sabían de estas ciencias por curiosidad, y que por esto eran más estimados aunque no las usaban en público.

VIII
Llegada de los Tutul-Xiu y alianza que hicieron con los señores de Mayapán.— Tiranía de Cocom, ruina de su poder y de la ciudad de Mayapán.

Que cuentan [los indígenas] que de la parte del mediodía vinieron a Yucatán muchas gentes con sus señores, y que parecen haber venido de Chiapas aunque [los indígenas] no lo saben; mas este autor lo conjetura porque muchos vocablos y composiciones de verbos son los mismos en Chiapas que en Yucatán; y hay grandes señales en la parte de Chiapas de lugares que han sido despoblados; y dicen que estas gentes anduvieron cuarenta años por los despoblados de Yucatán sin haber en ellos agua sino la que llueve; y que al fin de este tiempo aportaron a las sierras que caen algo enfrente de la ciudad de Mayapán, a diez leguas de ella, y que allí comenzaron a poblar y hacer muy buenos edificios en muchas partes; y que los de Mayapán tomaron mucha amistad con ellos y holgaron de que labrasen la tierra como naturales y que así estos Tutul Xiú se sujetaron a las leyes de Mayapán y emparentaron unos con otros; y que como el señor Xiú, de los Tutul Xiués, era tal, vino a ser muy estimado de todos.

Que estas gentes vivieron tan quietamente que no había pleito ninguno, ni usaban armas ni arcos aun para la caza, siendo ahora excelentes flecheros, y que sólo usaban lazos y trampas con los que tomaban mucha caza; y que los sacerdotes tenían cierto arte de tirar varas con un palo grueso como de tres dedos agujerado hacia la tercera parte y de seis palmos de largo y que con él y unos cordeles tiraban fuerte y certeramente.

Que tenían leyes contra los delincuentes y las aplicaban mucho, como contra el adúltero a quien entregaban al ofendido para que le matase soltándole una piedra grande desde lo alto sobre la cabeza, o lo perdonase si quería; y que a las adúlteras no daban otra pena más que la infamia, que entre ellos era cosa muy grave; y al que forzase doncella lo mataban a pedradas; y cuentan un caso: que el señor de los Tutul Xiués tenía un hermano que fue acusado de este crimen, y le hizo apedrear y después cubrir de un gran montón de piedras; y que dicen que tenían otra ley antes de la población de esta ciudad, que mandaba sacar las tripas por el ombligo a los adúlteros.

Que el gobernador Cocom entró en codicia de riquezas, y que para esto trató con la gente de guarnición que los reyes de México tenían en Tabasco y Xicalango que les entregaría la ciudad, y que así trajo gente mexicana a Mayapán y oprimió a los pobres e hizo muchos esclavos; y los señores le hubieran matado si no hubiesen tenido miedo a los mexicanos. Que el señor de los Tutul Xiués nunca consintió en esto y que viéndose (oprimidos) los de Yucatán, aprendieron de los mexicanos el arte de las armas y así salieron maestros del arco y flecha y de la lanza y hachuela, y sus rodelas y sacos fuertes de sal y algodón y de otros pertrechos de guerra, y que ya no se admiraban de los mexicanos ni los temían, antes hacían poca cuenta de ellos. Y que en esto pasaron algunos años.

Que aquel Cocom fue el primero que hizo esclavos, pero que de este mal siguió usar las armas con que se defendieron para que no fuesen esclavos todos.

Que entre los sucesores de la casa de Cocom hubo uno muy orgulloso e imitador de Cocom, y éste hizo otra liga con los de Tabasco y metió más mexicanos dentro de la ciudad y comenzó a tiranizar y a hacer esclavos a la gente menuda y que por esto se juntaron los señores en el bando de Tutul Xiú, que era gran republicano como sus pasados, y se concertaron para matar a Cocom y así lo hicieron, matando también a todos sus hijos sin dejar más que uno que estaba ausente, y le saquearon la casa y tomaron las heredades que tenía en cacao y otras frutas, diciendo que con ellas se pagaban de lo que les había robado; y que duraron tanto los bandos entre los Cocomes—que decían ser echados injustamente—, y los Xiués que después de haber estado en aquella ciudad más de 500 años la desampararon y despoblaron, yéndose cada uno a su tierra.

IX
Monumentos cronológicos de Mayapán.— Fundación del reino de Zotuta.— Origen de los C[h]eles.— Los tres reinos principales de Yucatán.

Que conforme a la cuenta de [los indígenas], hará 120 años que se despobló Mayapán, y que se hallan en la plaza de aquella ciudad siete u ocho piedras de a diez pies de largo cada una, redondas por una parte, bien labradas, y que tienen algunos caracteres que ellos usan y que, desgastados por el agua, no se pueden leer; mas piensan que es memoria de la fundación y destrucción de aquella ciudad. Otras semejantes están en Zilán, pueblo de la costa, aunque más altas, y preguntados los naturales qué cosa eran, respondieron que acostumbraban erigir de 20 en 20 años, que es el número que tienen de contar sus edades, una piedra de aquellas. Mas parece (que esta explicación) no lleva camino, porque según esto habría muchas más, principalmente que no las hay en otros pueblos sino en Mayapán y Zilán.

Que lo principal que llevaron a sus tierras estos señores que desampararon Mayapán fueron los libros de sus ciencias porque siempre fueron muy sujetos a los consejos de sus sacerdotes, y que por esto hay tantos templos en aquellas provincias.

Que el hijo de Cocom que escapó de la muerte por estar ausente en sus contrataciones en tierra de Ulúa, que es adelante de la villa de Salamanca, al saber la muerte de su padre y el desbarato de la ciudad, vino muy presto y se juntó con los parientes y vasallos y pobló un lugar que llamó Tibulón, que quiere decir jugados fuimos; y que edificaron otros muchos pueblos en aquellos montes reuniéndose muchas familias de estos Cocomes. La provincia donde manda este señor se llama Zututa.

Que estos señores de Mayapán no tomaron venganza de los mexicanos que ayudaron a Cocom porque fueron persuadidos por el gobernador de la tierra y porque eran extranjeros, y que así los dejaron dándoles facultad para que poblasen un pueblo apartado, para sí solos, o se fuesen de la tierra no pudiéndose casar con las naturales de ella, sino entre ellos. Y que escogieran quedarse en Yucatán y no volver a las lagunas y mosquitos de Tabasco, y poblaron la provincia de Canul que les fue señalada y que allí duraron hasta las segundas guerras de los españoles.

Dicen que entre los doce sacerdotes de Mayapán hubo uno muy sabio que tuvo una sola hija a quien casó con un mancebo noble llamado Ah Chel, el cual hubo hijos que se llamaron como el padre conforme a la usanza de esta tierra; y dicen que este sacerdote avisó a su yerno de la destrucción de aquella ciudad y que éste supo mucho en las ciencias de su suegro, el cual, dicen, le escribió ciertas letras en la tabla del brazo izquierdo, de gran importancia para ser estimado; y con esta gracia pobló en la costa hasta que vino a hacer asiento en Tikoch siguiéndole gran número de gentes, y que así fue muy insigne población aquella de los Cheles, y poblaron la más insigne provincia de Yucatán, a la cual llamaron, por aquel nombre, la provincia de Ah Kin Chel, y es la de Ytzamal, donde residieron estos Cheles y se multiplicaron en Yucatán hasta la entrada del adelantado Montejo.

Que entre tres casas de señores principales, que eran los Cocomes, Xiués, y Cheles, hubo grandes bandos y enemistades y hoy en día, con ser cristianos, aún las hay. Los Cocomes decían a los Xiués que eran extranjeros y traidores al matar a su señor natural robándole su hacienda. Los Xiués decían ser tan buenos como ellos, tan antiguos y tan señores, y que no fueron traidores sino libertadores de la patria matando al tirano. El Chel decía que era tan bueno como ellos en linaje, por ser nieto de un sacerdote, el más estimado de Mayapán, y que por su persona era mejor que ellos pues había sabido hacerse tan señor como ellos, y que con esto se hacían desabrimiento en los mantenimientos porque el Chel, que estaba en la costa, no quería dar pescado ni sal al Cocom, haciéndole ir muy lejos por ello, y el Cocom no dejaba sacar caza ni frutas al Chel.

X
Varias calamidades sufridas en Yucatán en el siglo anterior a la conquista: huracanes, pestilencias, guerras, etc.

Que estas gentes tuvieron más de 20 años de abundancia y de salud y se multiplicaron tanto que toda la tierra parecía un pueblo; y que entonces se labraron los templos en tanta muchedumbre como se ve hoy en día por todas partes, y que atravesando los montes se ven entre las arboledas asientos de casas y edificios labrados a maravilla.

Que después de esta felicidad, una noche, por invierno, vino un aire como a las seis de la tarde y fue creciendo, haciéndose huracán de cuatro vientos, y que este aire derribó todos los árboles crecidos, lo cual hizo gran matanza en todo género de caza y derribó todas las casas altas las cuales, como son de paja y tenían lumbre dentro por el frío, se incendiaron y abrasaron a gran parte de la gente, y si algunos escapaban quedaban hechos pedazos de los golpes de la madera; y que duró este huracán hasta el otro día a las doce en que se vio que habían escapado quienes moraban en casas pequeñas, entre ellos los mozos recién casados que allí acostumbraban a hacer unas casillas enfrente de las de sus padres o suegros donde moran los primeros años; y que así perdió entonces la tierra el nombre a la que solían llamar de los venados y pavos, y tan sin árboles quedó, que los que ahora hay parece que se plantaron juntos según están nacidos a la igual, pues mirando la tierra desde algunas partes altas, parece que toda está cortada con una tijera.

Que quienes escaparon se animaron a edificar y cultivar la tierra y se multiplicaron mucho viniéndoles 16 años de salud y buenos temporales y que el último fue el más fértil de todos; y que queriendo comenzar a coger los frutos sobrevinieron por toda la tierra unas calenturas pestilenciales que duraban 24 horas, y después de cesadas se hinchaban (los enfermos) y reventaban llenos de gusanos, y que con esta pestilencia murió mucha gente y gran parte de los frutos quedó sin coger.

Que después de cesada la peste tuvieron otros 16 años buenos en los cuales se renovaron las pasiones y bandos, de manera que murieron en batallas ciento cincuenta mil hombres y que con esta matanza se sosegaron e hicieron la paz y descansaron por 20 años, después de los cuales les dio pestilencia de unos grandes granos que les pudría el cuerpo con gran hedor, de manera que se les caían los miembros a pedazos en cuatro o cinco días. Que habrá que pasó esta última plaga más de 50 años y que la mortandad de las guerras fue 20 años antes y la peste de la hinchazón y gusanos sería 16 años antes de las guerras y el huracán otros 16 antes que ésta y 22 ó 23 después de la destrucción de la ciudad de Mayapán. Que según esta cuenta, hace 125 años que se desbarató (la ciudad), dentro de los cuales años los de esta tierra han pasado las dichas miserias y otras muchas que comenzaron al entrar en ella los españoles, así por guerras como por otros castigos que Dios envía; de manera que es maravilla haber la gente que hay, aunque no es mucha.

XI
Profecías de la llegad de los españoles.— Biografía de Francisco de Montejo Primer Adelantado de Yucatán.

Que como la gente mexicana tuvo señales y profecías de la venida de los españoles y de la cesación de su mando y religión, también las tuvieron los de Yucatán algunos años antes que el adelantado Montejo los conquistase; y que en las sierras de Maní, que es en la provincia de Tutul Xiú, un indio llamado Ah Cambal, de oficio Chilán, que es el que tiene a su cargo dar las respuestas del demonio, les dijo públicamente que presto serían señoreados por gente extranjera, y les predicarían un Dios y la virtud de un palo que en su lengua llamó Vahomché, que quiere decir palo enhiesto de gran virtud contra los demonios.

Que el sucesor de los Cocomes, llamado don Juan Cocom, después de cristiano, fue hombre de gran reputación y muy sabio en sus cosas y bien sagaz y entendido en las naturales; y fue muy familiar del autor de este libro, fray Diego de Landa, y le contó muchas antigüedades y le mostró un libro que fue de su abuelo, hijo del Cocom que mataron en Mayapán, y en él estaba pintado un venado; y que aquel su abuelo le había dicho que cuando en aquella tierra entrasen venados grandes, que así llaman a las vacas, cesaría el culto de los Dioses; y que se había cumplido porque los españoles trajeron vacas grandes.

Que el adelantado Francisco de Montejo fue natural de Salamanca y que pasó a las Indias después de poblada la ciudad de Santo Domingo y la Isla Española, habiendo estado primero algún tiempo en Sevilla donde dejó un hijo niño que allí hubo; y que vino a la ciudad de Cuba donde ganó de comer y tuvo muchos amigos por su buena condición y entre ellos fueron Diego Velázquez, gobernador de la Isla, y Hernán Cortés; y que como el gobernador determinó enviar a Juan de Grijalva, su sobrino, a rescatar a tierras de Yucatán y a descubrir más tierra después de la nueva que Francisco Hernández de Córdoba trajo cuando la descubrió, que era tierra rica, determinó que Montejo fuese con Grijalva. (Montejo) como era rico, puso uno de los navíos y muchos bastimentos y fue así de los segundos españoles que descubrieron a Yucatán. Y que vista la costa de Yucatán tuvo deseos de enriquecerse allí antes que en Cuba, y vista la determinación de Hernán Cortés, le siguió con su hacienda y persona y Cortés le dio un navío a su cargo haciéndole capitán de él. Que en Yucatán recogieron a Gerónimo de Aguilar de quien Montejo entendió la lengua de aquella tierra y sus cosas, y que llegado Cortés a la Nueva España comenzó a poblar y al primer pueblo llamó la Veracruz conforme al blasón de su bandera; y que en este pueblo fue Montejo nombrado Alcalde del Rey, cargo en que se mantuvo discretamente y así lo publicó por tal Cortés cuando tomó por allí después del camino que hizo navegando la tierra a la redonda, y que por eso lo envió a España como uno de los procuradores de la Nueva España y para que llevase el quinto del rey con una relación de la tierra descubierta y de las cosas que comenzaban a hacerse en ella.

Que cuando Francisco de Montejo llegó a la corte de Castilla, era Presidente del Consejo de Indias Juan Rodríguez de Fonseca, obispo de Burgos, quien estaba mal informado contra Cortés por parte de Diego Velázquez, gobernador de Cuba, que pretendía también lo de Nueva España; y que estaban los más del Consejo contra los negocios de Cortés que parecía que no enviaba dineros al Rey sino que se los pedía, y entendiendo que por estar el Emperador en Flandes se negociaba mal, perseveró siete años desde que salió de las Indias, que fue en 1519, hasta que se embarcó, que fue en 26, y que con esta perseverancia recusó al Presidente y al Papa Adriano que era gobernador y habló al emperador, lo cual aprovechó mucho, pues se despachó lo de Cortés como era de razón.

XII

Montejo navega a Yucatán y toma posesión de la tierra.— Los Cheles le conceden el asiento de Chichén Itzá. [los indígenas] le obligan a que los deje.

Que en este tiempo que Montejo estuvo en la corte negoció para sí la conquista de Yucatán aunque pudo haber negociado otras cosas; le dieron el título de adelantado y se vino a Sevilla llevando a un sobrino suyo de trece años de edad y de su mismo nombre, y en Sevilla halló a su hijo de 28 años a quien llevó consigo. Trató palabras de casamiento con una señora de Sevilla, viuda rica, y así pudo juntar 500 hombres a quienes embarcó en tres navíos. Siguió su viaje y aportó a Cuzmil, isla de Yucatán, donde [los indígenas] no se alteraron porque estaban domesticados con los españoles de Cortés, y que allí procuró saber muchos vocablos de [los indígenas] para entenderse con ellos, y que de allí navegó a Yucatán y tomó posesión diciendo un alférez suyo con la bandera en la mano: "en nombre de Dios tomo la posesión de esta tierra por Dios y por el rey de Castilla".

Que de esta manera se fue costa abajo, que estaba bien poblada entonces, hasta llegar a Conil, pueblo de aquella costa, y que [los indígenas] se espantaban de ver tantos caballos y gente, que dieron aviso a toda la tierra de lo que pasaba, y esperaban el fin que tenían los españoles.

Que [los indígenas] señores de la provincia de Chicaca vinieron al adelantado, a visitarle en paz y fueron bien recibidos; entre ellos había un hombre de grandes fuerzas, quien quitó un alfanje a un negrillo que lo llevaba detrás de su amo y quiso matar con él al adelantado quien se defendió, y se llegaron españoles y se apaciguó el ruido, y entendieron que era menester andar sobre aviso.

Que el adelantado procuró saber cuál era la mayor población y supo que la de Tekoch en donde eran señores los Cheles, la cual estaba en la costa tierra abajo por el camino que los españoles llevaban; y que [los indígenas], pensando que caminaban para salirse de la tierra, no se alteraban ni les estorbaban el camino y de esta manera llegaron a Tekoch al que hallaron ser pueblo mayor y mejor de lo que habían pensado. (Y el adelantado) fue dichoso de que no fuesen señores de aquella tierra los Couohes de Champotón, que siempre fueron de más coraje que los Cheles, quienes con el sacerdocio que les dura hasta hoy no son tan orgullosos como otros y por ello concedieron al adelantado que pudiese hacer un pueblo para su gente y les dieron para ello el asiento de Chichenizá, a siete leguas de allí, que es muy excelente, y que desde allí fue conquistando la tierra lo cual hizo fácilmente porque los de Ah Kin Chel no le resistieron y los de Tutul Xiú le ayudaron; y con esto, los demás hicieron poca resistencia.

Que de esta manera pidió el adelantado gente para edificar en Chichenizá y en breve edificó un pueblo haciendo las casas de madera y la cobertura de ciertas palmas y paja larga, al uso de [los indígenas]. Y que así, viendo que [los indígenas] servían sin pesadumbre contó la gente de la tierra, que era mucha, y repartió los pueblos entre los españoles y, según dicen, a quien menos cabía alcanzaban dos o tres mil [indígenas] de repartimiento; y así comenzó a dar orden a los naturales de cómo habían de servir a aquella su ciudad, y que no agradó mucho a [los indígenas], aunque disimularon por entonces.

XIII

Montejo deja Yucatán con su gente y va a México.— Su hijo Francisco de Montejo, pacifica después la tierra.

Que el adelantado Montejo no pobló a propósito de quien tiene enemigos porque estaba muy lejos de la mar para tener entrada y salida a México y para las cosas de España; y que [los indígenas], pareciéndoles cosa dura servir a extranjeros donde ellos eran señores, comenzaron a ofenderle por todas partes; aunque él se defendía con sus caballos y gente, y les mataba muchos, [los indígenas] se reforzaban cada día de manera que les vino a faltar la comida. Que al fin una noche dejaron la ciudad poniendo un perro atado al badajo de la campana y un poco de pan apartado para que no lo pudiese alcanzar, y que cansaron el día antes a [los indígenas] con escaramuzas para que no los siguiesen y el perro repicaba la campana para alcanzar el pan lo cual maravilló mucho a [los indígenas] pensando que querían salir a ellos; mas después de sabido estaban muy corridos de la burla y acordaron seguir a los españoles por muchas partes porque no sabían el camino que llevaban. La gente que fue por aquel camino alcanzó a los españoles dándoles mucha grita, como a gente que huía, por lo cual seis de a caballo los esperaron en un raso y alancearon a muchos de ellos. Uno de [los indígenas] asió a un caballo por la pierna y le detuvo como si fuese un carnero. Los españoles llegaron a Zilán que era muy hermoso pueblo cuyo señor era un mancebo de los Cheles, ya cristiano y amigo de españoles, quien los trató bien. Zilán estaba muy cerca de Tikoch la cual, y todos los otros pueblos de aquella costa, estaban en obediencia de los Cheles: y así les dejaron estar seguros algunos meses.

Que el adelantado viendo que desde allí no se podía socorrer de las cosas de España, y que si [los indígenas] tornaban sobre ellos serían perdidos, acordó irse a Campeche y (de allí) a México, dejando a Yucatán sin gente. Había desde Zilán a Campeche cuarenta y ocho leguas muy pobladas de gente. Dieron arte a Namux Chel, señor de Zilán, y él se ofreció a asegurarles el camino y acompañarlos. El adelantado trató con el tío de éste, que era señor de Yobain, que le diese dos hijos bien dispuestos que tenía para que le acompañasen, de manera que con tres mancebos primos hermanos, dos en colleras y el de Zilán a caballo, llegaron seguros a Campeche donde fueron recibidos en paz. Los Cheles se despidieron y volviendo a sus pueblos cayó muerto el de Zilán. Desde allí partieron para México donde Cortés había señalado repartimiento de [indígenas] al adelantado, aunque estaba ausente.

Que llegado el adelantado a México con su hijo y sobrino, llegó luego en busca suya doña Beatriz de Herrera, su mujer, y una hija que en ella tenía llamada doña Catalina de Montejo. El adelantado se había casado clandestinamente en Sevilla con doña Beatriz de Herrera y dicen algunos que la negaba, pero don Antonio de Mendoza, Virrey de la Nueva España, se puso de por medio y así la recibió y a él lo envió el mismo Virrey por gobernador de Honduras, donde casó a su hija con el licenciado Alonso Maldonado, Presidente de la Audiencia de los Confines; y que después de algunos años le pasaron a Chiapa desde donde envió a su hijo a Yucatán, con poderes, y lo conquistó y pacificó.

Que este don Francisco, hijo del adelantado, se crió en la corte del rey católico y le trajo su padre cuando volvió a las Indias, a la conquista de Yucatán, y de allí fue con él a México; y que el Virrey don Antonio y el marqués don Hernán Cortés le quisieron bien y fue con el marqués a la jornada de California. Y que tornado, le proveyó el Virrey para regir Tabasco y se desposó con una señora llamada doña Andrea del Castillo, que había pasado doncella a México con parientes suyos.

XIII
Estado de Yucatán después de la salida del los españoles.— Don Francisco, hijo del adelantado, restablece el gobierno español en Yucatán.

Que salidos los españoles de Yucatán faltó el agua en la tierra, y que por haber gastado sin orden su maíz en las guerras de los españoles, les sobrevino gran hambre; tanta, que vinieron a comer cortezas de árboles, en especial uno que llaman cumché, que es fofo y blando por dentro. Que por esta hambre, los Xiués, que son los señores de Maní, acordaron hacer un sacrificio solemne a los ídolos llevando ciertos esclavos y esclavas a echar en el pozo de Chichenizá. Mas como habían de pasar por el pueblo de los señores Cocomes, sus capitales enemigos, y pensando que en tal tiempo se renovarían las viejas pasiones, les enviaron a rogar que los dejasen pasar por su tierra. Los Cocomes los engañaron con buena respuesta y dándoles posada a todos juntos en una gran casa les pegaron fuego y mataron a los que escapaban; y por esto hubo grandes guerras. (Además) se les recreció la langosta por espacio de cinco años, que no les dejaba cosa verde; y vinieron a tanta hambre que se caían muertos por los caminos, de manera que cuando los españoles volvieron no conocían la tierra aunque con otros cuatro años buenos después de la langosta, se había mejorado algo.

Que este don Francisco se partió para Yucatán por los ríos de Tabasco y entró por las lagunas de Dos Bocas y que el primer pueblo que tocó fue Champotón con cuyo señor, llamado Mochcouoh les fue mal a Francisco Hernández y a Grijalva; mas por ser ya muerto no hubo allí resistencia, antes bien, los de este pueblo sustentaron a don Francisco y su gente dos años en cuyo tiempo no pudo pasar adelante por la mucha resistencia que hallaba. Que después pasó a Campeche y vino a tener mucha amistad con los de aquel pueblo. De manera que con su ayuda y la de los de Champotón acabó la conquista prometiéndoles que serían remunerados por el rey por su mucha fidelidad, aunque hasta ahora el rey no lo ha cumplido.

Que la resistencia no fue bastante para que don Francisco dejase de llegar con su ejercito a Tihó donde se pobló la ciudad de Mérida; y que dejando el bagaje en Mérida prosiguieron la conquista enviando capitanes a diversas partes. Don Francisco envió a su primo Francisco de Montejo a la villa de Valladolid para pacificar los pueblos que estaban algo rebeldes y para poblar aquella villa como ahora está. Pobló en Chectemal la villa de Salamanca y ya tenía poblado Campeche. (Entonces) dio orden para el servicio de [los indígenas] y el gobierno de los españoles hasta que el adelantado, su padre, vino a gobernar desde Chiapa con su mujer y casa; y fue bien recibido en Campeche llamando a esa villa de San Francisco por su nombre. Después pasó a la ciudad de Mérida.

XV
Crueldades de los españoles con los naturales.—Como se disculpan.

Que [los indígenas] recibían pesadamente el yugo de la servidumbre, mas los españoles tenían bien repartidos los pueblos que abrazaban la tierra, aunque no faltaba entre [los indígenas] quien los alterase, sobre lo cual se hicieron castigos muy crueles que fueron a causa de que apocase la gente. Quemaron vivos a algunos principales de la provincia de Cupul y ahorcaron a otros. Hízose información contra los de Yobain, pueblo de los Cheles, y prendieron a la gente principal y, en cepos, la metieron en una casa a la que prendieron fuego abrasándola viva con la mayor inhumanidad del mundo, y dice este Diego de Landa que él vio un gran árbol cerca del pueblo en el cual un capitán ahorcó muchas mujeres indígenas de las ramas y de los pies de ellas a los niños, sus hijos. Y en este mismo pueblo y en otro que dicen Verey, a dos leguas de él, ahorcaron a dos mujeres indígenas, una doncella y la otra recién casada, no por otra culpa sino porque eran muy hermosas y temían que se revolviera el real de los españoles sobre ellas y porque pensasen [los indígenas] que a los españoles no les importaban las mujeres; de estas dos hay mucha memoria entre [indígenas] y españoles por su gran hermosura y por la crueldad con que las mataron.

Que se alteraron [los indígenas] de la provincia de Cochua y Chectemal y los españoles los apaciguaron de tal manera que, siendo esas dos provincias las más pobladas y llenas de gente, quedaron las más desventuradas de toda aquella tierra. Hicieron (en [los indígenas]) crueldades inauditas cortando narices, brazos y piernas, y a las mujeres los pechos y las echaban en lagunas hondas con calabazas atadas a los pies; daban estocadas a los niños porque no andaban tanto como las madres, y si los llevaban en colleras y enfermaban, o no andaban tanto como los otros, cortábanles las cabezas por no pararse a soltarlos. Y trajeron gran número de mujeres y hombres cautivos para su servicio con semejantes tratamientos. Se afirma que don Francisco de Montejo no hizo ninguna de estas crueldades ni se halló en ellas, antes bien le parecieron muy mal, pero que no pudo (evitarlas).

Que los españoles se disculpaban con decir que siendo pocos no podían sujetar tanta gente sin meterles miedo con castigos terribles, y traen a ejemplo la historia de los hebreos y el paso a la tierra de promisión (en que se cometieron) grandes crueldades por mandato de Dios; y por otra parte tenían razón [los indígenas] al defender su libertad y confiar en los capitanes muy valientes que tenían para entre ellos y pensaban que así serían contra los españoles.

Que cuentan de un ballestero español y de un flechero indio que por ser muy diestros el uno y el otro se procuraban matar y no podían cogerse descuidados; el español fingió descuidarse puesta una rodilla en tierra y el indio le dio un flechazo en la mano que le subió brazo arriba y le apartó las canillas una de otra; pero al mismo tiempo soltó el español la ballesta y dio al indio por el pecho y sintiéndose herido de muerte, porque no dijesen que un español le había muerto, cortó un bejuco, que es como mimbre aunque mucho más largo, y se ahorcó con él a la vista de todos. De estas valentías hay muchos ejemplos.

XVI
Estado del país antes de la conquista.— Una sublevación.— Cédula real a favor de [los indígenas].— Muerte del adelantado.— Sus descendientes.

Que antes que los españoles ganasen aquella tierra vivían los naturales juntos en pueblos, con mucha policía, y tenían la tierra muy limpia y desmontada de malas plantas y puestos muy buenos árboles; y que su habitación era de esta manera: en medio del pueblo estaban los templos con hermosas plazas y en torno de los templos estaban las casas de los señores y de los sacerdotes, y luego la gente más principal, y así iban los más ricos y estimados más cercanos a éstas y a los fines del pueblo estaban las casas de la gente más baja. Los pozos, donde había pocos, estaban cerca de las casas de los señores, y que tenían sus heredades plantadas de los árboles de vino y sembraban algodón, pimienta y maíz, y vivían en estas congregaciones por miedo de sus enemigos que los cautivaban, y que por las guerras de los españoles se dispersaron por los montes.

Que [los indígenas] de Valladolid por sus malas costumbres o por el mal tratamiento de los españoles, se conjuraron para matar a los españoles cuando se dividían a cobrar sus tributos; y que en un día mataron diecisiete españoles y cuatrocientos criados de los muertos y de los que quedaron vivos; y luego enviaron algunos brazos y pies por toda la tierra en señal de lo que habían hecho, para que se alzasen, mas no lo quisieron hacer y con esto pudo el adelantado socorrer a los españoles de Valladolid y castigar a [los indígenas].

Que el adelantado tuvo desasosiegos con los de Mérida y mucho mayores con la cédula del emperador con la cual privó de [indígenas] a todos los gobernadores, y fue un receptor a Yucatán y quitó al adelantado [los indígenas] y los puso en cabeza del rey, y que tras esto, la Audiencia Real de México le tomó residencia, remitiéndolo al Consejo Real de Indias, en España, donde murió lleno de días y trabajos, y dejó en Yucatán a su mujer doña Beatriz más rica que él murió, y a don Francisco de Montejo, su hijo, casado en Yucatán y a su hija doña Catalina, casada con el licenciado Alonso Maldonado, Presidente de las Audiencias de Honduras y Santo Domingo, de la Isla Española, y a don Juan Montejo, español, y a don Diego, mestizo que hubo en una india.

Que este don Francisco después que dejó el gobierno a su padre el adelantado, vivió en su casa como un vecino particular en cuanto al gobierno, aunque muy respetado de todos por haber conquistado, repartido y regido aquella tierra. Fue a Guatemala con su residencia y tornó a su casa. Tuvo por hijos a Don Juan de Montejo, que casó con doña Isabel, natural de Salamanca; a doña Beatriz de Montejo, con su tío, primo hermano de su padre; y a doña Francisca de Montejo, que casó con don Carlos de Arellano, natural de Guadalajara; murió de larga enfermedad después de haberíos visto a todos casados.

XVII
Llegada de los frailes franciscanos españoles a Yucatán.— Protección que dispensaron a los indígenas.— Sus luchas con los encomenderos.

Que fray Jacobo de Testera, franciscano, pasó a Yucatán y comenzó a adoctrinar a los hijos de [los indígenas], y que los soldados españoles querían servirse tanto de los mozos que no les quedaba tiempo para aprender la doctrina; y que por otra parte disgustaban a los frailes cuando los reprendían del mal que les hacían a [los indígenas] y que por esto, fray Jacobo se tornó a México donde murió. Después fray Toribio Motolinia envió desde Guatemala frailes, y de México fray Martín de Hojacastro envió más y todos tomaron su asiento en Campeche y Mérida con favor del adelantado y de su hijo don Francisco, los cuales les edificaron un monasterio en Mérida, como está dicho, y que procuraron saber la lengua, lo cual era dificultoso.

El que más supo fue fray Luis de Villalpando, que comenzó a saberla por señas y pedrezuelas y la redujo a alguna manera de arte y escribió una doctrina cristiana en aquella lengua, aunque había muchos estorbos de parte de los españoles que eran absolutos señores y querían que se hiciese todo enderezado a su ganancia y tributos, y de parte de [los indígenas] que procuraban estarse en sus idolatrías y borracheras; principalmente era gran trabajo por estar tan derramados por los montes.

Que los españoles tomaban pesar de ver que los frailes hiciesen monasterios y ahuyentaban a los hijos de [los indígenas] de sus repartimientos, para que no viniesen a la doctrina; y quemaron dos veces el monasterio de Valladolid con su iglesia, que era de madera y paja, tanto que fue necesario a los frailes irse a vivir entre [los indígenas]; y cuando se alzaron [los indígenas] de aquella provincia escribieron al virrey don Antonio que se habían alzado por amor a los frailes y el virrey hizo diligencia y averiguó que al tiempo que se alzaron aún no eran llegados los frailes a aquella provincia; (aun los encomenderos) velaban de noche a los frailes con escándalo de [los indígenas] y hacían inquisición de sus vidas y les quitaban las limosnas.

Que los frailes viendo este peligro enviaron al muy singular juez Cerrato, Presidente de Guatemala, un religioso que le diese cuenta de lo que pasaba, el cual, visto el desorden y mala cristiandad de los españoles, que se llevaban absolutamente los tributos y cuanto podían sin orden del rey (y obligaban a [los indígenas]) al servicio personal en todo género de trabajo, hasta alquilarlos para llevar cargas, proveyó cierta tasación, harto larga aunque pasadera, en que señalaba qué cosas eran del indio después de pagado el tributo a su encomendero, y que no fuese todo absolutamente del español. (Los encomenderos) suplicaron de esto y con temor de la tasa sacaban a [los indígenas] más que hasta allí, y entonces los frailes tornaron a la Audiencia y reclamaron en España e hicieron tanto que la Audiencia de Guatemala envió a un oidor, el cual tasó la tierra y quitó el servicio personal e hizo casar a algunos, quitándoles las casas que tenían llenas de mujeres. Éste fue el licenciado Tomás López natural de Tendilla, y ello causó que aborreciesen mucho más a los frailes, haciéndoles libelos infamatorios y cesando de oír sus misas.

Que este aborrecimiento causó que [los indígenas] estuviesen muy bien con los frailes considerando los trabajos que tomaban sin interés ninguno para darles libertad, tanto que ninguna cosa hacían sin dar parte a los frailes y tomar su consejo, y esto dio causa a los españoles para que por envidia dijesen que los frailes habían hecho esto para gobernar las Indias y gozar de lo que a ellos se había quitado.

XVIII
Vicios de [los indígenas].— Los frailes estudian la lengua del país. Sus enseñanzas a las naturales.— Castigos a los apóstatas.

Que los vicios de [los indígenas] eran idolatrías y repudios y borracheras públicas y vender y comprar esclavos; y que por apartarlos de estas cosas vinieron a aborrecer a los frailes; pero que entre los españoles los que más fatigaron a los religiosos, aunque encubiertamente, fueron los sacerdotes, como gente que había perdido su oficio y los provechos de él.

Que la manera que se tuvo para adoctrinar a [los indígenas] fue recoger a los hijos pequeños de los señores y gente más principal, poniéndolos en torno de los monasterios en casas que cada pueblo hacía para los suyos, donde estaban juntos todos los de cada lugar, cuyos padres y parientes les traían de comer; y con estos niños se recogían los que venían a la doctrina, y con tal frecuentación muchos con devoción, pidieron el bautismo; y estos niños, después de enseñados, tenían cuidado de avisar a los frailes de las idolatrías y borracheras y rompían los ídolos aunque fuesen de sus padres, y exhortaban a las repudiadas; y a los huérfanos, si los hacían esclavos que se quejasen a los frailes y aunque fueron amenazados por los suyos, no por eso cesaban, antes respondían que les hacían honra pues era por el bien de sus almas. Y que el adelantado y los jueces del rey siempre han dado fiscales a los frailes para recoger [los indígenas] a la doctrina y castigar a los que se tornaban a la vida pasada. Al principio daban los señores de mala gana sus hijos, pensando que los querían hacer esclavos como habían hecho los españoles y por esta causa daban muchos esclavillos en lugar de sus hijos; mas como comprendieron el negocio, los daban de buena gana.

Que de esta manera aprovecharon tanto los mozos en las escuelas y la otra gente en la doctrina, que era cosa admirable.

Que aprendieron a leer y escribir en la lengua de [los indígenas] la cual se redujo tanto a un arte que se estudiaba como la latina y que se halló que no usaban de seis letras nuestras que son D, F, G, Q, R y S que para cosa ninguna las han menester; pero tienen necesidad de doblar y añadir otras para entender las muchas significaciones de algunos vocablos, porque Pa quiere decir abrir, y PPa, apretando mucho los labios, quiere decir quebrar; y Tan es cal o ceniza, y Than, dicho recio, entre la lengua y los dientes altos, quiere decir palabra o hablar; y así en otras dicciones, y puesto que ellos para estas cosas tenían diferentes caracteres no fue menester inventar nuevas figuras de letras sino aprovecharse de las latinas para que fuesen comunes a todos. Dióseles también orden para que dejasen los asientos que tenían en los montes y se juntasen como antes en buenas poblaciones, para que más fácilmente fuesen enseñados y no tuviesen tanto trabajo los religiosos para cuya sustentación les hacían limosnas las pascuas y otras fiestas; y hacían limosnas a las iglesias por medio de dos [indígenas] ancianos nombrados, para esto, con lo cual daban lo necesario a los frailes cuando andaban visitándoles, y también aderezaban las iglesias de ornamentos.

Que estando esta gente instruida en la religión y los mozos aprovechados, como dijimos, fueron pervertidos por los sacerdotes que en su idolatría tenían y por los señores, y tornaron a idolatrar y hacer sacrificios no sólo de sahumerios sino de sangre humana, sobre lo cual los frailes hicieron inquisición y pidieron la ayuda del alcalde mayor prendiendo a muchos y haciéndoles procesos; y se celebró un auto en que pusieron muchos en cadalsos encorozados, y azotados y trasquilados y algunos ensambenitados por algún tiempo; y otros, de tristeza, engañados por el demonio, se ahorcaron, y en común mostraron todos mucho arrepentimiento y voluntad de ser buenos cristianos.

XIX

Llegada del obispo Toral.— Suelta a [los indígenas] arbitrariamente presos.— Viaje de Landa a España para justificar la conducta de los franciscanos.

Que a esta sazón llegó a Campeche don fray Francisco Toral, franciscano, natural de Úbeda, que había estado 20 años en lo de México y venía por obispo de Yucatán, el cual, por las informaciones de los españoles y por las quejas de [los indígenas], deshizo lo que los frailes tenían hecho y mandó soltar los presos y que sobre esto se agravió al provincial quien determinó ir a España quejándose primero en México y que así vino a Madrid donde los del Consejo de las Indias le afearon mucho que hubiese usurpado el oficio de obispo y de inquisidor, para descargo de lo cual alegaba la facultad que su orden tenía para en aquellas artes, concedida por el Papa Adriano a instancias del emperador, y el auxilio que la Audiencia Real de las Indias le mandó dar conforme a como se daba a los obispos; y que los del Consejo se enojaron más por estas disculpas y acordaron remitirle con sus papeles y los que el obispo había enviado contra los frailes, a fray Pedro Bobadilla, provincial de Castilla, a quien el rey escribió mandándole que los viese e hiciese justicia. Y que este fray Pedro, por estar enfermo, sometió el examen de los procesos a fray Pedro de Guzmán, de su orden, hombre docto y experimentado en cosas de inquisición, y se presentaron los pareceres de siete personas doctas del reino de Toledo, que fueron fray Francisco de Medina, fray Francisco Dorantes, de la orden de San Francisco; el maestro fray Alonso de la Cruz, fraile de San Agustín que había estado 30 años en las Indias; y el licenciado Tomás López que fue oidor en Guatemala en el nuevo reino y fue juez en Yucatán; y don Hurtado, catedrático de cánones; y don Méndez, catedrático de sagrada escritura; y don Martínez, catedrático de Scoto en Alcalá, los cuales dijeron que el provincial hizo justamente el auto y las otras cosas en castigo de [los indígenas], lo cual, visto por fray Francisco de Guzmán, escribió largamente sobre ello al provincial fray Pedro de Bobadilla.

Que [los indígenas] de Yucatán merecen que el rey los favorezca por muchas cosas y por la voluntad que mostraron a su servicio. Estando necesitado en Flandes, envió la princesa doña Juana, su hermana, que entonces era gobernadora del reino, una cédula pidiendo ayuda a los de las Indias; célula que llevó a Yucatán un oidor de Guatemala y para esto juntó a los señores y ordenó que un fraile les predicase lo que debían a su majestad y lo que entonces les pedía. Concluida la platica se levantaron dos [indígenas] en pie y respondieron que bien sabían lo que eran obligados a Dios por haberles dado tan noble y cristianísimo rey y que les pesaba no vivir en parte donde le pudieran servir con sus personas y por tanto que viese lo que de su pobreza quería, que le servirían con ello y que si no bastase, venderían a sus hijos y mujeres.

XX

Manera de fabricar las casa en Yucatán.— Obediencia y respeto de [los indígenas] a sus señores.— Modo de ornar sus cabezas y de llevar sus vestidos.

Que la manera (que [los indígenas] tenían de) hacer sus casas era cubrirlas de paja, que tienen muy buena y mucha, o con hojas de palma, que es propia para esto; y que tenían muy grandes corrientes para que no se lluevan, y que después echan una pared de por medio y a lo largo, que divide toda la casa y en esta pared dejan algunas puertas para la mitad que llaman las espaldas de la casa, donde tienen sus camas y la otra mitad blanquean de muy gentil encalado y los señores las tienen pintadas de muchas galanterías; y esta mitad es el recibimiento y aposento de los huéspedes y no tiene puerta sino toda es abierta conforme al largo de la casa y baja mucho la corriente delantera por temor de los soles y aguas, y dicen que también para enseñorearse de los enemigos de la parte de dentro en tiempo de necesidad. El pueblo menudo hacía a su costa las casas de los señores; y que con no tener puertas tenían por grave delito hacer mal a casas ajenas. Tenían una portecilla atrás para el servicio necesario y unas camas de varillas y encima una serilla donde duermen cubiertos por sus mantas de algodón; en verano duermen comúnmente en los encalados con una de aquellas serillas especialmente los hombres. Allende de la casa hacía todo el pueblo a los señores sus sementeras, y se las beneficiaban y cogían en cantidad que les bastaba a él y a su casa; y cuando había caza o pesca, o era tiempo de traer sal, siempre daban parte al señor porque estas cosas siempre las hacían en comunidad. Si moría el señor, aunque le sucediese el hijo mayor, eran siempre los demás hijos muy acatados y ayudados y tenidos por señores.

A los demás principales inferiores del señor ayudaban en todas estas cosas conforme a quienes eran, o al favor que el señor les daba. Los sacerdotes vivían de sus oficios y ofrendas.

Los señores regían el pueblo concertando los litigios, ordenando y concertando las cosas de sus repúblicas, todo lo cual hacían por manos de los más principales, que eran muy obedecidos y estimados, especialmente de gente rica, a quienes visitaban; tenían palacio en sus casas donde concertaban las cosas y negocios, principalmente de noche; y si los señores salían del pueblo llevaban mucha compañía, lo mismo que cuando salían de sus casas.

Que [los indígenas] de Yucatán son gente bien dispuesta, altos, recios y de muchas fuerzas y comúnmente todos estevados porque en su niñez, cuando las madres los llevan de una parte a otra van a horcajadas en los cuadriles. Tenían por gala ser bizcos, lo cual hacían por arte las madres colgándoles del pelo desde niños, un pelotillo que les llegaba al medio de las cejas; y como les andaba allí jugando, ellos alzaban siempre los ojos y venían a quedar bizcos. Y que tenían las cabezas y frentes llanas, hecho también por sus madres, por industria, desde niños, que traían las orejas horadadas para zarcillos y muy arpadas de los sacrificios. No criaban barbas y decían que les quemaban los rostros sus madres con paños calientes siendo niños, para que no les naciesen. Y que ahora crían barbas aunque muy ásperas como cerdas de rocines.

Que criaban cabello como las mujeres: por lo alto quemaban como una buena corona y así crecía mucho lo de debajo y lo de la corona quedaba corto y que lo trenzaban y hacían una guirnalda de ello en torno de la cabeza dejando la colilla atrás como borlas.

Que todos los hombres usaban espejos y no las mujeres; y que para llamarse cornudos decían que su mujer les había puesto el espejo en el cabello sobrante del colodrillo.

Que se bañaban mucho, no curando de cubrirse de las mujeres sino cuanto podía cubrir la mano.

Que eran amigos de buenos olores y que por eso usan ramilletes de flores y yerbas olorosas, muy curiosos y labrados.

Que usaban pintarse de colorado el rostro y el cuerpo y les parecía muy mal, pero teníanlo por gran gala.

Que su vestido era un listón de una mano de ancho que les servía de bragas y calzas y que se daban con él algunas vueltas por la cintura de manera que uno de los cabos colgaba adelante y el otro detrás, y que estos cabos los hacían sus mujeres con curiosidad y labores de pluma, y que traían mantas largas y cuadradas y las ataban en los hombros; y que traían sandalias de cáñamo o cuero de venado por curtir, seco, y no usaban otro vestido.

XXI
Comidas y bebidas de [los indígenas] de Yucatán.

Que el mantenimiento principal es el maíz, del cual hacen diversos manjares y bebidas, y aun bebido como lo beben, les sirve de comida y bebida, y que las mujeres indígenas echan el maíz a remojar en cal y agua una noche antes, y que a la mañana está blando y medio cocido y de esta manera se le quita el hollejo y pezón; y que lo muelen en piedras y que de lo medio molido dan a los trabajadores, caminantes y navegantes grandes pelotas y cargas y que dura algunos meses con sólo acedarse; y que de aquello toman una pella y deslíenla en un vaso de la cáscara de una fruta que cría un árbol con el cual les proveyó Dios de vasos; y que se beben aquella sustancia y se comen lo demás y que es sabroso y de gran mantenimiento; y que de lo más molido sacan leche y la cuajan al fuego y hacen como poleadas para las mañanas y que lo beben caliente; y que en lo que sobra de las mañanas echan agua para beber en el día porque no acostumbran beber agua sola. Que también tuestan el maíz, lo muelen y deslíen en agua, que es muy fresca bebida, echándole un poco de pimienta de Indias o cacao.

Que hacen del maíz y cacao molido una manera de espuma muy sabrosa con que celebran sus fiestas y que sacan del cacao una grasa que parece mantequilla y que de esto y del maíz hacen otra bebida sabrosa y estimada; y que hacen otra bebida de la substancia del maíz molido así crudo, que es muy fresca y sabrosa.

Que hacen pan de muchas maneras, bueno y sano, salvo que es malo de comer cuando está frío; y así pasan las mujeres indígenas trabajo en hacerlo dos veces al día. Que no se ha podido acertar a hacer harina que se amase como la del trigo, y que si alguna vez se hace como pan de trigo no vale nada.

Que hacen guisados de legumbres y carne de venados y aves monteses y domésticas, que hay muchas, y de pescados, que hay muchos, y que así tienen buenos mantenimientos, principalmente después de que crían puercos y aves de Castilla.

Que por la mañana toman la bebida caliente con pimienta, como está dicho, y entre día, las otras frías, y a la noche los guisados; y que si no hay carne, hacen sus salsas de la pimienta y legumbres. No acostumbraban comer los hombres con las mujeres; ellos comían por sí en el suelo o cuando mucho sobre una serilla por mesa, y comen bien cuando tienen, y cuando no, sufren muy bien el hambre y pasan con muy poco. Se lavan las manos y la boca después de comer.

XXII
Pintura y labrado de [los indígenas].— Sus borracheras, banquetes, farsas, músicas y bailes.

Labrábanse los cuerpos, y cuanto más, tanto más valientes y bravos se tenían, porque el labrarse era gran tormento, que era de esta manera: los oficiales de ello labraban la parte que querían con tinta y después sajábanle delicadamente las pinturas y así, con la sangre y tinta, quedaban en el cuerpo las señales; y que se labraban poco a poco por el grande tormento que era, y también después se (ponían) malos porque se les enconaban las labores, y hacíase materia, y que con todo eso se mofaban de los que no se labraban. Y que se precian mucho de ser requebrados y tener gracias y habilidades naturales, y que ya comen y beben como nosotros.

Que [los indígenas] eran muy disolutos en beber y emborracharse, de lo cual les seguían muchos males como matarse unos a otros, violar las camas pensando las pobres mujeres recibir a sus maridos, también con padres y madres como en casa de sus enemigos, y pegar fuego a sus casas, y que con todo eso se perdían por emborracharse. Y cuando la borrachera era general y de sacrificios, contribuían todos para ello, porque cuando era particular hacía el gasto el que la hacía con ayuda de sus parientes. Y que hacen el vino de miel y agua y cierta raíz de un árbol que para esto criaban, con lo cual se hacía el vino fuerte y muy hediondo; y que con bailes y regocijos comían sentados de dos en dos o de cuatro en cuatro, y que después de comido, los escanciadores, que no se solían emborrachar, sacaban unos grandes artesones de beber hasta que se hacía un zipizape; y las mujeres tenían mucha cuenta de volver borrachos a casa sus maridos.

Que muchas veces gastan en un banquete lo que en muchos días, mercadeando y trompeando, ganaban; y que tienen dos maneras de hacer estas fiestas. La primera, que es de los señores y gente principal, obliga a cada uno de los convidados a que hagan otro tal convite y que den a cada uno de los convidados una ave asada, pan y bebida de cacao en abundancia y al fin del convite suelen dar a cada uno una manta para cubrirse y un banquillo y el vaso más galano que pueden, y si muere alguno de ellos es obligada la casa o sus parientes a pagar el convite. La otra manera es entre parentelas, cuando casan a sus hijos o hacen memoria de las cosas de sus antepasados; y ésta no obliga a restitución, salvo que si cuando han convidado a un indio a una fiesta así, él convida a todos cuando hace fiesta o casa a sus hijos. Y sienten mucho la amistad y la conservan (aunque estén) lejos unos de otros, con estos convites; y que en estas fiestas les daban de beber mujeres hermosas las cuales, después de dado el vaso, volvían las espaldas al que lo tomaba hasta vaciado el vaso.

Que [los indígenas] tienen recreaciones muy donosas y principalmente farsantes que representan con mucho donaire; tanto, que éstos alquilan los españoles para que vean los chistes de los españoles que pasan con sus mozas, maridos o ellos propios, sobre el buen o mal servir, y lo representan después con tanto artificio como curiosidad. Tienen atabales pequeños que tañen con la mano, y otro atabal de palo hueco, de sonido pesado y triste, que tañen con un palo larguillo con leche de un árbol puesta al cabo; y tienen trompetas largas y delgadas, de palos huecos, y al cabo unas largas y tuertas calabazas; y tienen otro instrumento de la tortuga entera con sus conchas, y sacada la carne táñenlo con la palma de la mano y es su sonido lúgubre y triste.

Tienen silbatos de los huesos de cañas de venado y caracoles grandes, y flautas de cañas, y con estos instrumentos hacen són a los bailantes. Tienen especialmente dos bailes muy de hombre y de ver. El uno es un juego de cañas, y así le llaman ellos colomché, que lo quiere decir. Para jugarlo se junta una gran rueda de bailadores con su música que les hace son, y por su compás salen dos de la rueda: el uno con un manojo de bohordos y baila enhiesto con ellos; el otro baila en cuclillas, ambos con compás de la rueda, y el de los bohordos, con toda su fuerza, los tira al otro, el cual, con gran destreza, con un palo pequeño arrebátalos. Acabado de tirar vuelven con su compás a la rueda y salen otros a hacer lo mismo. Otro baile hay en que bailan ochocientos y más y menos [indígenas], con banderas pequeñas, con son y paso largo de guerra, entre los cuales no hay uno que salga de compás; y en sus bailes son pesados porque todo el día entero no cesan de bailar y allí les llevan de comer y beber. Los hombres no solían bailar con las mujeres.

XXIII
Industria, comercio y moneda.— Agricultura y semillas. Justicia y hospitalidad.

Que los oficios de [los indígenas] eran olleros y carpinteros, los cuales, por hacer los ídolos de barro y madera, con muchos ayunos y observancias, ganaban mucho. Habla también cirujanos o, por mejor decir, hechiceros, los cuales curaban con yerbas y muchas supersticiones; y así de todos los demás oficios. El oficio a que más inclinados estaban es el de mercaderes llevando sal, y ropa y esclavos a tierra de Ulúa y Tabasco, trocándolo todo por cacao y cuentas de piedra que eran su moneda, y con ésta solían comprar esclavos u otras cuentas con razón que eran finas y buenas, las cuales traían sobre sí los señores como joyas en las fiestas; y tenían por moneda y joyas de sus personas otras hechas de ciertas conchas coloradas, y las traían en sus bolsas de red que tenían, y en los mercados trataban todas cuantas cosas había en esa tierra. Fiaban, prestaban y pagaban cortésmente y sin usura, y sobre todos eran los labradores y los que se ponen a coger el maíz y las demás semillas, las cuales guardan en muy lindos silos y trojes para vender a su tiempo. Sus mulas y bueyes son la gente. Suelen, de costumbre, sembrar para cada casado con su mujer medida de 400 pies lo cual llaman hum uinic, medida con vara de 20 pies, 20 en ancho y 20 en largo.

Que [los indígenas] tienen la buena costumbre de ayudarse unos a otros en todos sus trabajos. En tiempo de sus sementeras, los que no tienen gente suya para hacerlas, júntanse de 20 en 20 o más o menos, y hacen todos juntos por su medida y tasa la labor de todos y no la dejan hasta cumplir con todos. Las tierras, por ahora, son de común y así el que primero las ocupa las posee. Siembran en muchas partes, por si una faltare supla la otra. En labrar la tierra no hacen sino coger la basura y quemarla para después sembrar, y desde mediados de enero hasta abril labran y entonces con las lluvias siembran, lo que hacen trayendo un taleguillo a cuestas, y con un palo puntiagudo hacen un agujero en la tierra y ponen allí cinco o seis granos que cubren con el mismo palo. Y en lloviendo, espanto es cómo nace. Júntanse también para la caza de cincuenta en cincuenta más o menos, y asan en parrillas la carne del venado para que no se les gaste y venidos al pueblo hacen sus presentes al señor y distribuyen (el resto) como amigos y lo mismo hacen con la pesca.

Que [los indígenas], en sus visitas, siempre llevan consigo don que dar según su calidad; y el visitado, con otro don, satisface al otro, y los terceros de estas visitas hablan y escuchan curiosamente conforme a la persona con quien hablan, no obstante que todos se llaman de tú porque en el progreso de sus pláticas, el menor, por curiosidad, suele repetir el nombre del oficio o dignidad del mayor. Y usan mucho ir ayudando a los que les dan los mensajes (con) un sonsonete hecho con la aspiración en la garganta, que es como decir hasta que o así que. Las mujeres son cortas en sus razonamientos y no acostumbran a negociar por sí, especialmente si son pobres, y por eso los señores se mofaban de los frailes que daban oído a pobres y ricos sin respeto.

Que los agravios que hacían unos a otros mandaba satisfacer el señor del pueblo del dañador; y si no, era ocasión e instrumento de más pasiones. Y si eran de un mismo pueblo lo comunicaban al juez que era árbitro. Y examinado el daño mandaban la satisfacción; y si no era suficiente para la satisfacción, los amigos y parientes le ayudaban. Las causas de que solían hacer estas satisfacciones eran si mataban a alguno casualmente, o cuando se ahorcaban la mujer o el marido con alguna culpa o haberle dado ocasión para ello, o cuando eran causa de algún incendio de casas o heredades, de colmenas o trojes de maíz. Los otros agravios hechos con malicia los satisfacían siempre con sangre y puñadas.

Que los Yucatánenses son muy partidos y hospitalarios porque no entra nadie en su casa a quien no den de la comida o bebida que tienen; de día de sus bebidas y de noche de sus comidas. Y si no tienen, búscanlo por la vecindad; y por los caminos, si se les junta gente, a toda han de dar aunque (a ellos) les queda, por eso, mucho menos.

XXIV
Manera de contar de los yucatecos.— Genealogías.— Herencias y tutela de los huérfanos.— Sucesión de los señores.

Que su contar es de 5 en 5 hasta 20, y de 20 en 20 hasta 100, y de 100 en 100 hasta 400, y de 400 en 400 hasta 8 mil; y de esta cuenta se servían mucho para la contratación del cacao. Tienen otras cuentas muy largas, y que las extienden ad infinitum contando 8 mil 20 veces, que son 160 mil, y tornando a duplicar por 20 estas 160 mil, y después de irlo así duplicando por 20 hasta que hacen un incontable número, cuentan en el suelo o cosa llana.

Que tienen mucha cuenta con saber el origen de sus linajes, especialmente si vienen de alguna casa de Mayapán y eso procuran saberlo de los sacerdotes, que es una de sus ciencias, y jáctanse mucho de los varones señalados que ha habido en sus linajes. Los nombres de los padres duran siempre en los hijos, en las hijas no. A sus hijos e hijas los llamaban siempre por el nombre del padre y de la madre, el del padre como propio, y el de la madre como apelativo; de esta manera, el hijo de Chel y Chan llamaban Nachanchel, que quiere decir hijos de fulanos y ésta es la causa (por la cual) dicen [los indígenas] que los de un nombre son deudos y se tratan por tales. Y por eso cuando vienen a parte no conocida (y se ven) necesitados acuden luego al nombre, y si hay alguien (que lo lleve), luego con toda caridad se reciben y tratan. Y así ninguna mujer u hombre se casaba con otro del mismo nombre porque era en ellos gran infamia. Llámanse ahora (por) los nombres de pila y los otros.

Que [los indígenas] no admitían que las hijas heredaran con los hermanos sino era por vía de piedad o voluntad; y entonces dábanles algo del montón y lo demás lo partían igualmente los hermanos, salvo que al que más notablemente había ayudado a allegar la hacienda, dábanle equivalencia; y si eran todas hijas, heredaban los hermanos (del padre) o (los) más propincuos; y si eran de edad que no se pudiera entregar la hacienda, dábanla a un tutor, deudo más cercano, el cual daba a la madre para criarlos porque no usaban dejar nada en poder de (las) madres, o quitábanles los niños, principalmente siendo los tutores hermanos del difunto. Estos tutores daban lo que así se les entregaba a los herederos cuando eran de edad, y no hacerlo era gran fealdad entre ellos y causa de muchas contiendas. Cuando así lo entregaban era delante de los señores y principales, quitando lo que habían dado para criarlos; y no daban de las cosechas de las heredades sino cuando eran colmenares y algunos árboles de cacao, porque decían que harto era tenerlas en pie. Si cuando el señor se moría no estaban los hijos (en edad) de regir y tenía hermanos, regía el mayor de los hermanos o el más desenvuelto, y mostraban al heredero sus costumbres y fiestas para cuando fuese hombre; y estos hermanos, aunque el heredero (tuviese ya la edad) para regir, mandaban toda su vida; y si no había hermanos, los sacerdotes y gente principal elegían un hombre suficiente para ello.

XXV
Matrimonios.— Repudios frecuentes entre los yucatecos.— Sus casamientos.

Que antiguamente se casaban de 20 años y ahora de 12 ó 13 y por eso ahora se repudian más fácilmente, como que se casan sin amor e ignaros de la vida matrimonial y del oficio de casados; y si los padres no podían persuadirlos de que volviesen con ellas, buscábanles otras y otras. Con la misma facilidad dejaban los hombres con hijos a sus mujeres, sin temor de que otro las tomase por mujeres o después volver a ellas; pero con todo eso son muy celosos y no llevan a paciencia que sus mujeres no les están honestas; y ahora en vista de que los españoles, sobre eso, matan a las suyas, empiezan a maltratarlas y aun a matarlas. Si cuando repudiaban (a sus mujeres) los hijos eran niños, dejábanlos a las madres; si grandes, los varones con los padres, y hembras con las madres.

Que aunque era tan común y familiar cosa repudiar, los ancianos y de mejores costumbres lo tenían por malo y muchos había que nunca habían tenido sino una (mujer), la cual ninguno tomaba de su nombre de parte de su padre porque era cosa muy fea entre ellos; y si algunos se casaban con las cuñadas, mujeres de sus hermanos, era tenido por malo. No se casaban con sus madrastras ni cuñadas, hermanas de sus mujeres, ni tías, hermanas de sus madres, y si alguno lo hacía era tenido (por) malo. Con todas las demás parientas de parte de su madre contraían (matrimonio), aunque fuese prima hermana.

Los padres tienen mucho cuidado de buscarles con tiempo a sus hijos, mujeres de su estado y condición, y si podían, en el mismo lugar; y poquedad era entre ellos buscar las mujeres para sí, y los padres casamiento para sus hijas; y para tratarlo buscaban casamenteros que lo acordasen. Concertado y tratado, concertaban las arras y dote, lo cual era muy poco y dábalo el padre del mozo al consuegro, y hacía la suegra, allende del dote, vestidos a la nuera e hijo; y venido el día se juntaban en casa del padre de la novia y allí, aparejada la comida, venían los convidados y el sacerdote, y reunidos los casados y consuegros trataba el sacerdote cuadrarles y si lo habían mirado bien los suegros y si les estaba bien; y así le daban su mujer al mozo esa noche si era para ello y luego se hacía la comida y convite y de ahí en adelante quedaba el yerno en casa del suegro, trabajando cinco o seis años para el mismo suegro, y si no lo hacía echábanle de la casa. Las madres trabajaban para que la mujer diese siempre de comer al marido en señal de casamiento. Los viudos y viudas se concertaban sin fiesta ni solemnidad y con sólo ir ellos a casa de ellas y admitirlos y darles de comer se hacía el casamiento; de lo cual nacía que (las mujeres) se dejaban con tanta facilidad como se tomaban. Nunca los Yucatánenses tomaron más de una como se ha hallado en otras partes tener muchas juntas, y los padres, algunas veces, contraen matrimonio por sus hijos niños hasta que sean venidos en edad, y se tratan como suegros.

XXVI
Manera de bautismo en Yucatán. Cómo lo celebran.

No se halla el bautismo en ninguna parte de las Indias sino en ésta de Yucatán y aun con vocablo que quiere decir nacer de nuevo u otra vez, que es lo mismo que en la lengua latina renacer, porque en la lengua de Yucatán zihil quiere decir nacer de nuevo u otra vez, y no se usa sino en composición de verbo: y así caputzihil quiere decir nacer de nuevo.

No hemos podido saber su origen sino que es cosa que han usado siempre y a la que tenían tanta devoción que nadie la dejaba de recibir, y tanta reverencia que los que tenían pecados, si eran para saberlos cometer, habían de manifestarlos, especialmente a los sacerdotes para recibirlo, y tanta fe en él que no lo iteraban en ninguna manera. Lo que pensaban (que) recibían en el (bautismo) era una previa disposición para ser buenos en sus costumbres y no ser dañados por los demonios en las cosas temporales, y venir, mediante él y su buena vida, a conseguir la gloria que ellos esperaban, en la cual, según en la de Mahoma, habían de usar de manjares y bebidas. Tenían, pues, esta costumbre para venir a hacer los bautismos, que criaban las mujeres indígenas a los niños hasta la edad de tres años, y a los varoncillos usaban siempre ponerles pegada a la cabeza, en los cabellos de la coronilla, una contezuela blanca, y a las muchachas traían ceñidas abajo de los riñones con un cordel delgado y en él una conchuela asida, que les venía a dar encima de la parte honesta, y de estas dos cosas era entre ellos pecado y cosa muy fea quitarla de las muchachas antes del bautismo, el cual les daban siempre desde la edad de tres años hasta la de doce, y nunca se casaban antes del bautismo. Cuando había alguno que quisiese bautizar a su hijo, iba al sacerdote y dábale parte de su intento; el sacerdote publicaba por el pueblo el bautismo y el día en que lo hacía ellos miraban siempre que no fuese aciago. Hecho esto, el que hacía la fiesta, que era el que movía la plática, elegía a su gusto un principal del pueblo para que le ayudase en su negocio y las cosas de él. Después tenían por costumbre elegir a otros cuatro hombres ancianos y honrados que ayudasen al sacerdote en las ceremonias el día de la fiesta, y a éstos los elegían juntamente a su gusto con el sacerdote, y en estas elecciones entendían siempre los padres de todos los niños que había que bautizar pues de todos era también la fiesta, y a éstos que escogían llamábanles chaces. Tres días antes de la fiesta ayunaban los padres de los muchachos y los oficiales, absteniéndose de las mujeres.

El día (del bautismo) juntábanse todos en casa del que hacía la fiesta y llevaban a todos los niños que habían de bautizar a los cuales ponían en orden, de un lado los muchachos y del otro las muchachas, en el patio o plaza de la casa que limpio y sembrado de hojas frescas tenían. A las niñas poníanles como madrina a una mujer anciana y a los niños un hombre que los tuviese a su cargo.

Hecho esto trataba el sacerdote de la purificación de la posada echando al demonio de ella. Para echarlo ponían cuatro banquillos en las cuatro esquinas del patio en los cuales se sentaban los cuatro chaces con un cordel largo del uno al otro, de manera que quedaban los niños acorralados en medio o dentro del cordel; después, pasando sobre el cordel, habían de entrar al circuito todos los padres de los niños, que habían ayunado. Después, o antes, ponían en medio otro banquillo donde el sacerdote se sentaba con un brasero, un poco de maíz molido y un poco de su incienso. Allí venían los niños y las niñas, por orden, y echábales el sacerdote un poco de maíz molido y del incienso en la mano, y ellos (lo echaban) en el brasero, y así hacían todos; y acabados estos sahumerios tomaban el brasero, en que los hacían y el cordel con que los chaces los tenían cercados y echaban en un vaso un poco de vino y dábanlo todo a un indio que lo llevase fuera del pueblo, avisándole no bebiese ni mirase atrás a la vuelta, y con esto decían que el demonio quedaba echado.

Ido el indio, barrían el patio y lo limpiaban de las hojas de árbol que tenía, (árbol) que se dice cihom y echaban otras de otro que llaman copó y ponían unas seras en tanto que el sacerdote se vestía. Vestido, salía con un saco de pluma colorado y labrado de otras plumas de colores y otras plumas largas colgando de los extremos (del saco) y una como coroza, de las mismas plumas, en la cabeza, y debajo del saco muchos listones de algodón (que llegaban) hasta el suelo, como colas, y con un hisopo en la mano, hecho de un palo corto muy labrado y por barbas o pelos del hisopo ciertas colas de unas culebras (que son) como cascabeles, y con no más ni menos gravedad que tendría un papa para coronar a un emperador, que era cosa notable la serenidad que les causaban los aparejos. Los chaces iban luego a los niños y ponían a todos, en las cabezas, sendos paños blancos que sus madres traían para ello. Preguntaban a los que eran grandecillos si habían hecho algún pecado o tocamiento feo, y si lo habían hecho confesábanlo y los separaban de los otros.

Hecho esto mandaba el sacerdote callar y sentar la gente y comenzaba él a bendecir con muchas oraciones a los muchachos y a santiguarlos con su hisopo y (todo ello) con mucha serenidad. Acabada su bendición se sentaba y levantábase el principal que los padres de los muchachos habían elegido para esta fiesta y con un hueso que el sacerdote le daba iba a los muchachos amagaba a cada uno nueve veces en la frente; después mojábale en un vaso de una agua que llevaba en la mano y untábales la frente y las facciones del rostro, y entre los dedos de los pies, y de las manos, a todos sin hablar palabra. Esta agua la hacían de ciertas flores y de cacao mojado y desleído con agua virgen, que ellos decían traída de los cóncavos de los árboles o de las piedras de los montes.

Acabada esta untura se levantaba el sacerdote y les quitaba los paños blancos de la cabeza y otros que tenían colgados a las espaldas en que cada uno traía atadas unas pocas plumas de unos pájaros muy hermosos y algunos cacaos todo lo cual recogía uno de los chaces, y luego el sacerdote cortaba a los niños, con una navaja de piedra, la cuenta que habían traído pegada en la cabeza; tras esto iban los demás ayudantes del sacerdote con un manojo de flores y un humazo que [los indígenas] usan chupar y amagaban con cada uno de ellos nueve veces a cada muchacho y después dábanles a oler las flores y a chupar el humazo. Luego recogían los presentes que las madres traían y daban de ellos a cada muchacho un poco para comer allí, que de comida eran los presentes, y tomaban un buen vaso de vino y puesto en medio ofrecíanlo a los dioses, y con devotas plegarias les rogaban recibiesen aquel don pequeño de aquellos muchachos y llamando a otro oficial que les ayudaba, que llamaban cayom, dábanle (el vino) a que lo bebiese, lo que hacía sin descansar, que dicen que era pecado.

Hecho esto se despedían primero las muchachas a las cuales iban sus madres a quitarles el hilo con que habían andado atadas por los riñones hasta entonces, y la conchuela que traían en la puridad lo cual era como una licencia de poderse casar cuando quiera que los padres quisiesen. Después despedían a los muchachos, e idos, venían los padres al montón de las mantillas que habían traído y repartíanlas, por su mano, a los circunstantes y oficiales. Acababa después la fiesta con comer y beber largo. Llamaban a esta fiesta imku, que quiere decir bajada de Dios. El que principalmente habíala hecho moviéndola y haciendo el gasto, después de los tres días en que por ayuno se había abstenido, se había de abstener nueve más y lo hacían invariablemente.

XXVII
Especie de confesión entre los yucatecos.— Abstinencias y supersticiones.— Diversidad y abundancia de ídolos.— Oficios de los sacerdotes.

Que los Yucaténenses naturalmente conocían que hacían mal, y porque creían que por el mal y pecado les venían muertes, enfermedades y tormentos, tenían por costumbre confesarse cuando ya estaban en ellos. De esta manera, cuando por enfermedad u otra cosa estaban en peligro de muerte, confesaban sus pecados y si se descuidaban traíanselos sus parientes más cercanos o amigos a la memoria, y así decían públicamente sus pecados, al sacerdote si estaba allí, y si no, a los padres y madres, las mujeres a los maridos y los maridos a las mujeres.

Los pecados de que comúnmente se acusaban eran el hurto, homicidio, de la carne y falso testimonio y con esto se creían salvos; y muchas veces, si escapaban (a la muerte), había revueltas entre marido y mujer por las desgracias que les habían sucedido y con los que las habían causado.

Ellos confesaban sus flaquezas salvo las que con sus esclavas, los que las tenían, habían cometido, porque decían que era lícito usar de sus cosas como querían. Los pecados de intención no confesaban aunque teníanlos por malos y en sus consejos y predicaciones aconsejaban evitarlos. Que las abstinencias que comúnmente hacían eran de sal en los guisados, y pimienta, lo cual les era grave; absteníanse de sus mujeres para la celebración de todas sus fiestas.

No se casaban hasta un año después de viudos por no conocer hombre o mujer en aquel tiempo; y a los que esto no guardaban tenían por poco templados y (creían) que por eso les vendría algún mal.

En algunos ayunos de sus fiestas no comían carne ni conocían sus mujeres; recibían los oficios de las fiestas siempre con ayunos y lo mismo los oficios de la república; y algunos (ayunos) eran tan largos que duraban tres años y era gran pecado quebrantarlos.

Que eran tan dados a sus idolátricas oraciones, que en tiempo de necesidad hasta las mujeres, muchachos y mozas entendían en esto de quemar incienso y suplicar a Dios les librase del mal y reprimiese al demonio que ello les causaba.

Y que aun los caminantes llevaban en sus caminos incienso y un platillo en que quemarlo, y así, por la noche, do quiera que llegaban, erigían tres piedras pequeñas y ponían en ellas sendos pocos del incienso y poníanles delante otras tres piedras llanas en las cuales echaban el incienso, rogando al dios que llamaban Ekchuah los volviese con bien a sus casas; y esto lo hacían cada noche hasta ser vueltos a sus casas donde no faltaba quien por ellos hiciese otro tanto y aun más.

Que tenían gran muchedumbre de ídolos y templos suntuosos a su manera, y aun sin los templos comunes tenían los señores sacerdotes y gente principal oratorios e ídolos en casa para sus oraciones y ofrendas particulares. Y que tenían a Cuzmil y el pozo de Chichenizá en tanta veneración como nosotros las romerías a Jerusalén y Roma y así los iban a visitar y ofrecer dones, principalmente a Cuzmil, como nosotros a los lugares santos, y cuando no iban, enviaban siempre sus ofrendas. Y los que iban tenían también la costumbre de entrar en los templos de relictos cuando pasaban por ellos a orar y quemar copal.

Tantos ídolos tenían que aún no les bastaban los de sus dioses, pero no había animal ni sabandija a los que no les hiciesen estatuas, y todas las hacían a la semejanza de sus dioses y diosas. Tenían algunos pocos ídolos de piedra y otros de madera y de bultos pequeños, pero no tantos como de barro. Los ídolos de madera eran tenidos en tanto, que se heredaban como lo principal de la herencia. Ídolos de metal no tenían porque no hay metal ahí. Bien sabían ellos que los ídolos eran obras suyas y muertas y sin deidad, mas los tenían en reverencia por lo que representaban y porque los habían hecho con muchas ceremonias, especialmente los de palo.

Los más idólatras eran los sacerdotes, chilanes, hechiceros y médicos, chaces y nacones. El oficio de los sacerdotes era tratar y enseñar sus ciencias y declarar las necesidades y sus remedios, predicar y echar las fiestas, hacer sacrificios y administrar sus sacramentos. El oficio de los chilanes era dar al pueblo las respuestas de los demonios y eran tenidos en tanto que acontecía llevarlos en hombros. Los hechiceros y médicos curaban con sangrías hechas en la parte donde dolía al enfermo y echaban suertes para adivinar en sus oficios y otras cosas. Los chaces eran cuatro hombres ancianos elegidos siempre de nuevo para ayudar al sacerdote a hacer bien y cumplidamente las fiestas. Nacones eran dos oficios: el uno perpetuo y poco honroso porque era el que abría los pechos a las personas que sacrificaban; el otro era una elección hecha de un capitán para la guerra y otras fiestas, que duraba tres años. Éste era de mucha honra.

XXVIII
Sacrificios y mortificaciones crueles y sucios de los yucatecos.— Víctimas humanas matadas a flechazos.

Que hacían sacrificios con su propia sangre cortándose unas veces las orejas a la redonda, por pedazos, y así las dejaban por señal. Otras veces se agujereaban las mejillas, otras los bezos bajos; otras se sajaban partes de sus cuerpos; otras se agujereaban las lenguas, al soslayo, por los lados, y pasaban por los agujeros unas pajas con grandísimo dolor; otras, se arpaban lo superfluo del miembro vergonzoso dejándolo como las orejas, con lo cual se engañó el historiador general de las Indias cuando dijo que se circuncidaban.

Otras veces hacían un sucio y penoso sacrificio, juntándose en el temple, los que lo hacían y puestos en regla se hacían sendos agujeros en los miembros viriles, al soslayo, por el lado, y hechos pasaban toda la mayor cantidad de hilo que podían, quedando así todos asidos y ensartados; también untaban con la sangre de todas estas partes al demonio, y el que más hacia era tenido por más valiente y sus hijos, desde pequeños, comenzaban a ocuparse en ello y es cosa espantable cuán aficionados eran a ello.

Las mujeres no usaban de estos derramamientos aunque eran harto santeras, mas siempre le embadurnaban el rostro al demonio con la sangre de las aves del cielo y animales de la tierra o pescados del agua y cosas que haber podían. Y ofrecían otras cosas que tenían. A algunos animales les sacaban el corazón y lo ofrecían; a otros, enteros, unos vivos, otros muertos, unos crudos, otros guisados, y hacían también grandes ofrendas de pan y vino y de todas las maneras de comidas y bebidas que usaban.

Para hacer estos sacrificios, había en los patios de los templos unos altos maderos labrados y enhiestos, y cerca de la escalera del templo tenían una peana redonda y ancha, y en medio una piedra de cuatro o cinco palmos de alto, enhiesta, algo delgada; arriba de las escaleras del templo había otra tal peana.

Que si en las fiestas, en las cuales para solemnizarlas se sacrificaban personas, también por alguna tribulación o necesidad les mandaba el sacerdote o chilanes sacrificar personas, y para esto contribuían todos para que se comprasen esclavos o por devoción daban sus hijitos, los cuales eran muy regalados hasta el día y fiesta de sus personas, y muy guardados (para) que no se huyesen o ensuciasen de algún pecado carnal, y mientras les llevaban de pueblo en pueblo con bailes, los sacerdotes ayunaban con los chilanes y oficiales.

Y llegado el día juntábanse en el patio del templo y si había (el esclavo) de ser sacrificado a saetazos, desnudábanle en cueros y untábanle el cuerpo de azul (poniéndole) una coroza en la cabeza, y después de echado el demonio, hacía la gente un solemne baile con él, todos con flechas y arcos alrededor del palo, y bailando subíanle en él y atábanle siempre bailando y mirándole todos. Subía el sucio del sacerdote vestido y con una flecha le hería en la parte verenda, fuese mujer u hombre, y sacaba sangre y bajábase y untaba con ella los rostros del demonio, y haciendo cierta señal a los bailadores, ellos, como bailando, pasaban de prisa y por orden le comenzaban a flechar el corazón el cual tenía señalado con una señal blanca; y de esta manera poníanle al punto los pechos como un erizo de flechas.

Si le habían de sacar el corazón, le traían al patio con gran aparato y compañía de gente y embadurnado de azul y su coroza puesta, le llevaban a la grada redonda que era el sacrificadero y después de que el sacerdote y sus oficiales untaban aquella piedra con color azul y echaban al demonio purificando el templo, tomaban los chaces al pobre que sacrificaban y con gran presteza le ponían de espaldas en aquella piedra y asíanle de las piernas y brazos todos cuatro que le partían por en medio. En esto llegaba el sayón nacón con un navajón de piedra y dábale con mucha destreza y crueldad una cuchillada entre las costillas, del lado izquierdo, debajo de la tetilla, y acudíale allí luego con la mano y echaba la mano al corazón como rabioso tigre arrancándoselo vivo, y puesto en un plato lo daba al sacerdote el cual iba muy de prisa y untaba a los ídolos los rostros con aquella sangre fresca.

Algunas veces hacían este sacrificio en la piedra y grada alta del templo y entonces echaban el cuerpo ya muerto a rodar gradas abajo y tomábanle abajo los oficiales y desollábanle todo el cuero entero, salvo los pies y las manos, y desnudo el sacerdote, en cueros vivos, se forraba con aquella piel y bailaban con él los demás, y esto era cosa de mucha solemnidad para ellos. A estos sacrificados comúnmente solían enterrar en el patio del templo, o si no, comíanselos repartiendo entre los señores y los que alcanzaban; y las manos y los pies y cabeza eran del sacerdote y oficiales; y a estos sacrificados tenían por santos. Si eran esclavos cautivados en guerra, su señor tomaba los huesos para sacarlos como divisa en los bailes, en señal de victoria. Algunas veces echaban personas vivas en el pozo de Chichenizá creyendo que salían al tercer día aunque nunca más parecían.

XXIX
Armas de los yucatecos.— Jefes militares.— Milicia y soldados; costumbres de guerra.

Que tienen armas ofensivas y defensivas. Las ofensivas eran arcos y flechas que llevaban en sus carcajes con pedernales por casquillos y dientes de pescados, muy agudos, las cuales tiran con gran destreza y fuerza. Los arcos son de un hermoso palo leonado y fuerte a maravilla, más derechos que curvos, y las cuerdas

La largura del arco es siempre algo menor que la de quien lo trae. Las flechas son de (unas) cañas muy delgadas que se crían en las lagunas y largas de más de cinco palmos; átanle a la caña un pedazo de palo delgado, muy fuerte, en que va insertado el pedernal. No usaban, ni lo saben poner ponzoña, aunque tienen harto de qué. Tenían hachuelas de cierto metal y de esta hechura [vea ilustración], las cuales encajaban en un mástil de palo y les servían de armas y para labrar la madera. Dábanles filo con una piedra, a porrazos, pues el metal es blando. Tenían lanzuelas cortas de un estado con los hierros de fuerte pedernal, y no tenían más armas que éstas.

Tenían para su defensa rodelas que hacían de cañas hendidas y muy tejidas, redondas y guarnecidas de cueros de venados. Hacían sacos de algodones acolchados y de sal por moler, acolchada en dos tandas o colchaduras, y éstos eran fortísimos. Algunos señores y capitanes tenían como morriones de palo, pero eran pocos, y con estas armas y plumajes y pellejos de tigres y leones puestos, iban a la guerra los que los tenían.

Tenían siempre dos capitanes: uno perpetuo (cuyo cargo) se heredaba, y otro elegido por tres años con muchas ceremonias para hacer la fiesta que celebraban en su mes de Pax, que cae el doce de mayo, o por capitán de la otra banda para la guerra.

A éste llamaban Nacón; no había, en estos tres años, conocer mujer ni aun la suya, ni comer carne; teníanle en mucha reverencia y dábanle a comer pescados e iguanas que son como lagartos; no se emborrachaba en este tiempo y tenía en su casa las vasijas y cosas de su servicio, apartadas, y no le servía mujer y no trataba mucho con el pueblo.

Pasados los tres años, (volvía a vivir) como antes. Estos dos capitanes trataban la guerra y ponían sus cosas en orden y para esto había en cada pueblo gente escogida como soldados que, cuando era menester, acudían con sus armas. A éstos llamaban holcanes, y no bastando éstos, recogían más gente y concertaban y repartían entre sí, y guiados con una bandera alta salían con mucho silencio del pueblo y así iban a arremeter a sus enemigos con grandes gritos y crueldades donde topaban descuidos.

En los caminos y pasos, los enemigos les ponían defensas de flechaderos de varazón y madera y comúnmente hechos de piedra. Después de la victoria quitaban a los muertos la quijada y limpia de la carne, poníansela en el brazo. Para su guerra hacían grandes ofrendas de los despojos y si cautivaban algún hombre señalado, le sacrificaban luego porque no querían dejar quien les dañase después. La demás gente era cautiva en poder del que la prendía. Que a esos holcanes si no era en tiempo de guerra, no daban soldada, y cuando había guerra los capitanes les daban cierta moneda, y poca, porque era de la suya, y si no bastaba, el pueblo ayudaba a ello. El pueblo dábales también la comida, y ésa la aderezaban las mujeres para ellos; la llevaban a cuestas por carecer de bestias y así les duraban poco las guerras. Acabada la guerra, los soldados hacían muchas vejaciones en sus pueblos (mientras) duraba el olor de la guerra y sobre ello hacíanse servir y regalar; y si alguno había matado algún capitán o señor, era muy honrado y festejado.

XXX
Penas y castigos a los adúlteros, homicidas y ladrones.— Educación de los mancebos.— Costumbre de allanar a la cabeza a los niños.

Que a esta gente les quedó de Mayapán (la) costumbre de castigar a los adúlteros de esta manera: hecha la pesquisa y convencido alguno del adulterio, se juntaban los principales en casa del señor, y traído el adúltero atábanle a un palo y le entregaban al marido de la mujer delincuente; si él le perdonaba, era libre; si no, le mataba con una piedra grande (que) dejábale (caer) en la cabeza desde una parte alta; a la mujer por satisfacción bastaba la infamia que era grande, y comúnmente por esto las dejaban.

La pena del homicida aunque fuese casual, era morir por insidias de los parientes, o si no, pagar el muerto. El hurto pagaban y castigaban, aunque fuese pequeño, con hacer esclavos, y por eso hacían tantos esclavos, principalmente en tiempo de hambre, y por eso fue que nosotros los frailes tanto trabajamos en el bautismo: para que les diesen libertad.

Y si eran señores o gente principal, juntábase el pueblo y prendido (el delincuente) le labraban el rostro desde la barba hasta la frente, por los dos lados, en castigo que tenían por grande infamia.

Que los mozos reverenciaban mucho a los viejos y tomaban sus consejos y así se jactaban de (ser) viejos y decían a los mozos que pues habían más visto que ellos, les habían de creer, lo cual si hacían los demás les daban más crédito. Eran tan extremados en esto, que los mozos no trataban con viejos sino en cosas inevitables y los mozos por casar con los casados, sino muy poco. Por eso usaban tener en cada pueblo una casa grande y encalada, abierta por todas partes, en la cual se juntaban los mozos para sus pasatiempos. Jugaban a la pelota y a un juego con unas habas como a los dados, y a otros muchos. Dormían aquí todos juntos casi siempre, hasta que se casaban.

Y dado que he oído que en otras partes de las Indias usaban en tales casas del nefando pecado, en esta tierra no he entendido que hiciesen tal, ni creo lo hacían porque los llagados de esta pestilencial miseria dicen que no son amigos de mujeres como eran éstos, que a esos lugares llevaban a las malas mujeres públicas y en ellos usaban de ellas, y las pobres que entre esta gente acertaban a tener este oficio, no obstante que recibían de ellos galardón, eran tantos los mozos que a ellas acudían, que las traían acosadas y muertas.

Embadurnábanse de color negro, hasta que se casaban y no se solían labrar hasta casados, sino poco. En las demás cosas acompañaban siempre a sus padres y así salían tan buenos idólatras como ellos y servíanles mucho en los trabajos.

Que las mujeres indígenas criaban a sus hijitos en toda la aspereza y desnudez del mundo, porque a los cuatro o cinco días de nacida la criaturita poníanla tendidita en un lecho pequeño, hecho de varillas, y allí, boca abajo, le ponían entre dos tablillas la cabeza: la una en el colodrillo y la otra en la frente entre las cuales se la apretaban tan reciamente y la tenían allí padeciendo hasta que acabados algunos días les quedaba la cabeza llana y enmoldada como la usaban todos ellos. Era tanta la molestia y el peligro de los pobres niños, que algunos peligraban, y el autor vio agujerársele a uno la cabeza por detrás de las orejas, y así debían hacer muchos.

Criábanlos en cueros, salvo que de 4 a 5 años les daban una mantilla para dormir y unos listoncillos para honestarse como sus padres, y a las muchachas las comenzaban a cubrir de la cintura para abajo. Mamaban mucho porque nunca dejaban, en pudiendo, de darles leche aunque fuesen de tres o cuatro años, de donde venía haber entre ellos tanta gente de buenas fuerzas.

Criábanse los dos primeros años a maravilla lindos y gordos. Después, con el continuo bañarlos las madres y los soles, se hacían morenos; pero eran todo el tiempo de la niñez bonicos y traviesos, que nunca paraban de andar con arcos y flechas y jugando unos con otros y así se criaban hasta que comenzaban a seguir el modo de vivir de los mancebos y tenerse en su manera en más, y dejar las cosas de niños.

XXXI
Vestidos y adornos de las mujeres indígenas de Yucatán.

Que las mujeres indígenas de Yucatán son en general de mejor disposición que las españolas y más grandes y bien hechas, que no son de tantos riñones como las negras. Préciase de hermosas las que lo son y a una mano no son feas; no son blancas sino de color moreno causado más por el sol y del continuo bañarse, que de su natural. No se adoban los rostros como nuestra nación, que eso lo tienen por liviandad. Tenían por costumbre aserrarse los dientes dejándolos como dientes de sierra y esto tenían por galantería y hacían este oficio unas viejas limándolos con ciertas piedras y agua.

Horadábanse las narices por la ternilla que divide las ventanas por en medio, para ponerse en el agujero una piedra de ámbar y teníanlo por gala. Horadábanse las orejas para ponerse zarcillos al modo de sus maridos; labrábanse el cuerpo de la cintura para arriba—salvo los pechos por el criar—, de labores más delicadas y hermosas que los hombres. Bañábanse muy a menudo con agua fría, como los hombres, y no lo hacían con sobrada honestidad porque acaecía desnudarse en cueros en el pozo donde iban por agua para ello. Acostumbraban, además, bañarse con agua caliente y fuego y de éste poco, y más por causa de salud que por limpieza.

Acostumbraban untarse, como sus maridos, con cierto ungüento colorado, y las que tenían posibilidad, echábanse cierta confección de una goma olorosa y muy pegajosa que creo que es liquidámbar que en su lengua llaman iztah-te y con esta confección untaban cierto ladrillo como de jabón que tenían labrado de galanas labores, y con aquel se untaban los pechos y brazos y espaldas y quedaban galanas y olorosas según les parecía; y durábales mucho sin quitarse según era bueno el ungüento.

Traían cabellos muy largos y hacían y hacen de ellos muy galán tocado partido en dos partes y trenzábanselos para otro modo de tocado. A las mozas por casar, suelen las madres curiosas curárselos con tanto cuidado que he visto muchas mujeres indígenas de tan curiosos cabellos como curiosas españolas. A las muchachas hasta que son grandecitas se los trenzan en cuatro cuernos y en dos, que les parecen muy bien.

Las mujeres indígenas de la costa y de las provincias de Bacalar y Campeche son muy honestas en su traje, porque allende de la cobertura que traían de la mitad para abajo, se cubrían los pechos atándoselos por debajo de los sobacos con una manta doblada; todas las demás no traían de vestidura más que un como saco largo y ancho, abierto por ambas partes y metidas en él hasta los cuadriles donde se los apretaban con el mismo ancho y no tenían más vestidura salvo que la manta con que siempre duermen que, cuando iban en camino, usaban llevar cubierta, doblada o enrollada, y así andaban.

XXXII
Castidad y educación de las mujeres indígenas de Yucatán.— Sus relevantes cualidades y su economía.— Su devoción y especiales costumbres en sus partos.

Preciábanse de buenas y tenían razón porque antes que conociesen nuestra nación, según los viejos ahora lloran, lo eran a maravilla y de esto traeré ejemplos: el capitán Alonso López de Ávila, cuñado del adelantado Montejo, prendió una moza india y bien dispuesta y gentil mujer, andando en la guerra de Bacalar. Ésta prometió a su marido, temiendo que en la guerra no le matasen, no conocer otro hombre sino él, y así no bastó persuasión con ella para que no se quitase la vida por no quedar en peligro de ser ensuciada por otro varón, por lo cual la hicieron aperrear.

A mi se me quejó una india por bautizar, de un indio bautizado, el cual andando enamorado de ella, que era hermosa, aguardó se ausentase su marido y se le fue una noche a su casa y después de manifestarle con muchos requiebros su intento y no bastarle, probó a dar dádivas que para ello llevaba, y como no aprovechasen, intentó forzarla; y con ser un gigantón y trabajar por ello toda la noche, no sacó de ella más que darle enojo tan grande que se me vino a quejar a mi de la maldad del indio, y era así lo que decía.

Acostumbraban volver las espaldas a los hombres cuando los topaban en alguna parte, y hacerles lugar para que pasasen, y lo mismo cuando les daban de beber, hasta que acababan de beber. Enseñan lo que saben a sus hijas y críanlas bien a su modo, que las riñen y las adoctrinan y hacen trabajar, y si hacen culpas las castigan dándoles pellizcos en las orejas y en los brazos. Si las ven alzar los ojos, las riñen mucho y se los untan con su pimienta, que es grave dolor; y si no son honestas, las aporrean y untan con la pimienta en otra parte, por castigo y afrenta. Dicen a las mozas indisciplinadas, por mucho baldón y grave represión, que parecen mujeres criadas sin madre.

Son celosas, y algunas tanto, que ponían las manos en quien tienen celos, y tan coléricas y enojadas aunque harto mansas, que algunas solían dar vuelta de pelo a los maridos con hacerlo ellos pocas veces. Son grandes trabajadoras y vividoras porque de ellas cuelgan los mayores y más trabajos de la sustentación de sus casas y educación de sus hijos y paga de sus tributos, y con todo eso, si es menester, llevan algunas veces carga mayor labrando y sembrando sus mantenimientos. Son a maravilla granjeras, velando de noche el rato que de servir sus casas les queda, yendo a los mercados a comprar y vender sus cosillas.

Crían aves de las suyas y las de Castilla para vender y para comer. Crían pájaros para su recreación y para las plumas, con las que hacen ropas galanas; y crían otros animales domésticos, de los cuales dan el pecho a los corzos, con lo que los crían tan mansos que no saben írseles al monte jamás, aunque los lleven y traigan por los montes y críen en ellos.

Tienen costumbre de ayudarse unas a otras al hilar las telas, y páganse estos trabajos como sus maridos los de sus heredades y en ellos tienen siempre sus chistes de mofar y contar nuevas, y a ratos un poco de murmuración. Tienen por gran fealdad mirar a los hombres y reírseles, y por tanto, que sólo esto bastaba para hacer cualquier fealdad, y sin más entremeses las hacían ruines. Bailaban por sí sus bailes y algunos con los hombres, en especial uno que llamaban Naual no muy honesto. Son muy fecundas y tempranas en parir y grandes criadoras, por dos razones: la una, porque la bebida de las mañanas que beben caliente, cría mucha leche, y el continuo moler maíz y no traer los pechos apretados les hace tenerlos muy grandes, de donde les viene tener mucha leche.

Emborrachábanse también ellas en los convites, aunque por sí, ya que comían solas, y no se emborrachaban tanto como los hombres. Son gente que desea muchos hijos; la que carece de ellos los pedía a sus ídolos con dones y oraciones, y ahora los piden a Dios. Son avisadas y Cortés es y conversables con quien se entienden, y a maravilla bien partidas. Tienen pocos secretos y son tan limpias en sus personas y en sus casas, por cuanto se lavan como los armiños.

Eran muy devotas y santeras, y así tenían muchas devociones con sus ídolos, quemándoles de sus inciensos, ofreciéndoles dones de ropa de algodón, comidas, bebidas, y teniendo ellas por oficio hacer las ofrendas de comidas y bebidas que en las fiestas de [los indígenas] ofrecían; pero con todo eso no tenían por costumbre derramar su sangre a los demonios, ni lo hacían jamás. Ni tampoco las dejaban llegar a los templos a los sacrificios, salvo en cierta fiesta a la que admitían a ciertas viejas para la celebración. Para sus partos acudían a las hechiceras, las cuales les hacían creer sus mentiras y les ponían debajo de la cama un ídolo de un demonio llamado Ixchel, que decían era la diosa de hacer las criaturas.

Nacidos los niños los bañan luego y cuando ya los habían quitado del tormento de allanarles las frentes y cabezas, iban con ellos a los sacerdotes para que les viese el hado y dijese el oficio que había de tener y pusiese el nombre que había de llevar el tiempo de su niñez, porque acostumbraban llamar a los niños por nombres diferentes hasta que se bautizaban o eran grandecillos; y después que dejaban aquéllos, comenzaban a llamarlos (por) el de los padres hasta que los casaban, que (entonces) se llamaban (por) el del padre y la madre.

XXXIII
Duelos.— Entierros de los sacerdotes.— Estatuas para conservar las cenizas de los señores.— Reverencia que les tributaban. Creencia acerca de una vida futura.

Que esta gente tenía mucho, excesivo temor a la muerte y lo mostraban en que todos los servicios que a sus dioses hacían no eran por otro fin ni para otra cosa sino para que les diesen salud y vida y mantenimientos. Pero, ya que venían a morir, era cosa de ver las lástimas y llantos que por sus difuntos hacían y la tristeza grande que les causaban. Llorábanlos de día en silencio y de noche a altos y muy dolorosos gritos que era lástima oírlos. Andaban a maravilla tristes muchos días. Hacían abstinencias y ayunos por el difunto, especialmente el marido o la mujer, y decían (del difunto) que se lo había llevado el diablo, porque de él pensaban que les venían todos los males, en especial la muerte.

Muertos, los amortajaban, llenándoles la boca de maíz molido, que es su comida y bebida que llaman koyem, y con ello algunas piedras de las que tienen por moneda, para que en la otra vida no les faltase de comer. Enterrábanlos dentro de sus casas o a las espaldas de ellas, echándoles en la sepultura algunos de sus ídolos; y si era sacerdote, algunos de sus libros; y si hechicero, sus piedras de hechizos y pertrechos. Comúnmente desamparaban la casa y la dejaban yerma después de enterrados, menos cuando había en ella mucha gente con cuya compañía perdían algo del miedo que les quedaba de la muerte.

A los señores y gente de mucha valía quemaban los cuerpos y ponían las cenizas en vasijas grandes, y edificaban templos sobre ellas, como muestran haber hecho antiguamente los que se hallaron en Izamal. Ahora, en este tiempo, se halló que echaban las cenizas en estatuas huecas, hechas de barro, cuando (los muertos) eran muy señores.

La demás gente principal hacía a sus padres estatuas de madera a las cuales dejaban hueco el colodrillo, y quemaban alguna parte de su cuerpo y echaban allí las cenizas y tapábanlo; y después desollaban al difunto el cuero del colodrillo y pegábanselo allí, enterrando los residuos como tenían de costumbre; guardaban estas estatuas con mucha reverencia entre sus ídolos. A los antiguos señores Cocom, habían cortado las cabezas cuando murieron, y cocidas las limpiaron de la carne y después aserraron la mitad de la coronilla para atrás, dejando lo de adelante con las quijadas y dientes. A estas medias calaveras suplieron lo que de carne

220

les faltaba con cierto betún y les dieron la perfección muy al propio de cuyas eran, y las tenían con las estatuas de las cenizas, todo lo cual tenían en los oratorios de las casas, con sus ídolos, en muy gran reverencia y acatamiento, y todos los días de sus fiestas y regocijos les hacían ofrendas de sus comidas para que no les faltase en la otra vida donde pensaban (que) sus almas descansaban y les aprovechaban sus dones.

Que esta gente ha creído siempre en la inmortalidad del alma más que otras muchas naciones aunque no haya sido de tanta policía, porque creían que después de la muerte había otra vida más excelente de la cual gozaba el alma en apartándose del cuerpo. Esta vida futura, decían que se dividía en buena y mala vida, en penosa y llena de descanso. La mala y penosa, decían, era para los viciosos, y la buena y deleitosa para los que hubiesen vivido bien en su manera de vivir; los descansos que decían habrían de alcanzar si eran buenos, eran ir a un lugar muy deleitable donde ninguna cosa les diese pena y donde hubiese abundancia de comidas y bebidas de mucha dulzura, y un árbol que allá llaman yaxché muy fresco y de gran sombra, que es (una) ceiba, debajo de cuyas ramas y sombra descansarían y holgarían todos siempre.

Las penas de la mala vida que decían habrían de tener los malos, eran ir a un lugar más bajo que el otro que llaman mitnal, que quiere decir infierno, y en él ser atormentados por los demonios, y de grandes necesidades de hambre y frío y cansancio y tristeza. También había en este lugar un demonio, príncipe de todos los demonios, al cual obedecían todos y llámanle en su lengua Hunhau; y decían (que) estas mala y buena vida no tenían fin, por no tenerlo el alma. Decían también, y lo tenían por muy cierto, (que) iban a esta su gloria los que se ahorcaban; y así había muchos que con pequeñas ocasiones de tristeza, trabajos o enfermedades, se ahorcaban para salir de ellas e ir a descansar a su gloria donde, decían, los venía a llevar la diosa de la horca que llamaban Ixtab. No tenían memoria de la resurrección de los cuerpos y no daban razón de quién hubieron noticia de esta su gloria e infierno.

XXXIV
Del año yucateco.— Caracteres de los días.— Los cuatro bacabes y sus nombres.— Los días aciagos.

No se esconde ni aparta tanto el sol de esta tierra de Yucatán, que vengan las noches, jamás, a ser mayores que los días; y cuando mayores vienen a ser, suelen ser iguales desde San Andrés a Santa Lucía, que comienzan a crecer los días. Regíanse de noche para conocer la hora que era por el lucero y las cabrillas y los astilejos. De día, por el medio día, y desde él al oriente y poniente, tenían puestos a pedazos nombres con los cuales se entendían y se regían para sus trabajos.

Tienen su año perfecto como el nuestro, de 365 días y 6 horas. Divídenlo en dos maneras de meses, los unos de a 30 días que se llaman U, que quiere decir luna, la cual contaban desde que salía nueva hasta que no parecía.

Otra manera de meses tenían de a 20 días, a los cuales llaman Uinal Hunekeh; de éstos tenía el año entero 18, más los cinco días y seis horas. De estas seis horas se hacía cada cuatro años un día, y así tenía de cuatro en cuatro años el año 366 días. Para estos 360 días tienen 20 letras o caracteres con que los nombran, dejando de poner nombre a los otros cinco, porque los tenían por aciagos y malos. Las letras son las que siguen y lleva cada una su nombre debajo para que se entienda en nuestra lengua:

Kan

Lamat

Chicchan

Muluc

Cimi

Oc

Manik

Chuen

Eb

Ezanab

Been

Cauac

Ix

Ahau

Men

Ymix

Cib

Ik

Caban

Akbal

Ya he dicho que el modo de contar de [los indígenas] es de cinco en cinco, y de cuatro cincos hacen veinte; así, en estos sus caracteres que son 20, sacan los primeros de los cuatro cincos de los 20 y éstos sirven, cada uno de ellos un año, de lo que nos sirven a nosotros nuestras letras dominicales para comenzar todos los primeros días de los meses de a 20 días.

Kan

Ix

Muluc

Cauac

Entre la muchedumbre de dioses que esta gente adoraba, adoraban cuatro llamados Bacab cada uno de ellos. Éstos, decían, eran cuatro hermanos a los cuales puso Dios, cuando crió el mundo, a las cuatro partes de él sustentando el cielo (para que) no se cayese. Decían también de estos bacabes que escaparon cuando el mundo fue destruido por el diluvio. Ponen a cada uno de éstos otros nombres y señálanle con ellos a la parte del mundo que dios le tenía puesto teniendo el cielo, y aprópianle una de las cuatro letras dominicales a él y a la parte que está; y tienen señaladas las miserias o felices sucesos que decían habían de suceder en el año de cada uno de éstos y de las letras con ellos.

Y el demonio, que en esto como en las demás cosas los engañaba, les señaló los servicios y ofrendas que para evadirse de las miserias le habían de hacer. Y así, si no les venían, decían (que) era por los servicios que le hacían; y si venían, los sacerdotes hacían entender y creer al pueblo (que) era por alguna culpa o falta de los servicios o de quienes los hacían.

La primera, pues, de las letras dominicales es Kan. El año que esta letra servía era el agüero del Bacab que por otros nombres llaman Hobnil, Kanalbacab, Kanpauahtun, Kanxibchac. A éste señalaban a la parte de medio día. La segunda letra es Muluc; señalábanla al oriente y su año era agüero el Bacab que llaman Canzicnal, Chacalbacab, Chacpauahtun, Chacxibchac. La tercera letra es Ix. Su año era agüero el Bacab que llaman Zaczini, Zacalbacab, Zacpauahtun, Zacxibcbac y señalábanle a la parte del norte. La cuarta letra es Cauac: su año era agüero el Bacab que llaman Hozanek, Ekelbacab, Ekpauaktun, Ekxibchac; a ésta señalaban a la parte del poniente.

En cualquiera fiesta o solemnidad que esta gente hacía a sus dioses comenzaban siempre por echar de sí al demonio para mejor hacerla. Y el echarle unas veces era con oraciones y bendiciones que para ello tenían, y otras con servicios y ofrendas y sacrificios que por esta razón le hacían. Para celebrar la solemnidad de su año nuevo, esta gente, con más regocijo y más dignamente, según su desventurada opinión, tomaba los cinco días aciagos que ellos tenían por tales antes del día primero de su nuevo año, y en ellos hacían muy grandes servicios a los bacabes citados arriba y al demonio al que llamaban por otros cuatro nombres, a saber, Kanuuayayab, Chacuuayayab, Zacuuayayab, Ekuuayayab; y acabados estos servicios y fiestas, y lanzado de sí, como veremos, el demonio, comenzaban su año y las fiestas de él.

XXXV
Fiestas de los días aciagos.— Sacrificios del principio del año nuevo en la letra de Kan.

Uso era en todos los pueblos de Yucatán tener hechos dos montones de piedras, uno frente a otro, a la entrada del pueblo y por las cuatro partes del mismo, a saber, oriente, poniente, septentrión y mediodía, para la celebración de las dos fiestas de los días aciagos las cuales hacían de esta manera cada año.

El año cuya letra dominical era Kan, era el agüero Hobnil, y según ellos decían reinaban ambos por la parte del medio día. Este año, pues, hacían una imagen o figura hueca de barro del demonio que llamaban Kanuuayayab, y llevábanla a los montones de piedra seca que tenían hechos por la parte del mediodía; elegían un príncipe del pueblo, en cuya casa se celebrara estos días la fiesta, y para celebrarla hacían una estatua de un demonio al que llamaban Bolonzacab, la que ponían en casa del príncipe, aderezada en lugar público y al que todos pudiesen llegar.

Hecho esto se juntaban los señores y el sacerdote, y el pueblo de los hombres, y teniendo limpio y con arcos y frescuras aderezado el camino, hasta el lugar de los montones de piedra en donde estaba la estatua, iban por ella todos juntos, con mucha devoción. Llegados, la sahumaba el sacerdote con cuarenta y nueve granos de maíz molido con su incienso, y ello lo arrojaban al brasero del demonio y le sahumaban. Llamaban al maíz molido solo zacab y a la (bebida) de los señores chabalté. Sahumada la imagen, degollaban una gallina y se la presentaban u ofrecían.

Hecho esto metían la imagen en un palo llamado kanté poniéndole a cuestas un ángel en señal de agua, y este año había de ser bueno y estos ángeles pintaban y hacían espantables; y así la llevaban con mucho regocijo y bailes a la casa del principal donde estaba la otra estatua de Bolonzacab. Sacaban de casa de este principal al camino, para los señores y sacerdotes, una bebida hecha de cuatrocientos quince granos de maíz tostados que llaman piculakakla, y bebían todos de ella; llegados a la casa del principal, ponían esta imagen frente a la estatua del demonio que allí tenían, y así le hacían muchas ofrendas de comidas y bebidas, de carne y pescado, y repartían estas ofrendas a los extranjeros que allí se hallaban, y daban al sacerdote una pierna de venado.

Otros derramaban sangre cortándose las orejas y untaban con ella una piedra que allí tenían de un demonio Kanalacantun. Hacían un corazón de pan y otro pan con pepitas de calabazas y ofrecíanlos a la imagen del demonio Kanuuayayab. Tenían así esta estatua e imagen estos días aciagos y sahumábanlas con su incienso y con los maíces molidos con incienso. Tenían creído que si no hacían estas ceremonias habían de tener ciertas enfermedades que ellos tienen en este año. Pasados estos días aciagos llevaban la estatua del demonio Bolonzacab al templo, y la imagen a la parte del oriente para ir allí al otro año por ella, y echábanla por ahí e íbanse a sus casas a entender en lo que le quedaba a cada uno por hacer en la celebración del año nuevo.

Terminadas las ceremonias y echado el demonio según su engaño, tenían este año por bueno pues reinaba con la letra Kan el bacab Hobnil, del que decían no había pecado como sus hermanos y por eso no les venían miserias en él. Pero porque muchas veces las había, proveyó el demonio que le hiciesen servicios para que así, cuando las hubiese, echasen la culpa a los servicios o servidores y quedasen siempre engañados y ciegos.

Mandábales, pues, hiciesen un ídolo que llamaban Izamnakauil y que le pusiesen en su templo y le quemasen en el patio del templo tres pelotas de una leche o resina llamada kik, y que le sacrificasen un perro o un hombre, lo cual ellos hacían guardando el orden que ya se dijo tenían con los que sacrificaban, salvo que el modo de sacrificar en esta fiesta era diferente, porque hacían en el patio del templo un gran montón de piedras y ponían al hombre o perro que habían de sacrificar en alguna cosa más alta que él, y echando atado al paciente de lo alto a las piedras, le arrebataban aquellos oficiales y con gran presteza le sacaban el corazón y le llevaban al nuevo ídolo, y se lo ofrecían entre dos platos. Ofrecían otros dones de comidas y en esta fiesta bailaban las viejas del pueblo que para ello tenían elegidas, vestidas de ciertas vestiduras. Decían que descendía un ángel y recibía este sacrificio.

XXXVI
Sacrificios del año nuevo de la letra Muluc.— Baile de los zancos. Danza de las viejas con perros de barro.

El año en que la letra dominical era Muluc, tenía el agüero de Canzienal y a su tiempo elegían, los señores y el sacerdote, un principal para hacer la fiesta, y después hacían la imagen del demonio como la del año pasado, a la cual llamaban Chacuuayayab, y llevábanla a los montones de piedra de hacia la parte del oriente, donde habían echado la pasada. Hacían una estatua al demonio llamado Kinchahau y poníanla en casa del principal en lugar conveniente, y desde allí, teniendo muy limpio y aderezado el camino, iban todos juntos con su acostumbrada devoción por la imagen del demonio Chacuuayayab.

Llegados, la sahumaba el sacerdote con cincuenta y tres granos de maíz molidos y su incienso, a lo cual llaman zacah. Daba el sacerdote a los señores que pusiesen en el brasero más incienso del que llamamos chabalté y después degollábanle la gallina, como al pasado, y tomando la imagen en un palo llamado chasté la llevaban, acompañándola todos con devoción y bailando unos bailes de guerra que llaman holcanokot batelokot. Sacaban al camino, a los señores y principales, su bebida de trescientos ochenta maíces tostados como la de atrás.

Llegados a casa del principal ponían esta imagen en frente de la estatua de Kinchahau y hacíanle todos sus ofrendas, las cuales repartían como las demás. Ofrecían a la imagen pan hecho con yemas de huevo, y otros con corazones de venados, y otro hecho con su pimienta desleída. Había muchos que derramaban sangre cortándose las orejas y untando con su sangre la piedra que allí tenían de un demonio que llamaban Chacacantun. Aquí tomaban muchachos y por fuerza les sacaban sangre de las orejas, dándoles cuchilladas en ellas. Tenían esta estatua e imagen hasta pasados los días aciagos y entretanto quemábanles sus inciensos. Pasados los días, llevaban la imagen a echar a la parte del norte donde otro año la habían de salir a recibir, y la otra al templo, y después íbanse a sus casas a entender en el aparejo de su año nuevo. Habían de tener, si no hacían las cosas dichas, mucho mal de ojos.

Este año en que la letra Muluc era dominical y reinaba el bacab Canzienal tenían por buen año porque decían que éste era el mejor y mayor de esos dioses Bacabes, y así le ponían el primero en sus oraciones. Pero con todo eso les hacía el demonio hiciesen un ídolo llamado Yaxcocahmut, y que lo pusiesen en el templo y quitasen las imágenes antiguas e hiciesen en el patio, delante del templo, un bulto de piedra en el cual quemaban de su incienso y una pelota de la resina o leche kik, haciendo allí oraciones al ídolo y pidiéndole remedio para las miserias que aquel año temían, las cuales eran poca agua y echar los maíces muchos hijos y cosas de esta manera, para cuyo remedio los mandaba el demonio ofrecerle ardillas y un paramento sin labores el cual tejiesen las viejas que tenían por oficio bailar en el templo para aplacar a Yaxcocahmut.

Tenían otras muchas miserias y malas señales aunque era bueno el año si no hacían los servicios que el demonio les mandaba, lo cual era hacer una fiesta y en ella bailar un baile con muy altos zancos y ofrecerle cabezas de pavos y pan y bebidas de maíz; habían de ofrecerle (también) perros hechos de barro con pan en las espaldas, y las viejas habían de bailar con ellos en las manos y sacrificarle un perrito que tuviese las espaldas negras y fuese virgen; y los devotos habían de derramar su sangre y untar con ella la piedra del demonio Chacacantun. Tenían este sacrificio y servicio por agradable a su dios Yaxcocahmut.

XXXVII
Sacrificios del año nuevo de la letra Ix.— Pronósticos malos y sus remedios.

El año en que la letra dominical era Ix y el agüero Zaczini, hecha la elección del principal que celebrase la fiesta, hacían la imagen del demonio llamado Zacuuayayab y llevábanla a los montones de piedra de la parte norte, donde el año pasado la habían echado. Hacían una estatua al demonio Yzamná y poníanla en casa del principal, todos juntos, y el camino aderezado, iban devotamente por la imagen de Zacuuayayab. Llegados la sahumaban como solían hacer y degollaban la gallina, y puesta la imagen en un palo llamado Zachia la traían con su devoción y bailes, los cuales llaman alcabtan Kamahau. Traíanles la bebida acostumbrada al camino y llegados a casa ponían esta imagen delante de la estatua de Izamná, y allí todos le ofrecían sus ofrendas y las repartían, y a la estatua de Zacuuayayab ofrecían la cabeza de un pavo y empanadas de codornices y otras cosas y su bebida.

Otros se sacaban sangre y untaban con ella la piedra del demonio Zacacantun, y teníanse así los ídolos los días que faltaban hasta el año nuevo, y sahumábanlos con sus sahumerios hasta que llegado el día postrero llevaban a Yzamná al templo y a Zacuuayayab a la parte del poniente, a echarle por ahí para recibirla otro año.

Las miserias que temían este año, si eran negligentes en estos servicios, eran desmayos y amortecimientos y mal de ojos; teníanlo por ruin año de pan y bueno de algodón. Este año en que la letra dominical era Ix y reinaba el bacab Zaczini tenían por ruin año porque decían que habían de tener en él muchas miserias como gran falta de agua y muchos soles, los cuales habían de secar los maizales, de lo que les seguiría gran hambre, y del hambre hurtos, de hurtos esclavos y vender a los que los hiciesen. De esto les vendrían discordias y guerras entre sí propios o con otros pueblos. También decían que habría mudanza en el mando de los señores o de los sacerdotes por razón de las guerras y las discordias.

Tenían también un pronóstico: que algunos de los que quisiesen ser señores no prevalecerían. Decían que habrían de tener langosta, y que se despoblarían mucho sus pueblos por el hambre. Lo que el demonio les mandaba hacer para remedio de estas miserias, las cuales todas o algunas de ellas entendían les vendrían, era un ídolo que llamaban Cinchahau Izamná, y ponerlo en el templo donde le hacían muchos sahumerios y muchas ofrendas y oraciones y derramamientos de su sangre, con la cual untaban la piedra del demonio Zacacantun. Hacían muchos bailes y bailaban las viejas como solían, y en esta fiesta hacían de nuevo un oratorio pequeño al demonio, o renovaban el viejo y en él se juntaban a hacer sacrificios y ofrendas al demonio y a hacer todos una solemne borrachera, pues era fiesta general y obligatoria. Había algunos santones que de su voluntad y por su devoción hacían otro ídolo como el de arriba y le ponían en otros templos donde se hacían ofrendas y borrachera. Estas borracheras y sacrificios tenían por muy gratos a sus ídolos, y como remedio para librarse de las miserias del pronóstico.

XXXVIII
Sacrificios del año nuevo de la letra Cauac.— Pronósticos malos y su remedio con el baile del fuego.

El año que la letra dominical era Cauac y el agüero Hozanek, hecha la elección del principal para celebrar la fiesta, hacían la imagen del demonio llamado Ekuuayayab y llevábanla a los montones de piedra de la parte del poniente, donde el año pasado la habían echado. Hacían también una estatua a un demonio llamado Uacmituanahau y poníanla en casa del principal, en lugar conveniente, y desde allí iban todos juntos al lugar donde la imagen de Ekuuayayab estaba, y tenían para ello el camino muy aderezado. Llegados a ella sahumábanla el sacerdote y los señores, como solían, y degollaban la gallina. Hecho esto tomaban la imagen en un palo que llamaban Yaxek, y ponían a cuestas de la imagen una calavera y un hombre muerto, y encima un pájaro carnicero llamado Kuch, en señal de mortandad grande, pues por muy mal año tenían éste.

Llevábanla después de esta manera, con su sentimiento y devoción, y bailando algunos bailes entre los cuales bailaban uno como cazcarientas [sic], y así le llamaban Xibalbaokot, que quiere decir baile del demonio. Llegaban al camino los escanciadores con la bebida de los señores, la cual bebida llevaban al lugar de la estatua Uacmitunahau, y poníanla allí frente a la imagen que traían. Luego comenzaban sus ofrendas, sahumerios y oraciones y muchos derramaban la sangre de muchas partes del cuerpo, y con ella untaban la piedra del demonio llamado Ekelacantun, y así pasaban estos días aciagos, al cabo de los cuales llevaban a Uacmitunahau al templo y a Ekuuayayab a la parte de medio día, para recibirla otro año.

Este año en que la letra era Cauac y reinaba el bacab Hozanek, tenían, además de la pronosticada mortandad, por ruin, pues decían que los muchos soles les habrían de matar los maizales, y las muchas hormigas y los pájaros comerse lo que sembrasen; y como esto no sería en todas partes, en algunas, con gran trabajo, habría comida. Obligábales el demonio, para remedio de estas miserias, (a) hacer cuatro demonios llamados Chicacchob, Ekbalamchac, Ahcanuolcab y Ahbulucbalam y ponerlos en el templo donde los sahumaban con sus sahumerios y les ofrecían para quemar dos pellas de una leche o resina de un árbol que llamaban kik, y ciertas iguanas y pan, y una mitra y un manojo de flores, y una piedra preciosa de las suyas. Además de esto, para la celebración de esta fiesta hacían en el patio una gran bóveda de madera y henchíanla de leña por lo alto y por los lados, dejándole en ellos puertas para poder entrar y salir. Después de hecho tomaban los más hombres sendos manojos de unas varillas muy secas y largas, atados, y puesto un cantor en lo alto de la leña, cantaba y hacía son con un tambor de los suyos; bailaban todos los de abajo con mucho concierto y devoción, entrando y saliendo por las puertas de aquella bóveda de madera, y así bailaban hasta la tarde en que dejando allí cada uno su manojo se iban a sus casas a descansar y a comer.

En anocheciendo volvían y con ellos mucha gente, porque entre ellos esta ceremonia era muy estimada, y tomando cada uno su hachón lo encendía y con él cada uno por su parte pegaba fuego a la leña la cual ardía mucho y se quemaba presto. Después de hecho todo brasa, la allanaban y tendían muy tendida y junto a los que habían bailado, había algunos que se ponían a pasar descalzos y desnudos, como ellos andaban, por encima de aquella brasa, de una parte a otra; y pasaban algunos sin lesión, otros abrasados y otros medio quemados y en esto creían que estaba el remedio de sus miserias y malos agüeros, y pensaban que éste era el servicio más agradable a los dioses. Hecho esto, se iban a beber y hacer cestos, pues así lo pedía la costumbre de la fiesta y el calor del fuego.

XXXIX
Explicación sobre el calendario.

Con las letras de [los indígenas] puestas atrás, ponían nombres a los días de sus meses y de todos los meses juntos hacían un modo de calendario, con el cual se regían así para sus fiestas como para sus cuentas, tratas y negocios, como nosotros nos regimos con el nuestro, salvo que no comenzaban su calendario el día primero de su año, sino muy adelante, lo cual hacían por la dificultad con que contaban los días de los meses, todos juntos, como se verá en el propio calendario que pondré aquí; porque aunque las letras y días para sus meses son 20, tienen costumbre de contarlas desde una hasta 13. Tornan a comenzar de una después de las 13, y así reparten los días del año en 27 treces y 9 días sin los aciagos.

Con estos retruécanos y embarazosa cuenta, es cosa de ver la liberalidad con que los que saben, cuentan y se entienden, y mucho de notar es que salga siempre la letra que es dominical en el primer día de su año, sin errar ni faltar, ni venir a salir allí otra de las 20. Usaban también de este modo de contar para sacar de estas letras cierto modo de contar que tenían para las edades y otras cosas que, aunque son para ellos curiosas, no nos hacen aquí mucho al propósito, y por eso se quedan, con decir que el carácter o letra con que comenzaban la cuenta de sus días o calendario se llama Hun Imix y es éste:

—el cual no tiene día cierto ni señalado en que caiga, porque cada uno le muda la propia cuenta y con todo eso no falta el salir la letra que viene por dominical el primero del año que se sigue.

El primer día del año de esta gente era siempre a 16 días de nuestro mes de julio, y primero de su mes de Pop, y no es de maravillar que esta gente, aunque simple en otras cosas, le hemos hallado curiosidad y opinión en ésta, como la han tenido otras naciones, pues según la glosa sobre Ezequiel, enero es, según los romanos, el principio del año; según los hebreos, abril; según los griegos, marzo; y según los orientales, octubre. Pero, aunque ellos comienzan su año en julio, yo no pondré aquí su calendario sino por el orden del nuestro y junto con el nuestro, de manera que irán señaladas nuestras letras y las suyas, nuestros meses y los suyos y su cuenta de los trece sobre dichos, puesta en cuenta de guarismos.

Y porque no haya necesidad de poner en una parte el calendario y en otra las fiestas, pondré en cada uno de sus meses sus fiestas y las observancias y ceremonias con que las celebraban y con esto cumpliré lo que en alguna parte de atrás he dicho: que haré su calendario y en él diré de sus ayunos y de las ceremonias con que hacían los ídolos de madera y otras cosas, todas las cuales y las demás aquí tratadas no es mi intento sirvan de más de materia de alabar a la bondad divina que tal ha sufrido y tal ha tenido por bien remediar en nuestros tiempos, para que advirtiéndolo con entrañas cristianas le supliquemos por su conservación y aprovechamiento en buena cristiandad y los que a su cargo lo tengan, los favorezcan y ayuden porque por los pecados de esta gente o los nuestros, no les falte la ayuda, o ellos no falten en lo comenzado y así vuelvan a sus miserias ni a sus yerros y les acaezcan cosas peores que las primeras, tornando los demonios a las casas de sus almas, de donde con trabajosos cuidados hemos procurado echarlos, limpiándoselas y barriéndolas de sus vicios y malas costumbres pasadas; y no es mucho temer esto viendo la perdición que hace tantos años hay en toda la grande y muy cristiana Asia, y en la buena y católica y augustísima África, y las miserias y calamidades que el día de hoy pasan en nuestra Europa y en nuestra nación y casas, por lo cual podríamos decir: se nos han cumplido las evangélicas profecías sobre Jerusalén de que la cercarían sus enemigos y la agostarían y apretarían tanto que la derrocasen por tierra; y esto ya lo habría permitido Dios, según somos, pero no puede faltar su iglesia ni lo del que dijo: Dominus reliquisset semen, sicut Sodoma fuissemus.

ENERO

Van con mucho temor, según decían, criando dioses. Acabados ya y puestos en perfección los ídolos, hacía el dueño de ellos un presente, el mejor que podía, de aves y caza y de su moneda para pagar con él el trabajo de quienes habían hecho los(ídolos), y los sacaban de la casilla poniéndolos en otra enramada para ello hecha en el patio, en la cual los bendecía el sacerdote con mucha solemnidad y abundancia de devotas oraciones, habiéndose quitado primero él y los oficiales el tizne, porque decían que ayunaban en tanto que hacían los (ídolos). Estando untado y echado el demonio como solían, y quemado el incienso bendito, ponían (el ídolo) en una petaquilla envuelto en un paño y lo entregaban al dueño, y él, con asaz devoción, lo recibía. Luego predicaba el buen sacerdote la excelencia del oficio de hacer dioses nuevos y peligro que corrían quienes los hacían si acaso no guardaban sus abstinencias y ayunos. Después comían muy bien y se emborrachaban mejor.

YAX

En cualquiera de los meses de Chen y Yax, y en el día que señalaba sacerdote, hacían una fiesta que llamaban Ocná, que quiere decir renovación del templo; esta fiesta la hacían en honra de los chaces que tenían por dioses de los maizales, y en ella miraban los pronósticos de los bacabes, como más largo queda dicho y conforme al orden puesto en su lugar. Dicha fiesta la hacían cada año y además de esto renovaban los ídolos de barro y sus braseros, que era costumbre tener cadaídolo un bracerito en que le quemasen su incienso, y si era menester, hacían de nuevo la casa o la renovaban y ponían en la pared la memoria de estas cosas con sus caracteres.

FEBRERO

Aquí comienza la cuenta del Calendario de [los indígenas] diciendo en su lengüita: Hun Imix.

ZAC

En un día de este mes de Zac que el sacerdote señalaba, hacían los cazadores otra fiesta como la del mes de Zip, la cual servía para aplacar en los dioses la ira que tenían contra ellos y sus sementeras; y las hacían(también) por la sangre que derramaban en la caza, porque tenían por cosa horrenda cualquier derramamiento de sangre si no era en sus sacrificios, y por esta causa siempre que iban de caza invocaban al demonio y le quemaban incienso; y si podían, le untaban el rostro con la sangre del corazón de la tal caza. En cualquier día que cayese este séptimo de Ahau, hacían una muy grande fiesta que duraba tres días, de sahumerios y ofrendas y su gentil borrachera; y porque esta fiesta es movible, tenían los cuidadosos sacerdotes cuidados de echarla con tiempo para que se ayunase debidamente.

MAC

CEH

MARZO

En cualquier día de este mes de Mac hacía la gente anciana y los más viejos, una fiesta a los chaces, dioses de los panes, y a Yzamná. Y un día o dos antes, hacían la siguiente ceremonia, a la cual llamaban en su lengua tuppkak: tenían busca dos animales y sabandijas del campo que podía haber y había en la tierra, y con esos se juntaban en el patio del templo en el cual se ponían los chaces y el sacerdote, sentados en las esquinas, como solían (hacer) para echar al demonio, con sendos cántaros de agila que allí les traían a cada uno. En medio ponían un gran manojo de varillas secas, atadas y enhiestas, y quemando primero de su incienso en el brasero, pegaban fuego a las varillas y en tanto que ardían, sacaban con liberalidad los corazones a las aves y animales, y echaban los a quemar en el fuego; y si no había animales grandes como tigres, leones o lagartos, hacían corazones con su incienso y si había animales y los mataban, traían sus corazones para aquel fuego. Quemados todos los corazones, mataban el fuego con los cántaros de agua de, los chaces. Hacían esto para alcanzar con ello y la siguiente fiesta, buen año de aguapara sus panes; luego celebraban la fiesta, diferentemente de las otras, pues para ella no ayunaban, salvo el muñidor de ella, que éste ayunaba su ayuno. Venidos, pues, a celebrar la fiesta, se juntaba el pueblo, los sacerdotes y los oficiales en el patio del templo donde tenían hecho un montón de piedras con sus escaleras, todo muy limpio y aderezado de frescuras. Daba el sacerdote incienso preparado por el muñidor, (incienso), que se quemaba en el brasero y así dizque huía el demonio. Hecho esto con su devoción acostumbrada, untaban el primer escalón del montón de las piedras con lodo del pozo, y los demás escalones con betún azul, y echaban muchos sahumerios e invocaban a los chaces y a Yzamná con sus oraciones y devociones, y ofrecían sus presentes. Esto acabado, se consolaban comiendo y bebiendo lo ofrecido y quedaban confiados del buen año con sus servicios e invocaciones.

MUAN

En el mes de Muan los que tenían cacahuates hacían una fiesta a los dioses Ekchuah, Chac y Hobnil, que eran sus abogados. Ibanla a hacer a alguna heredad de alguno de ellos, donde sacrificaban un perro manchado por el color del cacao y quemaban a los ídolos su incienso y ofrecíanles iguanas de las azules, y ciertas plumas de un pájaro y otras cazas, y daban a cada uno de los oficiales una mazorca de la fruta del cacao. Acabado el sacrificio y sus oraciones, comíanse los presentes y bebían dizque no más tres veces del vino, que no llegaban a más, e ibanse a casa del que tenía la fiesta a (su) cargo, y hacíanse unas pasas [sic] con regocijo.

PAX

En este mes de Pax hacían una fiesta llamada Pacumchac, para la cual se juntaban los señores y sacerdotes de los pueblos menores a los mayores, y así juntos, velaban cinco noches en el templo de Citchaccoh, con oraciones, ofrendas y sahumerios, como está dicho hacen en la fiesta de Kukulkán, en el mes de Xul, en noviembre. Antes de pasados estos días, iban todos a casa del capitán de sus guerras, llamado Nacón, del cual traté, y traíanle con gran pompa sahumándole como a ídolo de templo, y le sentaban quemándole incienso y así estaban él y ellos hasta pasados los cinco días, en los cuales comían y bebían de los dones que se ofrecían en el templo, y bailaban un baile a manera de paso largo de guerra, y así le llaman Holcanakot, que quiere decir baile de guerreros. Pasados los cinco días, venían a la fiesta, la cual porque era para cosas de guerra y alcanzar la victoria sobre los enemigos, era muy solemne. Hacían, pues, primero la ceremonia y sacrificios del fuego, como dije en el mes de Mac; después echabán al demonio con mucha solemnidad como solían, y hecho esto venía el orar y ofrecer dones y sahumerios, y en tanto que la gente hacía estas sus ofrendas y oraciones, los señores tomaban en hombros al Nacón y traíanlo sahumándole en torno del templo; y cuando volvían con él, los chaces sacrificaban un perro y sacábanle el corazón y enviábanlo entre dos platos al demonio, y los chaces quebraban sendas ollas grandes llenas de bebida y con esto acababan su fiesta. Acabada, comían y bebían los presentes que allí se habían ofrecido y llevaban al Nacón con mucha solemnidad a su casa, pero sin perfumes. Allá tenían gran fiesta y en ella se emborrachaban los señores, los sacerdotes y los principales, y la demás gente ibase a sus pueblos, salvo que el Nacón no se emborrachaba. Otro día, después de digerido el vino, se juntaban todos los señores y sacerdotes de los pueblos que se habían embriagado y quedado allí, encasa del señor, quien les repartía mucha cantidad de su incienso que tenía aparejado y bendito por aquellos benditos sacerdotes; y junto con ello les hacía una plática y con mucha eficacia les encomendaba las fiestas que, en sus pueblos, ellos habían de hacer a sus dioses para que el año fuese próspero de mantenimientos. Hecha la plática se despedían todos, unos de otros, con mucho amor y batahola y cada uno se iba a su pueblo y casa. Allá trataban de hacer sus fiestas, las cuales les duraban, según las hacían, hasta el mes de Pop, y llamábanlas Zabacilthan, y las hacían de esta manera: miraban en el pueblo, entre los más ricos, quién quería hacer esta fiesta y encomendábanle su día por tener más agasajo estos tres meses que había hasta su año nuevo; y lo que hacían era juntarse en casa del que hacía la fiesta, y allí hacer las ceremonias de echar al demonio y quemar copal y hacer ofrendas con regocijos y bailes, y hacerse unas botas de vino, y en esto paraba todo; y era tanto el exceso que había de estas fiestas durante los tres meses, que lástima grande era verlos, que unos andaban arañados, otros descalabrados, otros (con) los ojos encarnizados del mucho emborracharse, y con todo eso (tenían tanto) amor al vino, que se perdían por él.

JUNIO

KAYAB
CUMKU

JULIO

Dicho queda en pasados capítulos, [los indígenas] comenzaban sus años de estos días sin nombre, aparejándose en ellos como en la vigilia para la celebración de la fiesta de su año nuevo; y allende del aparejo que hacían con la fiesta del demonio Uuayayab, para la cual salían de sus casas; los demás aparejos eran salir muy poco de casa estos cinco días, y ofrecer, además de los dones de la fiesta general, cuentas a sus demonios y a los otros (ídolos) de sus templos. Estas cuentas que así ofrecían nunca (las) tomaban para sus usos, (como ninguna otra) cosa que al demonio ofreciesen, y de ellas (sólo) compraban incienso para quemar. En estos días no se peinaban ni lavaban, ni las mujeres ni los hombres (se) espulgaban, ni hacían cosa servil o trabajosa, porque temían que les sucediera algún mal si lo hacían.

POP

El primer día de Pop es el primero del primer mes de [los indígenas]; era su año nuevo y, entre ellos, fiesta muy celebrada porque era general y de todos; y así todo el pueblo junto, hacía fiesta a todos los ídolos. Para celebrarla con más solemnidad, renovaban en este día todas las cosas de su servicio, como platos, vasos, banquillos, y la ropa vieja y las mantillas en que tenían envueltos a los ídolos. Barrían sus casas y la basura y los trastos viejos echábanlos fuera del pueblo, al muladar, y nadie, aunque los hubiese menester, los tocaba. Para esta fiesta comenzaban un tiempo antes a ayunar y abstenerse de sus mujeres los señores, el sacerdote y la gente principal y los que más (así) lo querían por su devoción, según les parecía, que algunos comenzaban tres meses antes, otros dos, y otros como les parecía, pero ninguno menos de trece días; y en estos trece días añadían a la abstinencia de la mujer no comer en los manjares ni sal ni pimienta, lo que era tenido entre ellos por gran penitencia. En este tiempo elegían (a) los oficiales chaces para ayudar al sacerdote, y éste aparejaba muchas pelotillas de su incienso fresco en unas tablillas que tenían los sacerdotes; incienso que los abstinentes y ayunantes quemaban a los ídolos. Quienes comenzaban estos ayunos no osaban quebrantarlos porque creían que les vendría algún mal en sus personas o casas. Venido, pues, el año nuevo, se juntaban todos los varones en el patio del templo, solos, porque en ningún sacrificio o fiesta que en el templo se hacía habían de hallarse mujeres, salvo las viejas que habían de hacer sus bailes. En las fiestas que hacían en otras partes podían ir y hallarse las mujeres. Aquí iban limpios y galanos de sus unturas coloradas, y quitado el tizne negro de que andaban untados cuando ayunaban. Congregados todos y con muchos presentes de comidas y bebidas, y mucho vino que habían hecho, purgaba el sacerdote el templo sentándose en medio del patio, vestido de pontifical, (teniendo) cerca de sí un braserito y la stablillas del incienso. Sentábanse los chaces en las cuatro esquinas y tiraban un cordel nuevo de uno a otro lado, dentro del cual habían de entrar todos los que habían ayunado para echar al demonio. Echado el demonio, todos comenzaban sus devotas oraciones y los chaces sacaban lumbre nueva; quemaban el incienso al demonio y el sacerdote comenzaba a echar su incienso en el brasero, y venían todos por su orden, comenzando con los señores, a recibir incienso de la mano del sacerdote, lo cual él les daba con tanta mesura y devoción como si les diera reliquias, y ellos lo echaban poco a poco en el brasero aguardando hasta que se hubiese acabado de quemar. Después de este sahumerio, comían entre todos los dones y presentes, y andaba el vino hasta que se hacían unas cubas: y este era su año nuevo y servicio muy acept(ado) por sus ídolos. Había después algunos otros que dentro de este mes de Pop celebraban esta fiesta por su devoción (y) con sus amigos y con los señores y sacerdotes, que sus sacerdotes siempre eran los primeros en sus regocijos y bebidas.

UO

En el mes de Uo se comenzaban a aparejar con ayunos y las demás cosas, para celebrar la fiesta, los sacerdotes, los médicos y hechiceros, que era todo uno. Los cazadores y pescadores venían la a celebrar a siete de Zip; y celebrábanla por sí, cada uno de estos, en su día: primero los sacerdotes, (fiesta) a la cual llamaban Pocam. Se juntaban en casa del señor con sus aderezos, echaban antes al demonio, como solían hacerlo y después sacaban sus libros y los tendían sobre las frescuras que para ello tenían, e invocando con sus oraciones y su devoción a un ídolo que llamaban Cinchau-Izamná, del cual dicen fue el primer sacerdote, y ofrecíanle sus dones y presentes y quemábanle con la lumbre nueva sus pelotillas de incienso; entre tanto, deslían en su vaso un poco de su cardenillo, con agua virgen, que ellos decían, traída del monte donde no llegase mujer, y untaban con ello las tablas de los libros para su mundificación, y hecho esto abría el más docto de los sacerdotes un libro y miraba los pronósticos de aquel año y los declaraba a los presentes, y predicábales un poco encomendándoles los remedios; y en esta fiesta señalaba, para el otro año, al sacerdote o señor que había de hacerla; y si moría el que señalaban para hacerla, los hijos quedaban obligados a cumplir por el difunto. Hecho esto, comían todos los dones y comida que habían traído, y bebían hasta hacerse (unos) zaques y así acababa la fiesta en la cual bailaban algunas veces un baile que llaman Okotuil.

ZIP

SEPTIEMBRE

Al día siguiente se juntaban los médicos y hechiceros en casa de uno de ellos, con sus mujeres, y los sacerdotes echaban al demonio; hecho lo cual, sacaban los envoltorios de sus medicinas en que traían muchas niñerías y sendos idolillos de la diosa de la medicina que llamaban Ixchel, y así a esta fiesta llamaban Ihcil Ixchel, y unas pedrezuelas de las suertes que echaban y llamaban Am y con su mucha devoción invocaban con oraciones a los dioses de la medicina que decían Yzamná, Citbolontun y Ahau Chamahez, y dándoles los sacerdotes el incienso, lo quemaban en el brasero del fuego nuevo entre tanto los chaces embadurnábanlos con otro betún azul como el de los libros de los sacerdotes. Hecho esto envolvía cada uno las cosas de su oficio y tomando el envoltorio a cuestas bailaban todo un baile llamado Chantunyiah. Acabado el baile se sentaban de una parte los varones y de la otra las mujeres, y sorteando la fiesta para el otro año, comían de los presentes y emborrachábanse muy sin asco, salvo los sacerdotes que dicen que habían vergüenza y guardaban el vino para beber a solas y a su placer.

El día siguiente se juntaban los cazadores en una casa de uno de ellos y llevando consigo a sus mujeres como los demás, venían los sacerdotes y echaban el demonio como solían. Ya echado, ponían en medio el aderezo par a el sacrificio de incienso y fuego nuevo y betún azul. Y con su devoción invocaban los cazadores a los dioses de la caza, Acanum, Zuhuyzib Zipitabai y otros, y repartíanles el incienso, el cual echaban al brasero; y en tanto que ardía, sacaba cada uno una flecha y una calavera de venado, las cuales untaban los chaces con el betún azul. Yauntadas, bailaban con ellas en las manos; otros se horadaban las orejas, otros la lengua y pasaban por los agujeros siete hojas de una yerba, algo anchas, que llaman Ac. Habiendo hecho esto primero, el sacerdote y los oficiales de la fiesta ofrecían luego los dones, y así bailando, se escanciaba el vino y se emborrachaban hechos unos cestos.

Al día siguiente los pescadores hacían su fiesta por el orden de los demás, salvo quel o untado eran los aparejos de pescar y no se horadaban las orejas sino arpábanselas a la redonda y bailaban su baile llamado Chohom; y hecho todo bendecían un palo alto y gordo y poníanle enhiesto. Tenían costumbre, después de que habían hecho la fiesta en los pueblos, irla a hacer a la costa los señores y mucha gente; y allá hacían muy grandes pesquerías y regocijos y llevaban gran recado de redes y anzuelos y otras industrias con que pescan. Los dioses que en esta fiesta eran sus abogados son

Ahkaknexoi, Ahpua y Ahcitzamalcun.

ZODZ

En el mes de Zodz se aparejaban los señores de los colmenares para celebrar su fiesta en Tzec, y aunque el aparejo principal de estas fiestas era el ayuno, no obligaba más que al sacerdote y oficiales que le ayudaban; para los demás era voluntario.

TZEC

Venido el día de la fiesta se aparejaban en la casa en que ésta se celebraba y hacían todo lo que en las demás, salvo que no derramaban sangre. Tenían por abogados a los bacabes y especialmente a Hobnil. Hacían muchas ofrendas y en especial daban a los cuatro chaces cuatro platos con sendas pelotas de incienso en medio de cada uno y pintadas a la redonda unas figuras de miel, que para la abundancia de ella era esta fiesta. Concluían la con vino, como solían, y harto, porque daban para ello en abundancia los dueños de las colmenas de miel.

XUL

NOVIEMBRE

Queda dicha la ida de Kukulkán, de Yucatán, después de la cual hubo entre [los indígenas] algunos que dijeron se había ido al cielo con los dioses, y por eso le tuvieron por dios y le señalaron templo en que como a tal le celebrasen su fiesta, y se la celebró toda la tierra hasta la destrucción de Mayapán. Después de esta destrucción, dicha fiesta se celebraba sólo en la provincia de Maní; y las demás, en reconocimiento de lo que debían a Kukulkán, presentaban a Mani una un año y otra en el otro año, o a las veces, cinco muy galanas banderas de pluma, con las cuales hacían la fiesta en esta manera y no como las pasadas: a 16 de Xul se juntaban todos los señores y sacerdotes en Maní, con ellos gran gentío de los pueblos, el cual venía ya preparado de ayunos y abstinencias. Aquel día, en la tarde, salían con gran procesión de gente, y con muchos de sus farsantes, de casa del señor donde se habían juntado, e iban con gran sosiego al templo de Kukulkán, el cual tenían muy aderezado; y llegados, hacían sus oraciones, ponían las banderas en lo alto del templo y abajo, en el patio, tendían todos cada uno de sus ídolos sobre hojas de árboles que para ello había, y sacada la lumbre nueva comenzaban a quemar en muchas partes incienso y a hacer ofrendas de comidas guisadas sin sal ni pimienta, y de bebidas de sus habas y pepitas de calabaza; y quemando siempre copal, sin volver los señores a sus Casas, (ni quienes) los habían ayudado, pasaban cinco días y cinco noches en oraciones y en algunos bailes devotos. Hasta el primer día de Yaxkin andaban los farsantes estos cinco días por las casas principales haciendo farsas, y recogían los presentes que les daban y todo lo llevaban al templo, donde acabados de pasar los cinco días repartían los dones entre los señores, sacerdotes y bailadores y cogían las banderas e ídolos y se volvían a casa del señor y de allí cada cual a la suya. Decían y tenían muy creído, que el postrer día bajaba Kukulkán del cielo y recibía los servicios, vigilias y ofrendas. Llamaban a esta fiesta Chickabán.

YAXKIN

En este mes de Yaxkin se comenzaban a aparejar como solían, para, una fiesta general que hacían en Mol, en el día que señalaba el sacerdote; (esta fiesta estaba dedicada) a todos los dioses. Llamábanla Olob-Zab-Kamyax. Lo que pretendían, después de juntos en el templo y hechas las ceremonias y sahumerios como en las fiestas pasadas, era untar con el betún azul que hacían, todos los instrumentos de todos los oficios. desde (los) del sacerdote hasta los huesos de las mujeres y los postes de las casas. Para esta fiesta juntaban todos los niños y niñas del pueblo y en vez de embadurnamientos y ceremonias, les daban en las coyunturas de las manos, por la parte de fuera, unos golpeculos; a las niñas se los daba una vieja vestida con un hábito de plumas, misma que allí las llevaba y por eso la llamaban Ixmol, que quiere decir la allegadera. Dábanles estos golpes para que saliesen expertos oficiales en los oficios de sus padres y madres. La conclusión era con buena borrachera, ya comidas las ofrendas, salvo que es de creer que aquella devota vieja llevaría con qué emborracharse en casa para no perder las plumas del oficio en el camino.

DICIEMBRE

MOL

En este mes tornaban los colmeneros a hacer otra fiesta como la de Tze, para que los dioses proveyesen de flores a las abejas. Una de las cosas que estos pobres tenían por más ardua y dificultosa era hacer ídolos de palo, a lo cual llamaban hacer dioses; y así tenían señalado tiempo particular para hacerlos, y éste era el mes de Mol u otro, si el sacerdote les decía que bastaba. Los que querían hacer los consultaban primero al sacerdote y tomando su consejo iban al oficial de ellos, y dicen que siempre se excusaban los oficiales porque temían que ellos o alguno de sus casas se habían de morir o venirles enfermedades de muerte. Si aceptaban, los chaces, que para esto también elegían, comenzaban sus ayunos. En tanto que ellos ayunaban, aquel cuyos eran los ídolos, iba o enviaba al monte por la madera que siempre era de cedro. Venida la madera, hacían una casilla de paja, cercada, donde la metían y una tinaja para echar a los ídolos y allí tenerlos tapados según los fuesen haciendo; metían incienso para quemarle a cuatro demonios llamados Acantunes, que ponían a las cuatro partes del mundo. Metían con qué cortarse o sacarse sangre de las orejas y la herramienta para labrar los negros dioses y con estos aderezos se encerraban en la casilla los chaces, el sacerdote y el oficial y comenzaban su labor de dioses cortándose a menudo las orejas y untando con la sangre aquellos demonios y quemándoles su incienso y así perseveraban hasta acabar, dándoles (entonces) de comer. Y no habían de conocer a sus mujeres ni por pienso, ni aun llegar nadie a aquel lugar donde ellos estaban.

CHEN

Calendario Maya

Número de los meses.	1	2	3	4	5	6	7	8	9	10	11	12	13	14	15	16	17	18
Cauac	1	8	2	9	3	10	4	11	5	12	6	13	7	1	8	2	9	3
Ahau	2	9	3	10	4	11	5	12	6	13	7	1	8	2	9	3	10	4
Ymix	3	10	4	11	5	12	6	13	7	1	8	2	9	3	10	4	11	5
Ik	4	11	5	12	6	13	7	1	8	2	9	3	10	4	11	5	12	6
Akbal	5	12	6	13	7	1	8	2	9	3	10	4	11	5	12	6	13	7
Kan	6	13	7	1	8	2	9	3	10	4	11	5	12	6	13	7	1	8
Chicchan	7	1	8	2	9	3	10	4	11	5	12	6	13	7	1	8	2	9
Cimi	8	2	9	3	10	4	11	5	12	6	13	7	1	8	2	9	3	10
Manik	9	3	10	4	11	5	12	6	13	7	1	8	2	9	3	10	4	11
Lamat	10	4	11	5	12	6	13	7	1	8	2	9	3	10	4	11	5	12
Muluc	11	5	12	6	13	7	1	8	2	9	3	10	4	11	5	12	6	13
Oc	12	6	13	7	1	8	2	9	3	10	4	11	5	12	6	13	7	1
Chuen	13	7	1	8	2	9	3	10	4	11	5	12	6	13	7	1	8	2
Eb	1	8	2	9	3	10	4	11	5	12	6	13	7	1	8	2	9	3
Been	2	9	3	10	4	11	5	12	6	13	7	1	8	2	9	3	10	4
Ix	3	10	4	11	5	12	6	13	7	1	8	2	9	3	10	4	11	5
Men	4	11	5	12	6	13	7	1	8	2	9	3	10	4	11	5	12	6
Cib	5	12	6	13	7	1	8	2	9	3	10	4	11	5	12	6	13	7
Caban	6	13	7	1	8	2	9	3	10	4	11	5	12	6	13	7	1	8
Ezanab	7	1	8	2	9	3	10	4	11	5	12	6	13	7	1	8	2	9

No sólo tenían [los indígenas] cuenta del año y de los meses, como queda dicho y señalado atrás, sino que tenían cierto modo de contar los tiempos y sus cosas por edades, las cuales hacían de veinte en vente años, contando 13 veintes con una de las 20 letras de los días que llaman *Ahua*, sin orden sino retrucadas como aparecen en el siguiente círculo:

LLámanles a estos en su lengua *Katunes*, y con ellos tenían, a maravilla, cuenta de sus edades, y le fue así fácil al viejo de quien en el primer capítulo dije, había trescientos años después, acordarse de ellos. Y si yo no supiera de estas sus cuentas, no creyera se pudiese así acordar de tanta edad.[81]

Quien esta cuenta de los Katunes ordenó, si fue el demonio, hizo lo que suele ordenándola a su honor; y si fue hombre, debía ser buen idólatra porque con estos sus *Katunes* añadió todos los principales engaños y agüeros y embaucamientos con que esta gente andaba allende de sus miserias del todo embaucada, y así, esta era la ciencia a que ellos daban más crédito y la que en más tenían y de la que no todos los

---

[81] Fray Diego de Landa no menciona a ningún viejo en el capítulo primero. Es posible que sea omission del amanuense.

sacerdotes sabían dar cuenta. El orden que tenían en contar sus cosas y hacer sus adivinaciones con esta cuenta era que tenían en el templo dos ídolos dedicados a dos de estos caracteres. Al primero, conforme a la cruz del círculo arriba contenido, adoraban y hacían servicios y sacrificios para remedio de las plagas de sus 20 años y en los 10 años que faltaban de los 20 primeros, no hacían sino quemarle incienso y reverenciarle.

Cumplido los 20 años del primero comenzaban a seguirse por los hados del segundo y hacerle sus sacrificios, y quitando aquel primer ídolo ponían otro para venerarle otros diez años.

Verbi gratia: dicen [los indígenas] que acabaron de llegar los españoles a la ciudad de Mérida el año de la Natividad del Señor de 1541, que era en punto el primer año de la era *Buluc-Ahau* que es el que está en la casa donde está la cruz, y llegaron el mismo mes de *Pop* que es el primer mes de su año. Si no hubiera españoles ellos hubiense adorado el ídolo de *Buluc-Ahau* y honrábanle siguiéndose por los pronósticos de *Bolon-Ahau* hasta el año de 61, y entonces quitáranle del templo y pusieran al ídolo *Uuc-Ahau*, y siguiéranle por los pronósticos de *Bolon-Ahau* otros 10 años; y así daban vuelta a todos. De manera que veneraban a estos sus Katunes 20 años y 10 se regían por sus supersticiones y engaños, los cuales eran tantos y tan bastantes para engañar a gente simple que admira, aunque no a los que saben de las cosas naturales y la experiencia que de ellas tiene el demonio.

Usaba también esta gente de ciertos caracteres o letras con las cuales escribían en sus libros sus cosas antiguas y sus ciencias, y con estas figuras y algunas señales de las mismas, entendían sus cosas y las daban a entender y enseñaban. Llallámosles gran número de libros de estas sus letras, y porque no tenían cosa en que no hubiese superstición y falsedades del demonio, se los quemamos todos, lo cual sintieron a maravilla y les dio mucha pena.

De sus letras pondré aquí un a, b, c, que no permite su pesadumbre más, porque usan para todas las aspiraciones de las letras de un carácter, y después, júntanle parte de otro y así vienen a ser *in infinitum*, como se podrá ver en el siguiente ejemplo. *Le* quiere decir *lazo y cazar con él*; para escribir le con sus caracteres, habiéndoles nosotros hecho entender que son dos letras, lo escribían ellos con tres poniendo a la aspiración de la *l*, la vocal *e*, que antes de si trae, y en esto no yerran aunque usen (otra) *e*, si quieren ellos, por curiosidad. Ejemplo:

e l e lé

Después, al cabo, le pegan la parte junta.

Ha que quiere decir agua, porque la *h* tiene *a* antes de sí la ponen ellos al principio con *a*, y al cabo de esta manera:

a   ha

También lo escriben por partes, pero de una y otra manera que no pusiera aquí sino por dar cuenta entera de las cosas de esta gente: *Ma in kati* quiere decir *no quiero* y ellos lo escriben por partes de esta manera:

ma   i   n   ka   ti

Siguese su a, b, c:

De las letras que faltan carece esta lengua y tienen otras añadidas de la nuestra para otras cosas que las ha menester y ya no usan de estos sus caracteres, especialmente la gente moza que ha aprendido los nuestros.

[Copia de esta página como aparece en la relación de Diego de Landa:]

A   A   A   B   B   C   T

E   H   I   CA   K   L   L

M   N   O   O   PP   CU   KU

X   X   U   P   U   Z

XLII
Multitud de edificios de Yucatán.— Los de Izamal, Mérida y Chichén Itzá.

Si Yucatán hubiere de cobrar nombre y reputación con muchedumbre, grandeza y hermosura de edificios, como lo han alcanzado otras partes de las Indias, con oro, plata y riquezas, ella hubiera extendídose tanto como el Perú y la Nueva España, porque es así en esto de edificios y muchedumbre de ellos, la más señalada cosa de cuantas hasta hoy en las Indias se han descubierto, porque son tantos y tantas las partes donde los hay y tan bien edificados de cantería, a su modo, que espanta, y porque esta tierra no es tal al presente, aunque es buena tierra, como parece haber sido en el tiempo próspero en que en ella tanto y tan señalado edificio se labró, con no haber en ella ningún género de metal con que labrarlos; pondré aquí las razones que he visto dar a los que dichos edificios han mirado. Las cuales son que estas gentes debieron estar sujetas a algunos señores amigos de ocuparlos mucho y que los ocuparon en esto, y que como ellos han sido tan buenos honradores de los ídolos, se señalaban de comunidad hacerles templos; y por algunas causas, se mudaban las poblaciones y así donde poblaban edificaban siempre de nuevo sus templos, santuarios y casas a su usanza para los señores, que ellos siempre las han usado de madera cubierta de paja; o que el grande aparejo que hay de piedra, cal y cierta tierra blanca excelente para edificios, les ha llevado a hacer tantos, que si no es a quienes los han visto, parecerá burla hablar de ellos; o la tierra tiene algún secreto que si hasta ahora no se le ha alcanzado ni a la gente natural de ella, en estos tiempos tampoco ha alcanzado. Porque decir los hayan edificado otras naciones sujetando a [los indígenas], no es así, por las señales que hay de haber sido edificados por gente indiana y desnuda, como se ve en uno de los muchos y muy grandes edificios que allí hay, en las paredes de los bastiones, en las cuales aún duran señales de hombres en carnes y honestados de unos largos listones que llaman Ex en su lengua, y de otras divisas que [los indígenas] de estos tiempos traían, todo hecho de argamasa muy fuerte. Y morando yo allí se halló en un edificio que desbaratamos un cántaro grande con tres asas y pintado por fuera de unos fuegos plateados, dentro del cual estaban las cenizas de un cuerpo quemado y entre ellas hallamos tres cuentas buenas de piedra, del arte de las que [los indígenas] ahora tienen por moneda, todo lo cual muestra haber sido [indígenas]. Bien sea, que si lo fueron, era gente de más ser que los de ahora y muy de mayores cuerpos y fuerzas, y aún se ve esto más aquí en Izamal que en otra parte, en los bultos de media talla que digo están hoy día de argamasa en los bastiones, que son de hombres crecidos; y los extremos de los brazos y piernas del hombre cuyas eran las cenizas del cántaro que hallamos en el edificio, que estaban a maravilla por quemar y muy gruesos. Se ve también en las escaleras de los edificios, que son más de dos buenos palmos de alto, y esto aquí sólo en Izamal y en Mérida.

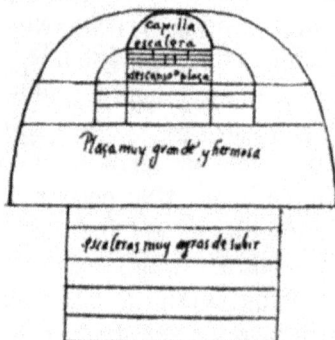

Hay aquí en Izamal un edificio entre los otros, de tanta altura y hermosura que espanta, el cual se verá en esta figura y en esta razón de ella: Tiene 20 gradas de a más de dos buenos palmos de alto y ancho cada una, y tendrán más de cien pies de largo. Son estas gradas de muy grandes piedras labradas, aunque con el mucho tiempo y estar expuestas al agua, están ya feas y maltratadas. Tiene después labrado en torno, como señala la raya redonda, una muy fuerte pared de cantería en la cual, como a estado y medio de alto, sale una ceja de hermosas piedras, todo a la redonda, y desde ellas se torna después a seguir la obra hasta igualar con la altura de la plaza que se hace después de la primera escalera. Después de la cual plaza, se hace otra escalera como la primera, aunque no tan larga ni de tantos escalones, siguiendo siempre a la redonda la obra de la pared. Encima de estos escalones se hace otra buena placeta y en ella, algo pegado a la pared, está hecho un cerro bien alto con su escalera al mediodía, donde caen las escaleras grandes, y encima está una hermosa capilla de cantería bien labrada. Yo subí a lo alto de esta capilla y, como Yucatán es tierra llana, se ve desde ella a maravilla tanta tierra cuanto la vista puede alcanzar, y se ve la mar. Estos edificios de Izamal eran once o doce por todos, aunque éste es el mayor, y están muy cerca unos de otros. No hay memoria de los fundadores y parecen haber sido los primeros. Están a ocho leguas de la mar en muy hermoso sitio y buena tierra y comarca de gente, por lo cual [los indígenas], con harta insistencia, nos hicieron poblar una casa en uno de estos edificios que llamamos San Antonio, el año de 1549, en la cual y en todo lo de la redonda se les ha ayudado mucho para su cristiandad y así se han poblado en este asiento dos buenos pueblos, aparte uno del otro.

Los segundos edificios que en esta tierra son más principales y antiguos—tanto que no hay memoria de sus fundadores—, son los de T-ho; están a trece leguas de los de Izamal y a ocho de la mar como los otros; y hay señales hoy en día de haber habido una muy hermosa calzada de los unos a los otros. Los españoles poblaron aquí una ciudad y llamáronla Mérida por la extrañeza y grandeza de los edificios, el principal de los cuales señalaré aquí como pudiere e hice (con el) de Izamal, para que mejor se pueda ver lo que es.

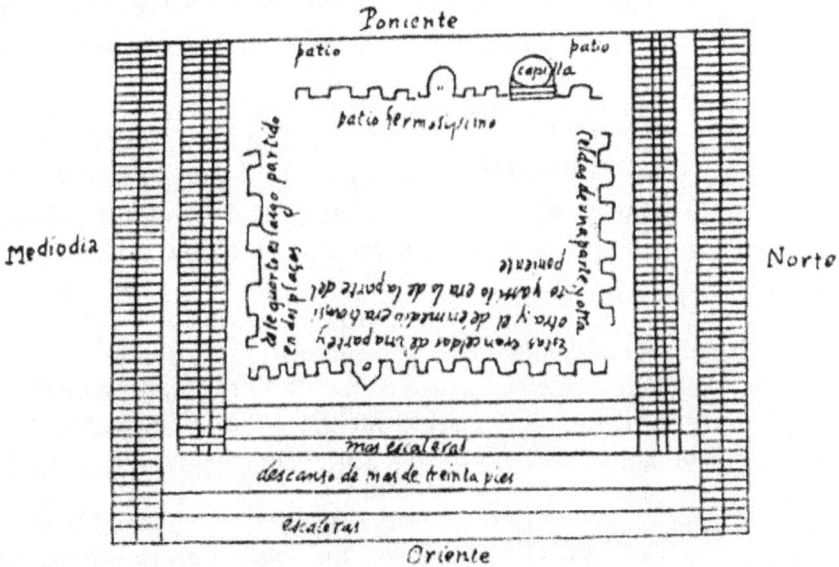

Éste es el borrón que he podido sacar del edificio, para cuyo entendimiento se ha de saber que éste es un asiento quebrado, de mucha grandeza, porque tiene más de dos carreras de caballo desde la parte del oriente. Comienza luego la escalera desde el suelo, y esta escalera será de siete escalones de la altura de los de Izamal. Las demás partes del mediodía, poniente y norte, se siguen de una pared fuerte y muy ancha. Todo aquel henchimiento del cuadro es de piedra seca, y en la parte llana torna a comenzar otra escalera por la misma parte del oriente, a mi parecer de veintiocho o treinta pies recogida dentro de otros tantos escalones igual de grandes. Hace el mismo recogimiento hacia la parte del mediodía y del norte, no del poniente, y síguense dos paredes fuertes hasta encontrar o juntarse con las del cuadro por la parte del poniente y así llegan hasta el peso de las escaleras, haciendo todo el henchimiento de en medio de piedra seca, que espanta tal altura y grandeza como allí hay de henchimiento a mano.

Después, en lo llano arriba, comienzan los edificios de esta manera: por parte del oriente se sigue un cuarto a la larga, recogido adentro hasta seis pies que no llega a los cabos, labrado de muy buena cantería y todo de celdas de una parte y de otra; de a 12 pies de largo y 8 de ancho; las puertas, en medio de cada una, no tienen señal de batientes ni manera de quicios para cerrarse, sino llanas, de su piedra muy labrada, y la obra trabada a maravilla y cerradas por lo alto todas las puertas, con tezas de piedra enteriza; tiene en medio un tránsito como arco de puente y por encima de las puertas de las celdas sale un releje de piedra labrada que (corre) a lo largo de todo el cuarto, sobre el cual salen hasta lo alto unos pilarejos, la mitad de ellos labrados redondos y la mitad metidos en la pared. Estos pilarejos seguían hasta lo alto de las bóvedas de que las celdas estaban hechas y cerradas por arriba. Por encima de estos pilaritos salía otro releje enrededor de todo el cuarto. Lo alto era de terrado, encalado muy fuerte como allá se hace con cierta agua de corteza de un árbol. Por la parte del norte había otro cuarto de celdas, tales como estas otras, salvo que el cuarto, con casi la mitad no era tan largo. Al poniente se seguían otra vez las celdas, y (cada) cuatro o cinco había un arco que atravesaba, como el de en medio del cuarto de oriente, todo el edificio, y luego un edificio redondo, algo alto, y luego otro arco, y lo demás eran celdas como las restantes. Este cuarto atraviesa todo el patio grande en buena parte menos de la mitad y así forma dos patios, uno por detrás, al poniente, y otro a su oriente, que viene a estar cercado de cuatro cuartos, el último de los cuales es muy diferente porque está hecho hacia el mediodía, de dos piezas cerradas con bóveda como las demás a la larga; la delantera de las cuales tiene un corredor de muy gruesos pilares cerrados por arriba con muy hermosas piedras labradas y enterizas. Por en medio va una pared sobre la que carga la bóveda de ambos cuartos, con dos puertas para entrar al otro cuarto. De manera que todo lo cierra por arriba un encalado.

Tiene este edificio, apartado de sí como dos buenos tiros de piedra, otro muy alto y hermoso patio en el cual hay tres cerros que de mampostería estaban bien labrados; y encima sus muy buenas capillas de la bóveda como solían y sabían ellos hacer. Tiene bien apartado de sí un tan grande y hermoso cerro que, con haberse edificado gran parte de la ciudad (con piedras) de él (para hacer las casas con) que la poblaron a la redonda, no sé si ha de verse jamás acabado.

El primer edificio de los cuatro cuartos nos dio el Adelantado Montejo a nosotros, hecho un monte áspero; limpiámosle y hemos hecho en él, con su propia piedra, un razonable monasterio todo de piedra, y una buena iglesia que llamamos la Madre de Dios. Hubo tanta piedra de los cuartos, que (aún) está entero el del mediodía y en parte los de los lados, y dimos mucha piedra a los españoles para sus casas, en especial para sus puertas y ventanas; tanta era su abundancia.

Los edificios del pueblo de Tikoh no son muchos ni tan suntuosos como algunos de estos otros, aunque eran buenos y lucidos, ni aquí yo hiciera mención de ellos salvo por haber habido en él una gran población de que adelante necesariamente se ha de hablar, y por eso se dejará ahora. Están estos edificios a tres leguas de Izamal al oriente, y a siete de Chicheniza.

Es pues Chicheniza un asiento muy bueno a diez leguas de Izamal y once de Valladolid, en la cual, según dicen los antiguos [indígenas], reinaron tres señores hermanos los cuales, según se acuerdan haber oído de sus pasados, vinieron a aquella tierra de la parte del poniente y juntaron en estos asientos gran población de pueblos y gentes, la cual rigieron algunos años en mucha paz y justicia.

Eran muy honradores de su dios y así edificaron muchos edificios y muy galanos, en especial uno, el mayor, cuya figura pintaré aquí como la pinté estando en él, para que mejor se entienda. Estos señores, dicen, vivieron sin mujeres, y en muy grande honestidad, y todo el tiempo que vivieron así, fueron muy estimados y obedecidos de todos. Después, andando el tiempo, faltó uno de ellos, el cual se debió morir, aunque [los indígenas] dicen que saltó de la tierra por la parte de Bac halal. Hizo la ausencia de éste, como quiera que ella fuese, tanta falta en los que después de él regían, que comenzaron luego a ser parciales en la república, y en sus costumbres tan deshonestos y desenfrenados que el pueblo los vino a aborrecer, en tal manera que los mataron y desbarataron y despoblaron dejando los edificios y el asiento harto hermoso porque está cerca de la mar, a diez leguas. Tiene muy fértiles tierras y provincias a la redonda. La figura del principal edificio es la siguiente:

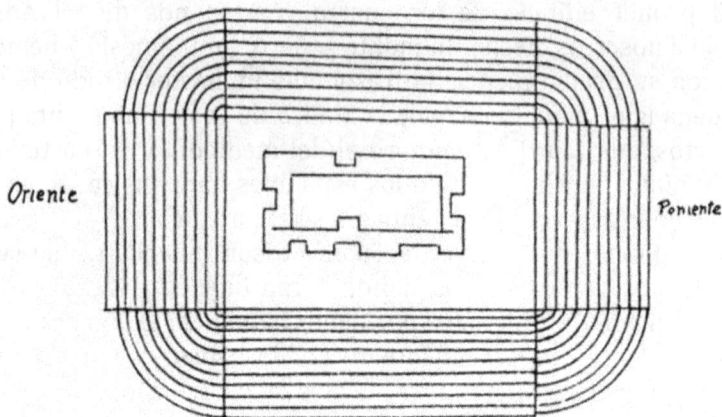

Este edificio tiene cuatro escaleras que miran a las cuatro partes del mundo, de treinta y tres pies de ancho y de noventa y un escalones cada una, que es muerte subirlas. Tienen en los escalones la misma anchura y altura que nosotros damos a los nuestros. Cada escalera tiene dos pasamanos bajos, al igual de los escalones, de dos pies de ancho, de buena cantería como lo es todo el edificio. Éste no está esquinado porque desde la halda del suelo, desde los pasamanos al contrario, se comienzan a labrar, como están pintados, unos cubos redondos que van subiendo a trechos y estrechando el edificio por muy galano orden. Había, cuando yo, le vi, al pie de cada pasamano, una fiera roca de sierpe de una pieza bien curiosamente labrada. Acabadas de esta manera las escaleras, queda en lo alto una placeta llana en la cual está un edificio hecho de cuatro cuartos. Los tres se andan a la redonda sin impedimento, y tiene cada uno puerta en medio, y están cerrados de bóveda. El cuarto del norte se anda por sí con un corredor de pilares gruesos. El de en medio, que había de ser como el patinico que hace el orden de los paños del edificio, tiene una puerta que sale al corredor del norte y está por arriba cerrado de madera y en él se quemaban los sahumerios. Hay en la entrada de esta puerta o del corredor, un a modo de armas esculpidas en una piedra que no pude entender bien.

Tenía este edificio otros muchos, y tiene hoy día a la redonda de sí, bien hechos y grandes, y todo el suelo que va de él a ellos encalado, y aún hay, en partes, memoria de los encalados, tan fuerte es la argamasa de que los hacen.

Tenía delante la escalera del norte, algo aparte, dos teatros de cantería, pequeños, de cuatro escaleras, enlosados por arriba, en que dicen representaban las farsas y comedias para solaz del pueblo. Va desde el patio, enfrente de estos teatros, una hermosa y ancha calzada

12

hasta un pozo como a dos tiros de piedra. En este pozo han tenido y tenían entonces, costumbre de echar hombres vivos en sacrificio a los dioses, en tiempo de seca, y pensaban que no morían aunque no los veían más. Echaban también otras muchas cosas de piedras de valor y que tenían preciadas. Y así, si esta tierra hubiera tenido oro fuera este pozo el que más parte de ello tuviera, según le han sido devotos [los indígenas]. Es pozo que tiene siete estados largos de hondo hasta el agua, de ancho más de cien pies, y redondo y de una peña tajada hasta el agua que es maravilla. Parece que tiene el agua muy verde y creo lo causan las arboledas de que está cercado, y es muy hondo; tiene encima de él, junto a la boca, un edificio pequeño donde hallé ídolos hechos a honra de todos los dioses principales de la tierra, casi como el Panteón de Roma. No sé si era esta invención antigua o de los modernos para toparse con sus ídolos cuando fuesen con ofrendas a aquel pozo. Hallé leones labrados de bulto, y jarras y otras cosas que no sé como nadie dirá que no tuvieron herramientas estas gentes. También hallé dos hombres de grandes estaturas, labrados de piedra, cada uno de una pieza, en carnes, cubierta su honestidad como se cubrían [los indígenas]. Tenían las cabezas por sí y con zarcillos en las orejas como los usaban [los indígenas], y hecha una espiga por detrás en el pescuezo que encajaba en un agujero hondo hecho para ello en el mismo pescuezo, y encajado, quedaba el bulto cumplido.

XLIII
Por qué cosas hacían otros sacrificios [los indígenas].

Las fiestas que en el calendario de esta gente atrás queda puesto, nos muestran cuáles y cuántas eran y para qué y cómo las celebraban. Pero porque eran sus fiestas sólo para tener gratos y propicios a sus dioses, sino era teniéndolos airados no (las) hacían más sangrientas; y creían estar airados cuando tenían necesidades o pestilencias o disensiones o esterilidades u otras semejantes necesidades; entonces no curaban de aplacar los demonios sacrificándoles animales, ni haciéndoles solamente ofrendas de sus comidas y bebidas o derramando su sangre y afligiéndose con velas y ayunos y abstinencias; mas olvidada toda natural piedad y toda ley de razón, les hacían sacrificios de personas humanas con tanta facilidad como si sacrificasen aves, y tantas veces cuantas los malvados sacerdotes o los chilanes les decían era menester, o a los señores se les antojaba o parecía. Y dado que en esta tierra, por no ser mucha la gente como en México, ni regirse ya después de la destrucción de Mayapán por una cabeza sino por muchas, no hacían así tan junta la matanza de hombres, ni por eso dejaban de morir miserablemente hartos, pues tenía cada pueblo autoridad de sacrificar los que el sacerdote o chilán o señor le parecía, y para hacerlo tenían sus públicos lugares en los templos como si fuera la cosa más necesaria del mundo a la conservación de la república. Después de matar en sus pueblos, tenían aquellos dos descomulgados santuarios de Chichenizá y Cuzmil donde infinitos pobres enviaban a sacrificar o despeñar al uno, y al otro a sacar los corazones; de las cuales miserias tenga a bien por siempre librarlos el señor piadoso que tuvo por bien hacerse sacrifico en la cruz al padre por todos.

¡Oh, señor, dios mío, hombre, ser y vida de mi alma, santa guía y camino cierto de mis costumbres, consuelo de mis consuelos, alegría interna de mis tristezas, refrigerio y descanso de mis trabajos! ¿Y qué me mandas tú, señor, que trabajo se puede llamar y no mucho mejor descanso? ¿A qué me obligas que yo no pueda muy cumplidamente hacer? ¿Por ventura, señor, ignoras la medida de mi vaso y la cantidad de mis miembros y la calidad de mis fuerzas? ¿Acaso, señor, me faltas tú en mis trabajos? ¿No eres tú cuidadoso padre de quien dice tu santo profeta en el salmo, "con él soy en la tribulación y trabajo, y yo le libraré de ella y le glorificaré"?

Señor, sí, tú eres, y tú eres aquel de quien dijo el profeta lleno de tu santísimo espíritu, que finges trabajo en tu mandamiento, y es así, señor, que los que no han gustado de la suavidad de la guarda y cumplimiento de tus preceptos, trabajo hallan en ellos; pero, señor, trabajo fingido es, trabajo temido es, trabajo de pusilánimes es, y témenlo los hombres que nunca acaban de poner la mano al arado de cumplirlos, que los que se disponen a la guarda de ellos, dulces los hallan, en pos del olor de sus ungüentos se van, su dulcedumbre los refrigera a cada paso, y muchos más gustos experimentan cada día (que les sabe discierne nadie), como otra reina de Saba; y así, señor, te suplico me des gracia que a ejemplo tuyo, dejada la casa de mi sensualidad y el reino de mis vicios y pecados, haga del todo experiencia de servirte y guardar tus santos mandamientos, para lo que en más me enseñare la experiencia de su guarda; que de sólo leerlos y tratarlos, halle yo el bien de tu gracia para mi alma, y así como creo ser tu yugo suave y leve, te hago gracias por haberme puesto debajo de su melena, y libre del (pecado) en que veo andan y han andado tantas muchedumbres de gentes, caminando para el infierno: lo cual es tan grave dolor que no sé a quién no quiebra el corazón ver la mortal pesadumbre e intolerable carga con que el demonio ha siempre llevado y lleva a los idólatras al infierno; y si esto, de parte del demonio que lo procura y hace, es crueldad grande, de parte de Dios es justísimamente permitido para que, pues si no se quieren regir por la luz de la razón que él les ha dado comiencen en esta vida a ser atormentados y a sentir parte del infierno que merecen, con los trabajosos servicios que al demonio de continuo hacen con muy largos ayunos y vigilias y abstinencias, con increíbles ofrendas y presentes de sus cosas y haciendas, con derramamientos continuos en su propia sangre, con graves dolores y heridas en sus cuerpos, y lo que es peor y más grave, con las vidas de sus prójimos y hermanos; y con todo esto nunca el demonio se harta y satisface de sus tormentos y trabajos, ni de llevarlos con ellos al infierno donde eternamente los atormenta; cierto, mejor se aplaca Dios y con menos tormentos y muertes se satisface: pues a voces dice y manda al Gran Patriarca Abraham que no extienda su mano para quitar la vida a su hijo, porque está su Majestad determinado a enviar al suyo al mundo y dejarle perder en la cruz la vida de veras, para que vean los hombres que para el hijo de Dios eterno es pesado el mandamiento de su padre, aunque a él (sea) muy dulce y fingido a los hombres de trabajo.

Por lo cual quiten ya los hombres la tibieza de sus corazones y el temor del trabajo de esta santa ley de Dios, pues es su trabajo fingido y en breve se vuelve dulcedumbre de las almas y de los cuerpos, cuanto más que, allende de que es digno Dios de ser muy servido y se lo debemos en justísima deuda, es todo para nuestro provecho, y no sólo eterno, sino aun temporal; y miremos todos los cristianos, especialmente los sacerdotes, que en esta vida es gran vergüenza y confusión, y en la venidera lo será mayor, ver que halle el demonio quien le sirva con increíbles trabajos para ir, en pago de ellos, al infierno, y que no halle

Dios apenas quien en guarda de tan suaves mandamientos le sirva fielmente para ir a la eterna gloria. Por lo cual, tú, sacerdote de Dios, dime si has mirado con advertencia el oficio de estos sacerdotes tristes del demonio, y de todos los que en las divinas letras hallamos lo fueron en los pasados tiempos, cuán enojosos y largos y muchos eran sus ayunos, más que los tuyos: qué tantos más continuos en las vigilias y en sus míseras oraciones que tú; cuán más curiosos y cuidadosos de las cosas de sus oficios que tú del tuyo; con cuánto mayor celo que tú entendían en enseñar sus pestíferas doctrinas, y si de esto te hallaras en alguna culpa, remédiala y mira que eres sacerdote del alto señor que con sólo el oficio te obliga a procurar vivir en limpieza y cuidado, limpieza del ángel cuanto más del hombre.

XLIV
Producción de la tierra.

Yucatán es una tierra la de menos tierra que yo he visto, porque toda ella es una viva laja, y tiene a maravilla poca tierra, tanto que habrá pocas partes donde se pueda cavar un estado sin dar en grandes bancos de lajas muy grandes. La piedra no es muy buena para labores delicadas, porque es dura y tosca; empero, tal cual es, ha sido para que de ella hayan hecho la muchedumbre de edificios que en aquella tierra hay; es muy buena para cal, de que hay mucha, y es cosa maravillosa que sea tanta la fertilidad de esta tierra sobre las piedras y entre ellas.

Todo lo que en ella hay y se da, se da mejor y más abundantemente entre las piedras que en la tierra, porque sobre la tierra que acierta a haber en algunas partes ni se dan árboles ni los hay, ni [los indígenas] en ella siembran sus simientes, ni hay sino yerbas; y entre las piedras y sobre ellas siembran y se dan todas sus semillas y se crían todos los árboles, y algunos tan grandes y hermosos que maravilla son de ver; la causa de esto creo que es haber más humedad y conservarse más en las piedras que en la tierra.

En esta tierra no se ha hallado hasta ahora ningún género de metal que ella de suyo tenga, y espanta (que) no habiendo con qué, se hayan labrado tantos edificios porque no dan [los indígenas] razón de las herramientas con que se labraron; pero ya que les faltaron metales, proveyolos Dios de una sierra de pedernal contigua a la sierra que según dije atraviesa la tierra, y de la cual sacaban piedras de que hacían los hierros de las lanzas para la guerra y los navajones para los sacrificios de los cuales tenían buen recaudo los sacerdotes; hacían los hierros para las saetas y aún los hacen, y así les servía el pedernal de metal. Tenían cierto azófar blanco con alguna poca mezcla de oro, de que hacían las hachuelas de fundición y unos cascabelazos con que bailaban, y una cierta manera de escoplillos con que hacían los ídolos y agujeraban las cerbatanas como esta figura del margen, que mucho usan la cerbatana y bien la tiran. Este azófar y otras planchas o láminas más duras, las traían a rescatar por sus cosas los de Tabasco para los ídolos, y no había entre ellos algún otro género de metal.

Según el sabio, una de las cosas a la vida del hombre más necesaria es el agua, y es tanto que sin ella ni la tierra produce sus frutos ni los hombres se pueden sustentar, y con haber faltado en Yucatán la abundancia de ríos que sus tierras vecinas tienen en mucha abundancia, porque sólo dos tienen, y el uno es el río de Lagartos que sale por un cabo de la tierra a la mar, y el otro el de Champotón, ambos salobres y de malas aguas, la proveyó Dios de muchas y muy lindas aguas, unas por industria y otras proveídas de naturaleza.

La naturaleza obró en esta tierra diferentemente en lo de los ríos y fuentes, que los ríos y las fuentes que en todo el mundo corren sobre la tierra, en ésta van y corren todos por sus meatos secretos por debajo de ella. Lo cual nos ha enseñado que casi toda la costa está llena de fuentes de agua dulce que nacen dentro en la mar y se puede de ellas, en muchas partes, coger agua como me ha acaecido a mí cuando de la menguante de la agua queda la orilla algo seca. En la tierra proveyó Dios de unas quebradas que [los indígenas] llaman zenotes, que llegan de peña tajada hasta el agua, en algunos de los cuales hay muy furiosas corrientes y acaece llevarse el ganado que cae en ellos, y todas estas salen a la mar de que se hacen las fuentes dichas.

Estos zenotes son de muy lindas aguas y muy de ver, que hay algunos de peña tajada hasta el agua y otros con algunas bocas que les creó Dios, o causaron algunos accidentes de rayos que suelen caer muchas veces, o de otra cosa; y por dentro con lindas bóvedas de peña fina y en la superficie sus árboles, de manera que en lo de arriba es monte y debajo zenotes, y hay algunos que puede caber y andar una carabela y otros más o menos. Los que éstos alcanzaban bebían de ellos; los que no, hacían pozos, y como se les había faltado herramienta para labrarlos, eran muy ruines. Pero ya no sólo les hemos dado industria para hacer buenos pozos sino muy lindas norias con estanques de donde, como en fuentes, toman el agua.

Hay también lagunas y todas son de agua salobre y ruin para beber y no son corrientes como zenotes. Tiene una cosa esta tierra en toda ella maravillosa en esto de los pozos, y es que en todas las partes de ella que se cave, salen muy buenas aguas de manantiales y algunos tan hermosos que se sume una lanza por ellos, y en todas las partes que se han cavado se ha hallado medio estado antes del agua un banco de conchas y caracolillos de la mar, de tantas diferencias y colores, grandes y chicos, como los que están a la orilla de la mar y la arena ya convertida en dura peña blanca. En Maní, pueblo del rey, cavamos un pozo grande para hacer una noria a [los indígenas] y al cabo de haber cavado siete u ocho estados en una peña fina, hallamos un sepulcro de siete buenos pies de largo, lleno de tierra bermeja muy fresca, y de huesos humanos, y todos estaban ya casi convertidos en piedra; faltaban dos o tres estados por llegar al agua y antes de ella había una bóveda hueca que crió allí Dios de manera que estaba el sepulcro metido dentro de la peña, y se podía andar por debajo hacia donde el agua; no pudimos entender cómo fuese esto si no es que digamos que aquel sepulcro se abrió allí por la parte de dentro, y después, con la humedad de la cueva y el mucho tiempo, vino a congelarse la peña y crecer y así cerrarse aquello.

Además de los dos ríos que he dicho hay en esta tierra, tiene una fuente a tres leguas de la mar, cerca de Campeche, y es salobre y no hay en toda la tierra otra ni otras aguas. [los indígenas] de hacia la sierra, por tener los pozos muy hondos, suelen en tiempo de las aguas hacer para sus casas concavidades en las peñas y allí recoger agua de la llovediza: porque en su tiempo llueven grandes y muy recios aguaceros y algunas veces con muchos truenos y relámpagos; los pozos todos y en especial los cercanos a la mar crecen y menguan cada día a la hora que crece y mengua la mar, lo cual muestra más claro ser todas las aguas ríos que corren debajo de la tierra hacia la mar.

Hay una ciénaga en Yucatán digna de memoria pues tiene más de setenta leguas de largo y es salina toda ella; comienza desde la costa de Ekab, que es cerca de la Isla de Mujeres, y síguese muy junto a la costa de la mar entre la misma costa y los montes, hasta cerca de Campeche; no es honda porque no le da lugar el no haber tierra, pero es mala de pasar yendo de los pueblos a la costa o viniendo de ella a los pueblos, por los árboles que tiene y mucho lodo. Esta ciénaga es salina que Dios ha criado allí de la mejor sal que yo he visto en mi vida, porque molida es muy blanca, y para sal dicen los que lo saben es tan buena, que sala más medio celemín de ella que uno de otras partes. Cría la sal Nuestro Señor en esta ciénaga del agua llovediza y no de la mar, que no le entra, porque entre la mar y la ciénaga va una costa de tierra a lo largo todo lo que dura ella, que la divide de la mar. En tiempo, pues, de aguas, se hincha esta ciénaga y se cuaja la sal dentro de la misma agua, en terrones grandes y pequeños que no parecen sino pedazos de azúcar cande. Después de pasadas las aguas cuatro meses o cinco, y ya que la laguna está algo enjuta, tenían [los indígenas] antiguamente costumbre de ir a sacar sal, la cual sacan cogiendo aquellos terrones dentro del agua y sacándolos a enjugar fuera. Tenían para esto sus lugares señalados en la propia laguna, que eran los más fértiles de sal y de menos lodo y agua, y acostumbraban a no hacer esta cosecha de la sal sin licencia de los señores, que a estos lugares de ella tenían, por cercanía, más acción; a los cuales todos los que por sal venían, hacían algún servizuelo o de la propia sal o de las cosas de sus tierras, y porque probó esto un principal llamado Francisco Euan, natural del pueblo de Caucel, y probó que el regimiento de la ciudad de Mayapán había puesto a sus antepasados en la costa, con cargo de ella y del repartimiento de la sal, la Audiencia de Guatemala les mandó, a los que a sus comarcas la fuesen a coger, dar ahora lo mismo. Cógese ya mucha en el tiempo de ella para llevar a México y a Honduras y a la Habana. Cría esta ciénaga, en algunas partes de ella, muy hermosos pescados y aunque no grandes, de muy buen sabor.

XLV
Peces de Yucatán.

No hay sólo pescado en la laguna pero es tanta la abundancia que en la costa hay, que casi no curan [los indígenas] de lo de la laguna, si no son los que no tienen aparejos de redes, que éstos suelen, con la flecha, como hay poca agua, matar mucho pescado; los demás hacen sus muy grandes pesquerías de que comen y venden pescado a toda la tierra.

Acostúmbranlo salar y asar y secar al sol sin sal, y tienen su cuenta cuál de estos beneficios ha menester cada género de pescado, y lo asado se conserva días, que se lleva a veinte y treinta leguas a vender, y para comerlo tórnanlo a guisar, y es sabroso y sano.

Los pescados que matan y hay en aquella costa son lisas muy excelentes y muy gordas; truchas, ni más ni menos en el color y pecas y sabor, y son más gordas y sabrosas de comer, y llámanse en la lengua uzcay; robalos muy buenos; sardinas, y con ellas acuden lenguados, sierras, caballas, mojarras e infinitas diversidades de otros pescados pequeños; hay muy buenos pulpos en la costa de Campeche; tres o cuatro castas de tollos muy buenos y sanos, y especialmente unos a maravilla sanos y en las cabezas diferentísimos de los otros que las tienen redondas y muy llanas que espanta, y por la parte de dentro la boca y en las orillas de lo redondo, los ojos: llámanse estos alipechpol. Matan unos pescados muy grandes que parecen mantas y hacen a trozos en salmuera en las orillas a la redonda, y es muy buena cosa (mas) no sé si es este pescado raya.

Hay muchos manatís en la costa entre Campeche y la Desconocida, de los cuales, allende del mucho pescado o carne que tienen, hacen mucha manteca y excelente para guisar de comer; de estos manatís se cuentan cosas de maravillar; en especial cuenta el autor de la Historia General de las Indias que crió en la Isla Española un señor indio uno en un lago, tan doméstico que venía a la orilla del agua en llamándolo por su nombre que le habían puesto, y que era "Matu". Lo que yo de ellos digo (es) que son tan grandes que se saca de ellos mucha más carne que de un buen becerro grande, y mucha manteca; engendran como los animales y tienen para ello sus miembros como hombre y mujer, y la hembra pare siempre dos y no más ni menos, y no pone huevos como los otros pescados; tienen dos alas como brazos fuertes con que nadan, el rostro tiene harto semejanza al buey y sácanle fuera del agua a pacer yerba a las orillas, y los suelen picar los murciélagos en una jeta redonda y llana que tienen, que les da vuelta al rostro, y mueren de ello porque son muy sanguíneos a maravilla y de cualquiera herida se desangran con el agua.

La carne es buena, especialmente fresca; con mostaza, es casi como buena vaca. Mátanlos [los indígenas] con arpones de esta manera: búscanlos en los esteros y partes bajas que no es pescado que sabe andar en hondo y llevan sus arpones atados en sus sogas con boyas al cabo; hallados, los arponean y suéltanles las sogas y las boyas y ellos con el dolor de las heridas huyen a una y otra parte por lo bajo y de poca agua, que jamás van a lo hondo de la mar ni saben, y como son tan grandes van turbando el cieno y tan sanguíneos vanse desangrando; y así con la señal del cieno los siguen en sus barquillas [los indígenas] y después los hallan con sus boyas y sacan. Es pesca de mucha recreación y provecho, porque son todos carne y manteca.

Hay otro pescado en esta costa al cual llaman ba, es ancho y redondo y bueno de comer, pero muy peligroso de matar o de topar con él, porque tampoco sabe andar en lo hondo y es amigo de andar en el cieno donde [los indígenas] lo matan con el arco y flecha; y si se descuidan andando con él o pisándolo en el agua, acude luego con la cola que la tiene larga y delgada y hiere con una sierra que tiene, tan fieramente, que no se puede sacar de donde la mete sin hacer muy mayor la herida, porque tiene los dientes al revés, de la manera que aquí está pintada.* De estas sierritas usaban [los indígenas] para cortar sus carnes en los sacrificios del demonio, y era oficio del sacerdote tenerlas, y así tenían muchas; son muy lindas porque son un hueso muy blanco y curioso hecho sierra así de aguda y delicada, que corta como cuchillo.

Hay un pescadillo pequeño tan ponzoñoso que nadie que lo come escapa de morir hinchado, todo muy en breve, y burla a algunos hartas veces, aunque es conocido en que es algo tardío en morir fuera del agua y se hincha mucho todo él. Hay muy gentiles ostiones en el río de Champotón y hay muchos tiburones en toda la costa.

XLVI
Iguanas y lagartos.

Demás de los pescados cuya morada son las aguas, hay algunas cosas que juntamente se sirven y viven en el agua y en tierra como son muchas iguanas, las cuales son como lagartos de España en la hechura y grandeza y en el color, aunque no son tan verdes; éstas ponen huevos en mucha cantidad y andan siempre cerca de la mar y de donde hay aguas, indiferentemente se guarecen en el agua y en la tierra, por lo cual las comen los españoles en tiempos de ayuno y la hallan muy singular comida y sana. Hay de éstas tantas, que ayudan a todos por la cuaresma; péscanlas [los indígenas] con lazos, encaramadas en los árboles y en agujeros de ellos, y es cosa increíble lo que sufren el hambre, que acaece estar vivas, después de tomadas, veinte y treinta días sin comer bocado y sin enflaquecer y he oído que hay experiencia hecha, que si les frotan las barrigas con arena engordan mucho. El estiércol de éstas es admirable medicina para curar nubes de los ojos, puesto fresco en ellas.

Hay tortugas a maravilla grandes, que las hay muy mayores que grandes rodelas y son de buen comer y tienen harto qué; ponen los huevos tan grandes como de gallina, y ponen ciento cincuenta y doscientos, haciendo en la arena, fuera del agua, un gran hoyo y cubriéndolos, después con la arena y allí salen las tortuguillas. Hay otras diferencias de tortugas en la tierra, por los montes secos y en las lagunas.

Un pescado vi en las costas, algunas veces, que por ser de concha todo, lo dejé para poner aquí. Es, pues, del grandor de una tortuga pequeña y cubierto por arriba de una concha delicada, redonda, de hermosa hechura y verde muy claro; tiene una cola de lo mismo de la concha, muy delgada, que parece punzón y larga como un jeme; por debajo tiene muchos pies y todo lleno de menudos huevos que no tiene qué comer de él sino huevos y cómenlos muchos [los indígenas]; llámanle en su lengua mex.

Hay muy fieros lagartos, los cuales aunque andan en el agua, salen y están mucho en tierra, y comen en tierra o la cabeza fuera del agua porque carecen de agallas y no pueden mascar dentro del agua. Es animal pesado y no se aparta mucho del agua y tiene furioso ímpetu en el acometer a algo, o en la huida. Es muy tragón, que cuentan de él cosas extrañas; y lo que yo sé es que uno nos mató, cerca de un monasterio, a un indio, bañándose en una laguna; y fue luego de allí a un rato un religioso con [los indígenas] a matarle a él y para matarle tomaron un perro no muy grande y metiéronle un fuerte palo por la boca hasta el sieso, hecho con sus puntas, y atáronle por las tripas del perro una muy

recia soga, y echando en la laguna el perro salió luego el lagarto y lo tomó
en los dientes y se lo tragó; y tragado tiró la gente que con el fraile iba y lo
sacaron con gran trabajo y dificultad atravesándosele el palo en el
cuerpo; abriéronle y halláronle la mitad del hombre en el buche a más del
perrillo. Estos lagartos engendran como los animales, y ponen huevos y
para ponerlos hacen grandes hoyos en la arena, muy cerca del agua, y
ponen trescientos huevos y más, grandes más que de aves, y déjanlos allí
hasta el tiempo que les ha Naturaleza enseñado que han de salir y
entonces ándanse por allí aguardando y salen los lagartillos de esta
manera: salen del huevo tan grandes como un palmo y están aguardando
la ola de la mar que bate cerca de ellos, y así como la sienten, saltan de su
lugar al agua y todos los que no alcanzan quedan muertos en la arena que
como son tan tiernos y ella está muy caliente del sol, abrásanse y mueren
luego. Los que alcanzan el agua escapan todos y comienzan luego a andar
por allí hasta que acudiendo los padres los siguen; de esta manera
escapan muy pocos aunque ponen tantos huevos, no sin divina
providencia que quiere sea más lo que nos aprovecha que lo que nos daña
y podría tanto perjudicar, como estas bestias, si todas saliesen a la luz.

XLVII
De la manera que hay de serpientes y otros animales ponzoñosos.

De culebras o serpientes es grande la diversidad que hay, de muchos colores y no dañosas; salvo dos castas de ellas que son muy ponzoñosas víboras, y mayores mucho que las de acá de España. Llámalas taxinchan. Otras hay también muy ponzoñas y muy grandes y con cascabel en las colas; otras muy grandes que se tragan un conejo o dos y no son dañosas, y es cosa de decir que hay [indígenas] que con facilidad toman unas y las otras sin recibir de ellas perjuicio.

Hay una casta de lagartijas mayores que las de acá, de las cuales es maravilla grande el temor que [los indígenas] tienen, porque según ellos dicen, en tocándola la persona, suda un sudorcillo el cual es mortal ponzoña. Hay muchos alacranes entre las piedras y no son tan ponzoñosos como los de acá de España. Hay un género de hormigas grandes cuya picada es mucho peor y duele y encona más que la de los alacranes, y tanto, que dura su enconación más del doble que la del alacrán, como yo he experimentado.

Hay dos géneros de arañas, la una muy pequeña y muy pestífera, la otra es muy grande y toda cubierta de espinitas muy delicadas, negras, que parecen vello y tiene en ellas la ponzoña, y así se guardan mucho de tocarlas [los indígenas] donde las hay.

Hay un gusanito colorado del cual se hace ungüento muy bueno, amarillo, para hinchazones y llagas, con no más de batirlos o amasarlos juntos y sirve de óleo para pintar los vasos y hace fuerte la pintura.

XLVIII
De las abejas y su miel y cera.

Hay dos castas de abejas y ambas son muy más pequeñas que las nuestras. Las mayores de ellas crían en colmenas, las cuales son muy chicas; no hacen panal como las nuestras sino ciertas vejiguitas como nueces de cera, todas juntas unas a otras, llenas de miel. Para castrarlas no hacen más que abrir la colmena y reventar con un palillo estas vejiguitas y así corre la miel y sacan la cera cuando les parece. Las demás crían en los montes, en concavidades de árboles y de piedras, y allí les buscan la cera de la cual y de miel abunda esta tierra mucho, y la miel es muy buena salvo que como es mucha la fertilidad del pasto de las abejas sale algo tocada del agua y es menester darle un hervor al fuego y con dárselo queda muy buena y de mucha duración. La cera es buena salvo que es muy humosa y nunca se ha acertado cual sea la causa, y en unas provincias es muy más amarilla por razón de las flores. No pican estas abejas ni hacen (nada) cuando las castran mal.

XLIX
La flora de Yucatán.

Mucha es, y muy de notar, la diversidad de yerbas y flores que a Yucatán ornan en sus tiempos, así en los árboles como en las yerbas y muchas de ellas a maravilla lindas y hermosas y de diversos colores y olores, las cuales, allende el ornato con que a los montes y campos atavían, dan abundantísimo mantenimiento a las abejitas para su miel y cera. Pero entre ellas pondré aquí algunas, así por su preciosidad de olor y hermosura, como por el provecho que de ellas los moradores de aquellas tierras tienen.

Hay ajenjos muy más frescos y olorosos que los de acá y de más largas y delgadas hojitas y críanlos [los indígenas] para sus olores y recreación, y he visto que se hacen más hermosos con echarles las mujeres indígenas, al pie, cernada.

Hay una yerba de muy anchas hojas y de altas y gordas ramas, de singular frescura y fertilidad, porque de pedazos de las ramas se dan tanto, que crecen [a] la manera y muchedumbre de las mimbreras, aunque en nada les son de comparar; tratada un poco la hoja entre las manos, tiene el verdadero olor del trébol, aunque lo pierde después de seca; es muy buena para frescura de los templos en las fiestas, y [para] esto sirve.

Hay tanta albahaca, que están los montes llenos de ella en algunas partes, y con nacer en aquellas peñas es muy fresca, hermosa y olorosa, aunque no se compara a la que se cría en las huertas, llevada de acá, que es cosa de ver lo que cría y ensancha cada pie.

Hay una flor que llaman *tixzula* del más delicado olor que yo he olido y mucho más que los jazmines; es blanca y la hay morada clara, y [como] su tronco es de cebollas gordas se podría traer a España. Es, pues de esta manera: echan sus cebollas unas espadañas altas y gruesas muy frescas, que duran todo el año y dan en medio una vez al año, un mástil verde ancho como de tres dedos, y gordo y tan largo como las espadañas; y en el cabo de este mástil salen las flores en un manojo, cada una de un jeme de largo con [todo y] pezón, abiertas, y ciérralas por lo bajo una tela blanca, delicada, y en medio tienen unas telitas amarillas [y estas flores son] a maravilla de hermosas de blanco y amarillo. Cortado este vástago y puesto en un jarro de agua, dura con suave olor muchos días, porque no se abren las flores juntas, sino poco a poco.

Hay unas azucenitas muy blancas y olorosas y que duran mucho en agua, y fáciles de traer acá, porque son también de cebolla y en todo semejantes a las azucenas, salvo que el olor es más suave y no dañoso a la cabeza, y no tienen en medio lo amarillo de las azucenas: Hay una rosa llamada *ixlaul* que me han dicho que es de mucha hermosura y olor.

Hay también un género de árboles que llaman *nicté* que llevan muchas rosas blancas y otras amarillas y otras, en medio, moradas: son de mucha frescura y olor y hacen de ellas galanos ramilletes y los que quieren, [hacen] letuario. Hay una flor que llaman *Kom*, la cual es de mucho olor y arde de gran calor cuando huele; podríase fácilmente traer acá, y son sus hojas a maravilla frescas y anchas. Sin estas flores y yerbas olorosas hay otras muy provechosas y medicinales entre las cuales hay dos maneras de yerba-mora muy fresca y muy linda.

Hay mucha doradilla y culantrillo y una yerba con cuyas hojas cocidas y agua se quitan a maravilla las hinchazones de los pies y piernas. Hay otra muy singular para curar llagas viejas que llaman *iaxpalialché*. Hay también otra que tiene el mismo sabor del hinojo y se come y es muy buena para cocer agua y para curar llagas, puesta así cruda como la pasada. Hay en lo de *Bac-halar* zarzaparrilla.

Tienen cierta yerba que crían en los pozos y en otras partes, triangulada como la juncia, pero muy más gorda, de la cual hacen sus ceras y la suelen teñir de colores y hácenlas muy lindas a maravilla. Tienen una yerba silvestre, que también la crían en sus casas, y es mejor, de la cual sacan su manera de cáñamo de que hacen infinitas cosas para su servicio. También crían en algunos árboles, sin ser de su cosecha, un cierto género de yerbas las cuales echan unas frutas como pequeños cohombros, de los cuales se hacen sus gomas o colas con que pegan lo que han menester.

Las simientes que para la humana sustentación tienen, son: muy buen maíz y de muchas diferencias y colores, de lo cual cogen mucho y hacen trojes y guardan en silos para los años estériles. Hay dos castas de habas pequeñas, las unas negras y las otras de diversos colores, y otra que han llevado los españoles, blanquillas y pequeñas. Hay de su pimienta; muchas diferencias de calabazas, algunas de las cuales son para sacar pepitas para hacer guisados, otras para comer asadas y cocidas y otras para vasos de sus servicios; tienen ya melones, y muy buenos, y calabazas de España; los hemos puesto a coger mijo, que es buen mantenimiento; tiene una fruta a maravilla fresca y sabrosa que se siembra y la fruta es la raíz que nace como nabo gordo y redondo: cómense crudas con sal; la otra raíz que nace debajo de tierra sembrándola, que es grande mantenimiento, y es de muchas diferencias, que hay moradas, amarillas y blancas, cómense cocidas y asadas y son buena comida, y tiran algo a castañas, y ayudan, asadas, a beber. Hay otros dos géneros de raíces y son mantenimiento de [los indígenas]. Otras dos raíces silvestres hay que se parecen algo a las dos que primero he dicho, y ayudan en tiempos de necesidad de hambre a [los indígenas], que sin ella no curan de ellas. Tienen un arbolillo de blandas ramas y que tiene mucha leche, las hojas del cual se comen guisadas, y son como berzas de comer y buenas con mucho tocino gordo. Plántanlo [los indígenas] luego do quiera van a morar, y en todo el año tiene hoja que cogerle. Hay muy frescas achicorias, y criábanlas en las heredades aunque no las saben comer.

Cosa es de mucho alabar a Dios con el profeta que dice: "admirable es, Señor, tu nombre en toda la tierra", por la muchedumbre de árboles que en esta tierra Su Majestad crió, todos tan desemejantes de los nuestros, que hasta hoy [no se ha visto uno que conozca, digo en Yucatán, que fuera sí he visto, y de todos tienen sus servicios y provechos [los indígenas] y aun los españoles. Hay un árbol de cuya fruta, que es como una calabaza redonda hacen [los indígenas] sus vasos, y son muy buenos y hácenlos ellos muy pintados y galanos. De esta misma casta hay otro que lleva la fruta más pequeña y muy dura y hacen de ella otros vasillos para ungüentos y otros servicios. Hay otro, el cual lleva una frutilla como avellana de cuesco, de la cual se hacen buenas cuentas, y con la cáscara se lava la ropa como un jabón, y así hace su espuma.

Criaban mucho el árbol del incienso para los demonios, y sacábanselo hiriendo con una piedra el árbol en la corteza para que allí corriese aquella goma o resina; es árbol fresco, alto y de buena sombra y hoja, pero su flor hace negra la cera donde lo hay. Hay un árbol que crían en los pozos, muy hermoso de alto, y fresco de hoja, y que es maravilla lo que extiende sus ramas, las cuales nacen en el tronco por mucho orden, que nacen de tres en tres o más, a trozos, a la redonda del árbol, y así se van extendiendo ellas y la guía creciendo.

Hay cedros, aunque no de los finos. Hay una casta de palo algo amarillo y vetoso como encina, a maravilla fuerte y de mucha dur[ez]a y tan recio, que lo hallamos en las puertas de los edificios de Izamal, puesto por batientes y cargada la obra toda sobre él. Hay otro, fortísimo, y hacían de él los arcos y las lanzas y es de color leonado. Otro hay de color anaranjado oscuro, de que hacían bordones; es muy fuerte y creo se dice *esbrasil.* Hay muchos árboles de los que dicen son buenos para la enfermedad de bubas, y llámanle *zon.* Hay un árbol que lleva leche la cual es rejalgar y llaga cuanto toca, y su sombra es muy pestífera, especial [mente] si se duerme a ella. Hay otro que todo él está lleno de pares de espinas largas y muy duras y gordas, que no hay ave que en él repose jamás ni se pueda en él asentar; tiene unas espinas agujereadas por el tronco y llenas siempre de hormigas. Hay un árbol de muy gran altura y grandeza; lleva una fruta como algarrobas llena de unos piñones negros, y que en tiempo de necesidad hacen de ella comida [los indígenas], y con sus raíces hacen cubos para sacar agua de los pozos y norias.

Otros árboles hay de cuyas cortezas hacen [los indígenas] cubillos para sacar agua para sí, y otros de que hacen las sogas, y otros, de cuyas cortezas majadas, hacen un caldo para bruñir con él los encalados, y los hace muy fuertes. Hay muy hermosas moreras y es buena madera, y tienen otros tantos árboles y de todo servicio y provecho, que espanta. Tienen en los campos y montes muchas diferencias de mimbres, de los cuales hacen cestas de todas maneras y con los cuales atan sus casas y cuanto han menester, y es muy grande a maravilla el servicio que de esto tienen. Hay un árbol cuya leche es singular medicina para encarnar los dientes. Hay otro que lleva cierta fruta grande, llena de lana mejor para almohadas que las estopas de la Alcarria.

Temiendo hacer agravio a la fruta o sus árboles los he acordado poner por sí, y primero diré del vino como cosa que [los indígenas] mucho estimaban y por eso lo plantaban casi todos en sus corrales o espacios de sus casas. Es árbol feo y sin más fruto que hacer de sus raíces y miel y agua, su vino. Hay en esta tierra ciertas parras silvestres que llevan uvas comestibles; hay muchas en la costa de *Kupul*. Hay ciruelos de muchas diferencias de ciruelas y algunas muy sabrosas y sanas y diferentísimas de las nuestras, que tienen poca carne y gran cuesco, al revés de las que acá hay; a qué comprar [las] echa este árbol las frutas antes que las hojas; y sin flor, sino la fruta. Hay muchos plátanos y los han llevado los españoles, que no los había antes. Hay un árbol muy grande, el cual lleva una fruta grande, algo larga y gorda cuya carne es colorada, y muy buena de comer; no echa flor sino la propia fruta, muy pequeñita y va creciendo muy poco a poco. Hay otro árbol muy frondoso y hermoso y que nunca se le cae la hoja, y sin echar flor, echa una fruta de tanta y más dulzura que la de arriba, pequeña, muy golosa y gustosa de comer y muy delicada, y hay unos mejores que otros, y tanto mejores que serían muy preciados si los tuviésemos: llámanlos en la lengua *Ya*. Hay otro muy hermoso y fresco árbol que nunca pierde la hoja y lleva unos higuillos sabrosos que llaman *Ox*. Hay otro árbol a maravilla hermoso y fresco y lleva la fruta como huevos grandes. Cógenla verde [los indígenas] y madúranla en ceniza, y madura, queda a maravilla y al comerla es dulce y empalaga como yemas de huevo. Otro árbol lleva otra fruta así amarilla y no tan grande como esta otra y más blanda y dulce que ella, la cual comida, queda el cuesco como blando erizo todo, que es de ver. Hay otro muy fresco y hermoso árbol que lleva una fruta ni más ni menos que las avellanas con su cáscara; tienen debajo [de] aquella cáscara una fruta como guindas, y su cuesco [es] grande; llámanlas [los indígenas] *Vayam* y los españoles *Guayas*. Hay una fruta que los españoles han llevado, de buen comer y sana, que llaman *Guayabas*.

En las sierras hay dos géneros de árboles. El uno lleva unas frutas tan grandes como una buena pera, muy verdes, y de gorda corteza, las cuales maduran aporreándolas todas en una piedra, y son después de muy singular sabor. El otro lleva unas frutas muy grandes, de la hechura de las piñas, y tienen gustoso comer, que son aguanosas y acedas, y tienen muchos cuescos, pequeños, pero no son sanas. Hay un árbol el cual se da siempre en los rasos, y nunca entre los árboles sino solos ellos, cuya corteza es muy buena para adobar cueros y sirve [como] zumaque; lleva una frutilla amarilla sabrosa y golosa mucho para las mujeres. Hay un árbol muy grande y fresco al cual llaman [los indígenas] *On*; lleva una fruta como calabacillas grandezuelas de gran suavidad que parece a sabor de manteca y es mantecosa, y es de muy gran mantenimiento y substancia. Tiene gran cuesco y delicada cáscara, y cómese cortado [en] rebanadas como melón y con sal

Hay unos cardos muy espinosos y feos, y crecen a trozos siempre pegados a otros árboles, revueltos con ellos. Éstos llevan una fruta cuya corteza es colorada y semejante algo a la hechura de la alcachofa y blanda de quitar y sin ninguna espina. La carne que dentro tiene es blanca y llena de muy pequeños granos negros. Es dulce y delicada a maravilla y aguanosa que se deshace en la boca; cómese a ruedas como naranjas y con sal, y no hallan [los indígenas] tantas por los montes cuantas comen los españoles.

Hay un árbol fofo y feo aunque grande, que lleva cierta manera de fruta llena de tripas amarillas muy sabrosas y cosquezuelos como cañamones y muy mayores, los cuales son muy sanos para la orina. De esta fruta hacen buena conserva y echa el árbol la hoja después de pasada la fruta. Hay un árbol algo espinoso pequeño, el cual lleva una fruta de hechura de delgados pepinos y algo larga. Tiene alguna similitud su sabor con el cardo, y cómese así, con sal, partida en rebanadas, y los cuescos son como los del cohombro, muchos y tiernos. Si acierta a tener esta fruta algún agujero por algún accidente estando en el árbol, en el se le recoge una gomilla [de] muy fino olor de algalia. Hay otro árbol cuya flor es asaz de suave olor, y cuya fruta es la que acá en España llaman del manjar blanco, y hay muchas diversidades de ellos en el llevar fruta buena y mejor.

Hay un arbolito que suelen [los indígenas] criar en sus casas, el cual lleva unos erizos como las castañas, aunque no son tan grandes ni tan ásperos. Ábrense cuando están en sazón y tienen dentro unos granillos de los cuales usan; aun los españoles, para dar color a los guisados, como lo da el azafrán, y [es] tan fino el color que mancha mucho. Bien creo se me deben quedar más frutas, pero todavía diré de la de las palmas, de las cuales hay dos castas. Las unas sirven sus ramas [para] cubrir las casas, y son muy altas y delgadas, y llevan unos muy grandes racimos de una golosilla fruta negra como garbanzos [a las que] son muy aficionadas las mujeres indígenas. Las otras son unas palmas bajas y muy espinosas, y no sirve su hoja de nada, que es muy cortilla y rara. Llevan unos grandes racimos de una fruta redonda, verde, tan grande como huevos de paloma. Quitada la cáscara le queda un cuesco de gran dureza, y quebrado, sale de él una pepita redonda tan grande como una avellana, muy sabrosa y provechosa en tiempos estériles, que hacen de ella la comida caliente que beben en las mañanas, y a falta, se guisaría con su leche, que es como de las almendras, cualquier manjar.

Cógese mucho algodón a maravilla, y dáse en todas las partes de la tierra, de lo cual hay dos castas: la una siembran cada año, y no dura más que aquel año su arbolito, y es muy pequeño; la otra dura el árbol cinco o seis años y [en] todos da sus frutos, que son unos capullos como nueces con cáscara verde, los cuales se abren en cuatro partes a su tiempo y allí tiene el algodón.

Solíase coger grana, y dicen que era de la mejor de las Indias, por ser tierra seca, y todavía cogen en algunas partes alguna, [los indígenas]. Colores hay de muchas diversidades, hechos de tintas de algunos árboles, y de flores, y porque [los indígenas] no han sabido perfeccionarlos con las gomas para que les den el temple que han menester para que no desdigan, desdicen. Pero los que cogen la seda han ya buscado remedios y dicen se darán tan perfectos como en las partes que más perfectos se dan.

L
Aves de la tierra y el mar.

La abundancia que tiene esta tierra de aves esa maravilla grande, y tan diversas, que es mucho alabar al que de ellas las hinchió como de bendición. Tienen aves domésticas y que crían en las casas como son sus gallinas y gallos en mucha cantidad, aunque son penosos de criar. Hanse dado a criar aves de España, gallinas, y crían muchas a maravilla, y en todos los tiempos del año hay pollos de ellas. Crían algunas palomas mansas, de las nuestras, y (se) multiplican mucho. Crían para la pluma cierta casta de anadones blancos grandes, que creo les vinieron del Perú, y así les pelan muchas veces las barrigas, y quieren aquella pluma para las labores de sus ropas. Hay muchas diversidades de pájaros y muchos muy lindos, y entre ellos hay dos castas de tortolillas muy saladas, y las unas muy chiquitas y domésticas para criar, mansas. Hay un pajarito pequeño, de tan suave canto como el ruiseñor, que llaman Ixyalchamil; anda en las paredes de las casas que tienen huertas y en los árboles de ellas. Hay otro pájaro grande y muy lindo, de color verde muy oscuro, que no tiene en la cola más de dos plumas largas, y con no más de la mitad, y al cabo, (unos) pelos en ellas, y su morar es en los edificios, y no anda sino a las mañanas. Hay otros pájaros que en las travesuras y cuerpo son como las picazas y grandes gritadores a la gente que pasa por los caminos, que no la dejan ir secreta(mente).Hay muchos avioncillos [sic] o golondrinas, y yo he creído que son aviones porque no crían en las casas como las golondrinas. Hay un pájaro grande y de muchos colores y hermosura el cual tiene gran pico y muy fuerte, y anda siempre en los árboles secos, asido con las uñas, agujereando las cortezas aherrojadas con el pico tan recio que se oye buena pieza, para sacar los gusanos de la carcoma, de los cuales se mantiene; y es tanto lo que agujerean estos pájaros, que están los árboles que crían estos gusanos, de arriba abajo, hechos una criba de agujeros. Hay muchas aves del campo, buenas todas para comer, que hay tres maneras de muy lindas palomitas pequeñas. Hay unas aves en todo semejantes a las perdices de España, salvo que son de muy altas piernas, aunque coloradas, y tienen ruin comer; son, empero, a maravilla domésticas, si se crían en casa. Hay muchas codornices a maravilla, y son algo mayores que las nuestras, y de singular comer; vuelan poco y tománlas [los indígenas] con perros, encaramadas en los árboles, con lazos que les echan al pescuezo, y es muy gustosa caza. Hay muchos faisanes pardillos y pintados y de razonable tamaño, y no tales para Comer como los de Italia. Hay un pájaro grande como las gallinas de allá que llaman Cambul, muy hermoso a maravilla y de gran denuedo y buen comer. Hay otro que llaman Cox, tan grande como él, de furioso paso y meneo, y son los machos negros todos como un azabache, y tienen unas coronas muy lindas de plumas, crespas, y los párpados de los ojos amarillos y muy lindos. Hay muchos pavos que aunque no son de tan hermosas plumas como los de acá de España, las tienen muy galanas y son a maravilla hermosos, y tan grandes como los gallos de [los indígenas] y de tan buen comer. A todas las grandes matan [los indígenas], en los árboles, con las flechas, y a todas les hurtan los huevos y los (empollan) sus gallinas, y se crían muy domésticas. Hay tres o cuatro castas de papagayos pequeños y grandes y tantas banda(da)s de ellos, que hacen mucho daño a las sementeras. Hay otras aves nocturnas, como son las lechuzas, mochuelos, y gallinas ciegas, que es cosa de pasatiempo caminar de noche pues se ven grandes piezas en el camino, poniéndose a vuelos delante de los hombres. Amohinan mucho a [los indígenas] y tienen las por agüero, y lo mismo tienen a otros pájaros. Hay unas aves muy carniceras que llaman los españoles auras y [los indígenas] kuch, las cuales son negras y tienen el pescuezo y cabeza como las gallinas de allá, y el pico larguillo con un garabato. Son muy sucias; casi siempre andan en los establos en lugares de la purgación del vientre comiéndolas y buscando carnes muertas para comer. Es cosa averiguada no habérsele hasta ahora conocido nido ni saber dónde crían por lo cual dicen algunos (que) viven vidas de doscientos años y más, y otros creen (que son) los verdaderos cuervos. Huelen tanto la carne muerta que para hallar [los indígenas] los venados que matan y se les huyen heridos, no tienen remedio sino subidos en altos árboles mirar adonde acuden estas aves, y es cierto hallar allí su caza. De aves de rapiña esa maravilla mucha la diversidad que hay, porque hay águilas pequeñas, hay muy lindos azores y muy grandes cazadores, hay gavilanes muy hermosos y mayores que los de acá de España. Hay alcotanes y sacres, y otros que, como no soy cazador, no tengo memoria. En el mar es cosa que admira la infinidad, la variedad y la diversidad y muchedumbre que hay de aves y pájaros, y la hermosura de cada una en sus géneros. Hay unos pájaros tan grandes como avestruces, pardos y de mayor pico; andan siempre en el agua buscando que pescar y así como sienten al pescado, álzanse en el aire y caen con gran ímpetu sobre la pesca con aquel picazo y pescuezo, y jamás echan lance vacío, y quédanse, en haciendo el golpe, nadando y tragando al pez vivo sin más lo guisar ni escamar. Hay unos pájaros grandes, flacos y que vuelan mucho y muy alto, los cuales dividen la cola en sus dos puntas, la enjundia de los cuales esa maravilla medicinal para señales de heridas y para pasmo de miembros por causa de heridas. Hay unos anadones que se sustentan grandísimo rato debajo del agua, para pescar de comer, y son muy sueltos y tienen en el pico un garfio con que pescan.

Hay otros andencitos pequeños y de mucha hermosura que se llaman Maxix; son muy mansitos y se crían en casa, y no se saben huir. Hay muchas maneras de garzas y garcetas, unas blancas, otras pardas, unas grandes, otras pequeñas; en las Lagunas de Términos hay muchas encarnadas muy claras que parecen de color de polvo de grana, y tantas maneras de pajarillos chicos y grandes, que porfíen admiración su muchedumbre y diversidad, y más el verlos a todos cuidadosos de buscar de comer en aquella playa, unos entrando tras la ola en la reventazón del mar, y después huyendo de ella, otros buscando comida a las orillas, otros quitándola a otros con llegar más presto a ella, y lo que más admira: ver que a todos los provee Dios (y) que los hinche de bendición.

De muchos animales han carecido [los indígenas]; y especialmente han carecido de los que más necesarios son para el servicio del hombre; pero tenían otros de los más, de los cuales se aprovechaban para su mantenimiento, y ninguno de ellos era doméstico salvo los perros, los cuales no saben ladrar ni hacer mal a los hombres, ya la caza sí, que encaraman las codornices y otras aves y siguen mucho (a) los venados y algunos son grandes rastreado res. Son pequeños y comían [los indígenas] por fiesta, y yo creo se afrentan y tienen (hoy) por poquedad comerlos. Dicen que tenían muy buen sabor. Hay dantas en sólo un cornijal de la tierra que está detrás de las sierras de Campeche; y hay muchas, y han me dicho [los indígenas] que son de muchos colores, que hay rucias y overas, bayas y castañas, y muy blancas y negras. Andan más en este pedazo de tierra que en toda ella, porque es animal muy amigo de(l) agua y hay por allí muchas lagunas de aquellos montes y sierras. Es animal del tamaño de medianas mulas, muy ligero y tiene zapata hendida como el buey, y una trompilla en el hocico en que guarda agua. Tenían [los indígenas] por gran valentía matarlas y duraba para memoria el pellejo, o partes de él, hasta los biznietos, como lo vi yo; llámanla Tzimin, y por ellas han puesto nombre a los caballos. Hay leoncillos y tigres, y matánlos [los indígenas] con el arco, encaramados en los árboles. Hay un cierto género de oso o quier [sic] que es de maravilla amigo de castrar colmenas. Es pardo con uñas manchas negras y largo de cuerpo y corto de piernas y cabecirredondo.

Hay cierta casta de cabrillas monteses, pequeñas y muy ligeras y hosquillas de color. Hay puercos, animales pequeños y muy diferentes de los nuestros, que tienen el ombligo en el lomo y hieden mucho. Hay muchos venados que es maravilla, y son pequeños y la carne de buen comer. Conejos hay infinitos en todo semejantes a los nuestros, salvo el hocico que lo tienen largo y no nada romo, sino como de carnero; son grandes y de muy buen comer. Hay un animalito tristísimo de su natural y anda siempre en las cavernas y escondrijos, y de noche; y para cazarlo le arman [los indígenas] cierta trampa y en ella le cogen; es semejante a la liebre y anda asaltos y encogido. Tiene los dientes delanteros muy largos y delgados, la colilla aun menor que la liebre y el color xeloso [sic] y muy sombrío y es de maravilla manso y amable y llámase Zub.

Hay otro animalito pequeño, como un lechoncillo recién nacido, y así (tiene) las manezuelas y el hocico y (es) gran hozeador, el cual está todo cubierto de graciosas conchas que no parece sino caballo encubertado, con sólo las orejuelas y los pies y manos fuera, y su pescuezo y testera cubiertos de conchas; es muy bueno de comer y tierno.

Hay otros animales como perrillos pequeños; tienen la cabeza de hechura de puerco y larga cola, y son de color ahumado y a maravilla torpes; tanto, que los toman muchas veces de la cola. Son muy golosos y andan de noche en las casas y no se les escapa gallina en poco a poco. Paren las hembras catorce y dieciocho hijuelos como coma rejuelas y sin ningún abrigo de pelo y a maravilla torpecillos; y proveyó Dios a las madres de una extraña bolsa en la barriga en que los amparan, porque le nace a todo lo largo en la barriga, por cada parte y encima de las tetas, un cuero, y cuando lo junta uno con otro, quedan cerradas las tetas, y cuando quiere lo abre, y allí reciben los hijos, cada uno, el pezón de la teta en la boca, y cuando los tienen todos asidos échales aquellas ijadas o cueros encima y apriétalos tan fuertemente que ninguno se le cae, y con ellos, así cargada, va por ahí a buscar de comer; cría los así hasta que tienen pelo y pueden andar.

Hay zorras en todo como las de acá, salvo que no son tan grandes ni tienen tan buena cola. Hay un animal que llaman Chu a maravilla travieso, tan grande como un perrillo, de hocico como lechón. Críanlo las mujeres indígenas, y no les dejan cosa que no les hozen y trastornen, y es cosa increíble que son a maravilla amigos de burla con las mujeres indígenas, y las espulgan y se llegan siempre a ellas, y no pueden ver al hombre más que a la muerte. Hay muchos de éstos y andan siempre a manadas en hilo, uno tras otro, encajados los hocicos (de) los unos debajo de la cola de los otros, y destruyen mucho la heredad de maíz donde entran.

Hay un animalito como ardilla, blanco y de unas conchitas amarillas oscuras cercado alrededor, que llaman Pay, el cual se defiende de los que le siguen o dañan con orinarse, y es de tan horrible hedor lo que echa, que no hay quien lo pueda sufrir ni cosa en que caiga se puede más traer. Hánme dicho que no es aquello orina sino un sudorcillo que trae en una bolsita detrás. Sea lo que fuere, sus armas le defienden, y por maravilla matan uno de ellos [los indígenas]. Hay muchas ardillas muy lindas, y topos y comadrejas y muchos ratones como los de España, salvo que sonde muy largos hocicos.

LII
Conclusión.

No han [los indígenas] perdido sino ganado mucho con la ida de la nación española, aun en lo que es menos, aunque es mucho, acrecentándoseles muchas cosas de las cuales han de venir, andando los tiempos, a gozar por fuerza, y ya comienzan a gozar y usar de muchas de ellas. Hay ya muchos y buenos caballos y muchas mulas y machos; los asnos se dan mal, y creo lo ha causado el regalarlos, porque sin falta es bestia recia y que la daña el regalo. Hay muchas y muy hermosas vacas, puercos muchos, carneros, ovejas, cabras y de nuestros perros que merecen su servicio, y que con ellos se ha, en las Indias, hecho contarlos entre las cosas provechosas. Gatos que son muy provechosos y allá necesarios, y los quieren mucho [los indígenas]. Gallinas y palomas, naranjas, limas, cidras, parras, granadas, higos, guayabos y dátiles, plátanos, melones y las demás legumbres; y sólo los melones y calabazas se dan de su simiente, que las demás es menester simiente fresca de México. Dáse ya seda y es muy buena.

Hanles ido herramientas y el uso de los oficios mecánicos, y dánseles muy bien. El uso de la moneda y de otras muchas cosas de España, que aunque [los indígenas] habían pasado y podido pasar sin ellas, viven sin comparación con ellas más como hombres y más ayudados a sus trabajos corporales y a la relevación de ellos que según la sentencia del filósofo, el arte ayuda a la naturaleza.

No ha dado Dios acrecentamiento a [los indígenas] con la nuestra nación española de las cosas dichas tan necesarias al servicio del hombre, que por solas ellas no pagan con lo que dan o darán a los españoles, tan solamente; pero les han ido sin paga las que no se pueden comprar ni merecer, que son la justicia y cristiandad y paz en que ya viven; por lo cual deben más a España y a sus españoles, y principalmente a los muy católicos reyes de ella—que con tan continuo cuidado y con tan grande cristiandad de estas dos cosas los han proveído y los proveen—, que a sus primeros fundadores, malos padres que los engendraron en pecado e hijos de ira, que la cristiandad los engendra en gracia y para gozar la vida eterna. Sus primeros fundadores no les supieron dar orden (para que) careciesen de (los) errores tantos y tales como en los que han vivido. La justicia los ha sacado de ellos mediante la predicación, y ella los ha de guardar no tornen a ellos; y si tornaren, los ha de sacar de ellos con razón, pues se puede gloriar España en Dios, pues la eligió entre otras naciones para remedio de tantas gentes, por lo cual ellas le deben mucho más que a sus fundadores ni genitores; que si como el bienaventurado

San Gregorio dice, no nos fuera de mucho provecho nacer si no viniéramos a ser de Cristo, bien nuestro, redimidos. Ni más ni menos ¿qué fruto—podemos decir con Anselmo— nos trae el ser redimidos si no conseguimos el fruto de la redención que es nuestra salvación? Y así, yerran mucho los que dicen que porque [los indígenas] han recibido agravios, vejaciones y malos ejemplos de los españoles, hubiera sido mejor no los haber descubierto, porque vejaciones y agravios mayores eran los que unos a otros se hacían perpetuamente matándose, haciéndose esclavos y sacrificándose a los demonios. Mal ejemplo, si lo han recibido o de algunos lo reciben ahora, el rey lo ha remediado y remedia cada día con sus justicias y con la continua predicación y perseverante contradicción de los religiosos a quienes los dan y han dado; y cuanto más es evangélica la doctrina, los malos ejemplos y los escándalos son necesarios, y así creo lo han sido entre esta gente para que ella supiese, apartando el oro del lodo y el grano de la paja, estimar la virtud como lo han hecho, viendo con el filósofo que resplandecen las virtudes entre los vicios y los virtuosos entre los viciosos, y el que mal ejemplo o escándalo les ha dado, tiene terrible aflicción si no los satisface con (algo) bueno; y tú, carísimo lector, pídelo así de tu parte a Dios y recibe mi poco de trabajo perdonando los defectos de él, y acordándote, cuando con ellos topares, que no sólo no les defiendo, como San Agustín dice decía de sí Tulio, el cual decía nunca había dicho palabra que la quisiese revocar, y no agradó el santo por ser tan propio el errar de los hombres; pero al principio, antes que los topes, los toparás revocados o confesados en mis introducciones o prólogos, y así juzgarás con el bienaventurado Agustín en la epístola a Marcela, la diferencia entre quien confiesa su yerro o falta y el que las defiende, y perdonarás las mías como dice el profeta hace Dios (con) las mías y las tuyas, diciendo: Señor, yo dije que confesaré mi maldad e injusticia, y luego tú la perdonaste.

El historiador de las cosas de las Indias, a quien se debe mucho en ellas por su trabajo y por la lumbre que les dio,* dice hablando de las cosas de Yucatán que usaban honda en la guerra y varas tostadas; y de las cosas que en la guerra usaban ya lo dejo dicho y no me espanto le pareciesen a Francisco Hernández de Córdoba y a Juan de Grijalva, de honda las pedradas que les tiraban [los indígenas], cuando en Champotón los desbarataron, pues se retiraban, pero no saben tirar con honda ni la conocen, aunque tiran muy certera y recia una piedra, y encaran con el brazo izquierdo y el dedo índice a lo que tiran. Dice también que son [los indígenas] retajados, y como sea esto ha de hallarse anteriormente. Dice hay liebres y cómo son las que hay hallarás en el último capítulo. Dice hay perdices y qué tales, y cómo sean hallarás también en el último capítulo. Dice más nuestro historiador: que hallaron en el cabo de Cotoch cruces entre muertos y los ídolos, y que no lo cree porque si fueran de los españoles que de España se despoblaron cuando se perdió, tocaran de fuerza primero en otras tierras, que hay muchas. Yo, no por esta razón que no me convence, no lo creo porque no se sabe de las otras partes que podían reconocer y a dónde antes que a Yucatán podían llegar, si llegaron o no, tampoco como en estas de Yucatán. Pero por lo que no lo creo es porque cuando Francisco Hernández y Grijalva llegaron a Cotoch, no andaban a desenterrar muertos sino a buscar oro entre los vivos, y también creo de la virtud de la cruz y de la malicia del demonio que no sufriera, ver cruz entre los ídolos, en peligro de que milagrosamente algún día su virtud se los quebrantara y a él le ahuyentara y confundiera como hizo a Dagón el arca del testamento con no estar consagrada con sangre del hijo de Dios y dignificada con sus divinos miembros, como la santa cruz. Pero con todo eso, diré lo que me dijo un señor de [los indígenas], hombre de muy buen entendimiento y de mucha reputación entre ellos: hablando en esta materia un día y preguntándole yo si había oído algún tiempo nuevas de Cristo, Nuestro Señor, o de su Cruz, díjome que no había oído jamás nada a sus antepasados de Cristo ni de la Cruz, mas de que desbaratando un edificio pequeño en cierta parte de la costa, habían hallado en unos sepulcros, sobre los cuerpos y huesos de los difuntos, unas cruces pequeñas de metal, y que no miraron en lo de la cruz hasta ahora que eran cristianos y la veían venerar y adorar, que habían creído lo debían ser aquellos difuntos que allí se habían enterrado. Si esto fue así, es posible haber allí llegado alguna poca gente de España y consumídose en breve, y no haber podido quedar, por eso, memoria de ellos.

FIN.

www.ingramcontent.com/pod-product-compliance
Lightning Source LLC
Chambersburg PA
CBHW031501270326
41930CB00006B/196